T0131611

WHAT IN THE
UNIVERSE
ARE WE DOING
HERE?

And What Are We Made Of?

DR. WILLIAM D. MEHRING
D.C., M.A.

BALBOA.
PRESS

A DIVISION OF HAY HOUSE

Balboa Press books may be ordered through booksellers or by contacting:

Balboa Press
A Division of Hay House
1663 Liberty Drive
Bloomington, IN 47403
www.balboapress.com
1 (877) 407-4847

Because of the dynamic nature of the Internet, any web addresses or links contained in this book may have changed since publication and may no longer be valid. The views expressed in this work are solely those of the author and do not necessarily reflect the views of the publisher, and the publisher hereby disclaims any responsibility for them.

The author of this book does not dispense medical advice or prescribe the use of any technique as a form of treatment for physical, emotional, or medical problems without the advice of a physician, either directly or indirectly. The intent of the author is only to offer information of a general nature to help you in your quest for emotional and spiritual well-being. In the event you use any of the information in this book for yourself, which is your constitutional right, the author and the publisher assume no responsibility for your actions.

Any people depicted in stock imagery provided by Thinkstock are models, and such images are being used for illustrative purposes only. Certain stock imagery © Thinkstock.

Print information available on the last page.

ISBN: 978-1-5043-6407-2 (sc)
ISBN: 978-1-5043-6409-6 (hc)
ISBN: 978-1-5043-6408-9 (e)

Library of Congress Control Number: 2016912893

Balboa Press rev. date: 12/08/2016

CONTENTS

INTRODUCTION

I wrote this book for people like me who like to contemplate humanity's perennial "Big Questions":

Who are we? Where did we come from? Why are we here? Where, if anywhere, are we going?

We may never solve these basic and ultimate inquiries, but I believe that if we keep questioning, we will move closer to the answers. There is another important goal in this quest that is even loftier than solving the mysteries beyond any doubt: to become aware of the amazing potential we hold within ourselves as we participate in the conversation. Over the course of these pages, we will explore:

1. Cosmology: the study of the structure and origin of the universe
2. Our purpose as human beings on Earth
3. What heaven might be like
4. The ways in which a multidimensional being might perceive and act simultaneously in our world and in the multiverse
5. The undiscovered marvels that may flourish just beyond our eyes and our conscious mind

We will also look at the central messages of several world religions and how those messages inform this quest. We'll examine, from an interfaith perspective, how the wisdom that men and women have received and cherished down through the ages helps us navigate life.

If you are looking for the statement of a single fixed and final truth, I'm afraid this is not the book for you. My intention and hope are to expand the understanding of a variety of intriguing possibilities, while remembering that what lies at the end of our search may be unknowable by human consciousness.

We shouldn't worry that our story's secret may finally reside beyond the farthest horizon of our conscious perceptions and abilities to reason. It's all right not to expect and demand perfect understanding, or feel the need to create reassuring descriptions and definitions of the seemingly ineffable, in order to placate our internal discomfort at remaining in doubt or only partial comprehension.

Remaining calm in the face of our inability to decipher the deepest enigmas keeps our minds and hearts open to new hypotheses and the continued development of human capacities that allow us to enter wider and richer areas of knowledge. Insisting on the discovery of a fixed, unchanging answer to all questions separates us from the very thing we seek. Seeking absolute certainty leads to a dead end, not a path to the complex and apparently inexplicable.

Our concepts of reality will expand as our consciousness and technological abilities continue to evolve. Testing things we can't see or sense and examining ideas and intuitions about what might possibly be true allow us to modify or jettison our theories. Sometimes, an analysis of the unthinkable produces spectacular results.

I invite you to be my companion, beginning from the beginning, as I retrace the different byways I took and what happened to me along my life journey that helped me form my best guesses about the nature of all that is and our purpose.

I hope that by joining me step by step, you can see the experiences I encountered and the assumptions that I drew from them as you compare your deductions with my own. You'll be able to generate your own thoughts and determine your own hierarchy of possible conclusions concerning the issues I considered and the hypotheses I later drew.

The person I am today and the beliefs I now hold have dramatically evolved since the days of my youth. Our consciousness changes as we grow older and continue to learn more about life and our deeper selves. I have witnessed too many unexpected and remarkable phenomena to allow my present views to be limited by my previous experiences, considerations, and conclusions.

Just as our individual consciousness evolves over time, so does the consciousness of all mankind develop and expand through the centuries as human knowledge increases and human societies evolve. We are not the same as our distant ancestors—thus we do not read or consider religious texts that describe God and mankind's appointed purpose on Earth in the same way they did. The religious ideas handed down to us through the ages were structured by the civilizations in which they first appeared, with concepts of God and humanity mirroring the earthly monarchies of the time that had absolute power over their subjects. The first religious teachings reflected and ratified the domination of the ruler, who was often considered God's representative on Earth. Though inequality and injustice certainly still exist in the contemporary world, most of us no longer live in societies dominated by kings and nobility, in which people endure a life of servitude.

Today, when inspired women and men write their descriptions of profound encounters with the Divine, the picture of God, Creation, and our purpose in the world is much different. I believe that contemporary visionaries experience God and the universe as a democratic, organic, and continually unfolding process in which every conscious being has an important part to play in the ongoing evolution of the cosmos. In other words, we all get to vote.

As our view of God, ourselves, and even reality changes and expands, we are no longer satisfied to accept on pure faith an earlier authoritarian and patriarchal culture's vision of who we are, how we got here, and what our earthly roles should be.

It is my present belief, based on a range of experiences as well as considerable study, that our understanding of all things will deepen and develop through two main avenues: increased scientific exploration and knowledge, and a better understanding of the Universal Consciousness inside each of us—the spirit that binds humanity and the universe in a mysterious, all-embracing unity.

Whatever we should discover about ourselves and the cosmos, I'm convinced that scientific advancements and inner psychological and spiritual work will bring us closer to contextualizing and answering the great eternal questions.

I am reminded of the Caribbean Indians' first encounter with Christopher Columbus, when more than five hundred years ago his three ships appeared off their shores. From historical accounts we learn that the Indians saw the disruptions in the water made by the strange ships as they moved and later anchored on the sea, but the islanders were completely unable to observe the sailing vessels. Yet the Indians knew well how the ocean moves, and they realized that something they could not see was disrupting its natural wave patterns.

The *Niña, Pinta,* and *Santa Maria* and the explorers onboard surely existed, and the Spaniards would soon make their very real presence known. But for now, the visitors and their large sailing ships from another world remained beyond the Indians' previous experience of reality and therefore beyond their present powers of sight.

For several days the native people stared at the pattern of obstructed waves without determining what power or being disturbed the sea. The mystery went unsolved until the tribe's shamans were asked to decipher the strange marine phenomena.

At first, the seers saw nothing but odd waves, but after unproductive physical observation they entered their spirit world, seeking a glimpse of what had so far lacked shape, size, and color.

In their visions, the shamans saw the ships and the men onboard. After they had received these inner images and related their discovery to the tribe, Columbus's ships and their crews began to appear to the other islanders. Because the shamans had seen them in trance and knew of their existence, the ships had gained actual existence in reality, and now were visible to the puzzled Indians who had sought the shamans' help.

Apparently, the "idea" that the ships existed somewhere allowed the Indians to perceive them in the here and now. The shamans' vision of the fleet allowed it to be perceived in waking reality.

The point of this intriguing true story is important: we can't see what we don't expect reality to contain, even when it appears before our eyes. Believing that something is possible sometimes allows it to register in our senses.

It is my hope that, through the discussion we're about to begin, we can enlarge our expectations of the width and depth of what is possible and gain a better view of what may already exist both within and all around us.

You may wish to read this book alone, with family or friends, or with new acquaintances. I invite you to think about and meditate on the views and experiences that I present in the following pages. I hope that you will share and discuss your responses with others who also desire to pierce the limiting illusions of the purely conscious mind. By opening our thoughts and feelings to new possibilities, perhaps we can increase our chances of glimpsing that living something we call "ultimate reality."

BACKGROUND AND FOUNDATIONAL EXPERIENCES

It is difficult to say where our journey begins and ends. I believe there is a fundamental curiosity in everyone, but like most human qualities, the need to understand the mysterious is stronger in some of us than in others. Many children at play, for example, are enthralled by play itself, the pure experience of joyfully interacting with the world. They are happy to accept nature as it appears to the senses and are unbothered by questions about the source and inner nature of things.

Other children inquire constantly, and to each answer they receive they always find another "Why?" And then another, and another.

I was a child who often wondered how the world had become the way it was, and for what reasons.

My father died when I was eight months old, so at a very early age I was led to thoughts of life and death and the connection between the two states of being. Where had my father's essence gone? Where were his experiences and knowledge? Was it possible that he could somehow sneak back into our world? Was there a door somewhere? I wanted to know what that gateway looked like. I imagined ways the on-off switch for life might work.

My need to ask and try to discover answers about human existence took a first important turn during a seemingly mundane event in junior high school.

Who's in There?

One day as a young teenager I was staring at myself in the mirror, noticing signs of unfolding puberty. I looked so different from the way I had before. It was as if I were changing into someone else. There was fuzz on my face. I was getting pimples. My muscles were growing. I realized I was becoming a new person physically.

For a long time, I looked deep into the pupils of my eyes, until their darkness seemed to turn into twin portals. I remember asking myself, *Who's in there? Who am I?*

I kept staring, waiting for the answer. The longer and harder I looked, the better I understood that "I" was not in my body. Instead, my body was a shell that housed my consciousness. This thought produced an eerie feeling and I hurried away from the mirror and out of the room.

My experience with the mirror created a dramatic shift in my sense of reality—the idea that *I wasn't my body but instead a consciousness inhabiting a body* was overwhelming to me. The insight wasn't a passing fantasy but became a deep-seated certainty that would not reverse itself, though I tiptoed around its ramifications for a long time.

Not the First

I was not the first person to ask who I really was and awaken to a new reality as a result. I believe it's an experience as old as humanity.

I've always been fascinated by biblical texts and their descriptions of human experience. They reveal that we are still asking the same questions people posed three thousand years ago. This questioning surely took place well before the invention of written language, perhaps fifty thousand years ago, and likely even before that.

Who are we? is a question whose possible answers have always opened doors to exploring deeper realities.

Many contemporary books and movies dare to ask and try to solve this riddle of identity that is apparently as ancient as mankind. Tom Shadyac, a well-known movie director, made a film called *I Am* after a near fatal bicycle accident set him on a journey toward a deeper understanding of humanity. He sought the answer to the simple and profound question "Who am I?"

Shadyac's accident is just one example of the kinds of openings that bring a person to search for hidden truths to the deep mysteries of life. Everyone's journey is both similar and unique. In many ways he did not find an exact answer but found one that can give us great comfort. He discovered a connection that unites all of humanity and that goes beyond the understanding we can gain from our five senses. Likewise, my experience of gazing into the endless dark within my own eyes was the beginning of my search.

My next life-changing discoveries occurred during my chiropractic education. I encountered new experiences that were truly eye opening and would develop my awareness of what might lie beyond the limitations of my five senses.

Muscle Testing

My first surprise in chiropractic school was an introduction to muscle testing, also known as applied kinesiology, a technique used to access the innate wisdom of the body. Here's how it works: you select a "test muscle" to work with and then ask the body's consciousness a question. The muscle will either stay strong or go weak, and in that way, answer yes or no.

You can use this technique to assess food allergies and sensitivities, something chiropractors have always diagnosed and treated. In this form of muscle testing, a patient places a bit of the suspect food in the mouth and if the observed muscle becomes weak on testing, it's a signal that the food does indeed produce negative effects. The same method is used to evaluate spinal dysfunction. The chiropractor palpates an area of the spine, and if the test muscle then becomes weak, he or she knows that portion of the spine is a problematic area.

Muscle testing has expanded beyond diagnosing physical ailments. Many chiropractors believe that asking questions of the patient's subconscious mind can tap into issues that are impairing the healing process.

As my experience with muscle testing grew, I became more and more astounded by the accuracy with which it answered diagnostic questions. The more I practiced the technique, the more convinced I became of its amazing benefits and the passages it opened to layers of the body and mind that usually remain hidden.

I thought long and hard about this strange, life-enhancing approach developed by Dr. George Goodhart, who discovered it in the course of his chiropractic practice. I became intrigued about what this technique might indicate about the human mind and body and their connection to one another—and perhaps to sources of conscious energy beyond the individual.

Where Does It Live?

I considered several possibilities that might explain the underlying mechanisms of muscle testing and unconscious knowledge. Was there a form of consciousness connected with the patient's body that superseded the knowledge of the conscious mind? In chiropractic philosophy this source of knowledge, consciousness, and well-being is known as "innate." This innate consciousness always has the best in mind for us. In fact, it seems eager to expand on a wide range of information that can return a person to health: physically, energetically, emotionally, and even spiritually.

My experience with patients suggested that this expanded consciousness apparently accesses or is in some other way part of a wide range of healing modalities, including pharmacology, herbs, and physical medicine—and for that matter, nearly everything in the human experience. Somehow, this innate consciousness knows what is helpful and what is detrimental to the body.

I also found that this alternate consciousness is not just connected to physical body issues but can provide accurate accounts of distant memories and knows exactly which past events were crucial to the patient's core psychological makeup.

Indeed, muscle testing appears to unearth a buried way of knowing. I regularly access this using my own therapeutic technique, "E3," Emotional Energetic Evolution, the topic of my previous book, *Finding Peace in Chaos.*[1]

As a student learning about the innate knowing within us and seeing the efficacy of muscle testing, I began to wonder about this connection to knowledge and memories. Another term that seemed to lend meaning to what I was experiencing was *Universal Consciousness.* Yet I still had so many questions. For example, where is this consciousness located?

Is it within the body? Is the body a conduit? Is it outside the body? Is this active, sentient consciousness *always* alive, or does it need a body in order to live and express itself?

At this point, there seemed no way around it: I had to question the very definition of what it is to be a living entity. It seemed to me quite reasonable that all living things shared at least a portion of an innate superconsciousness within themselves, or through themselves, emanating from a common source.

Not content to probe the mysteries of living things, I couldn't help but land on the next question: do inanimate objects have consciousness too? Perhaps all physical forms—which are, after all, made up of energy—inherently have consciousness. Was a creative spark of consciousness the seed that produced all physical things, living or not? If so, was this conscious energy an important clue to the universe's creation, the nature and meaning of the cosmos, and our existence on Earth?

Listening Hands

You would think my hands would be full as I grappled with these questions, but another enlightening experience during chiropractic training stretched my curiosity even further. One instructor asked us to determine the subtle movements of the vertebrae in our patients, something that requires intense focus and extreme sensitivity. You have to learn to quiet your mind, not construct or project thoughts about what you think may be happening but concentrate entirely on receiving tactile information—to listen with your hands.

We were also asked to run our hands down patients' spines, looking for any areas that felt hotter than others, which could indicate inflammation and possible spinal subluxations (the movement of one or more vertebrae out of position, which creates pressure on spinal nerves).

As I practiced these procedures, I became aware of another feeling in my hands and fingers. Without even touching the patient, but instead holding my hand above the back, I could get a sense of where energy was actively flowing and where it wasn't. I soon realized that areas that felt less energetic indicated where there were spinal subluxations. I began to further explore this phenomenon. When I found a spot with less energy, I would imagine how exactly the bone was fixated and the problems that might exist there.

I have to admit, this exercise started almost as a party trick more than anything else, and there were many wrong guesses at first, but my accuracy quickly increased. Soon other information about the health profile of the patient came into my awareness through this intuitive sense.

I had read many accounts of physicians who developed a second sense of their patients' conditions and illnesses. Initially, I'd believed this ability among doctors was the result of their years of experience treating patients. Then I began to realize that for some physicians, this diagnostic gift had more to do with pure intuition than experience. I came to believe that I was receiving hints about the nature of an innate medical wisdom and technique.

The Path Toward Connection and Understanding

I became very curious about the field of information I had learned to connect to. I realize now that I was in a unique situation where I was asked every day to focus my mind on feeling the subtle movements and information that might be available to me as a practitioner. As students, we all relied on our strongest senses in developing our diagnostic skills. For some of us, this was a refined sense of touch; others would listen or feel heat. There was also a group of us who learned to set aside the chaotic thinking of the conscious mind so we could receive information from our conversations with the innate. You can be naturally intuitive, but unless you exercise that ability like a muscle at the gym, it will not grow.

Later, I came to understand that part of this journey is to become more "right-brained." No one, of course, solely uses the right brain when accessing their intuitive senses, but there is much more activity on the right side when you are connecting to this expanded source of information. Any exercise that brings you into the present moment, without input from the ego, will put you on the right track. And you will know when the more left-brain ego is working because you will feel inadequate or fearful, or you will find yourself saying something to others that makes you look or feel better about yourself. The ego will monopolize your attention in its constant comparison of you with the rest of humanity.

The other conscious activity that shuts off intuition is continuously repeating some story or diatribe about yourself or others, something people who are depressed, angry, or hiding from their own truth often do. Letting the ego take charge and repeating stories both limit your experience to what your five senses have to offer.

The Portal of Intuition

During my time in chiropractic school and the years that followed, I became more and more intrigued by the portal of intuition I had discovered. The more I thought about the information I could access through it, as well as how and where it might be stored, the more it seemed that it had to be present in our midst, just invisible to the eye. I began to see this information superimposed upon all the space around me.

I was familiar with the concepts that humans are multidimensional beings and that somehow we might be able to reach into other dimensions where information flows freely. I was very excited about the potential, yet at the same time a little afraid to expose the application of the portal as anything more than a party trick. Despite these conflicting feelings, I continued to practice quieting my mind so I could create moments of emptiness in which to receive information in the form of feelings, pictures, or metaphors. I also believed that it was important to maintain this same quiet neutrality while doing muscle testing.

Brain Waves

Back in my high school days, I read a book called *Steppenwolf.* It was intriguing, laced with metaphors. I remember the main character traveling to different rooms that signified parts of his mind. I wondered then how a person could shift to have that capacity. I now believe the secret is in changing your brain wave state. Through hypnotherapy training, I learned that hypnosis shifts brain waves to theta or low alpha states. These states bypass our critical mind and open the portal to information we usually cannot retrieve while we're awake, very different from the brain state we are usually in as we go about the day. You can think of it like radio frequencies; it is a little like turning the dial from the AM band to the weather band—you receive completely different information. On AM you get background music, and on the weather station you get information you need before you set sail for the day.

There is more good news when you shift into an alpha or theta state: you become free of the fears and worries of the day. So it is a very relaxing thing to do, and it helps create homeostasis in your body, the state in which everything in your body reboots and focuses on self-healing and restoration.

As I relate these ideas to you, I realize that I have come to accept these mysterious aspects of life as true—they are true for me now. But the whole concept of working with the innate, trusting my intuition, and then "coming out of the closet" with it all was a bit of a struggle, a conflict between curiosity about how healing works and fear of what I would find, and how people might judge me. Luckily for me, my curiosity trumped my fear and I continued my search for answers. My chiropractic training and practice were the key avenues that led me to a multitude of experiences that changed the way I thought about the world and myself.

Doubt and Disbelief

After mulling over my childhood experiences and curiosity about my father's death, I assumed that when you died, you died. Yet my mother told me that my father had believed that consciousness was energy, and that energy could neither be created nor destroyed.

Both of my parents were raised with a Christian set of beliefs, but I grew up with a science-based, atheistic philosophy. My nonreligious perspective meant that I wasn't indoctrinated into any theology, nor had I given much thought to the idea of life after death or reincarnation. My father's view sounded like a kind of religious thought or faith, but for me it remained an abstract idea unattached to any formal, organized religion. And I couldn't see how his ideas about consciousness and energy were of any practical use. For years, I was wary and unconvinced of the religious certainties other people held.

A Dawning Light

But we all change our minds as we progress through life. We test boundaries by discovering which actions produce positive feelings deep within us and which ones cause pain. Seeking what brings pleasure and satisfaction and avoiding actions that hurt ourselves and others are the ways we learn to live and grow. This process can be hit or miss, but it allows us to determine true and false, whether in terms of personal behavior or religious knowledge. You could say that we really do learn by trial and error.

Healthy, functioning human beings live, grow, and change. What we believe in today may evolve, not just over time but through experience and expanding our thinking. Conversely, the things we disbelieve this year may become known facts in the future.

Though I didn't grow up with him physically present, I believe my father embraced the idea of growth and change, and that the purpose of human life is to find our humanity. He was sensitive to, and critical of, any actions or statements that suggested personal hypocrisy—the failure to put into practice what you preach no matter the cost. In my youth I began to ask my mother questions about religion, and my mom shared with me one of my father's views about the religion he was raised with: "There's nothing wrong with Christianity. It's just that no one has practiced it yet."

As abrasive as that sentiment might sound, it doesn't take away from Christian truths, or the truths of any other faith traditions. My father was by all accounts a wonderful teacher, a department head at the university where he worked. His coworkers and students have told me many stories about him, describing him as a man of his word, insightful, with a keen sense of justice and equality. I am sure he met many people who touted themselves as good Christians (or Muslims, or Buddhists) but didn't strive to live up to the values of their faith: equality for all, helping the downtrodden, and brotherly/sisterly love.

We all, at one time or another, find ourselves facing the same very human dilemma, struggling to find our truth and stick to it despite our selfish, hungry ego's need for instant gratification. And surely, as we can learn from both history and contemporary life, when religion is mixed with the needs of the ego and its thirst for power, control, and survival, a fertile field is created for human hypocrisy, particularly for people who are less self-aware than my father was.

I have shared my background in this chapter because I believe it's important that you understand where I come from and how my beliefs have evolved. Very few people who know me see me as a religious or even spiritual person, and I didn't start out that way. Yet my views have changed as a result of how my life has unfolded, and I look forward to sharing them with you.

Multiple Lives

The next defining moment in my search for answers about human consciousness was as unexpected as my previous experiences, but this time it came from reading a book: *Many Lives, Many Masters* by Dr. Brian Weiss.[1]

Dr. Weiss wrote about his clinical experiences suggesting that reincarnation is a real phenomenon. Because I'd had no Christian upbringing, I was able to be open to the possibility of multiple lives, and I was particularly struck by the case history of a woman who had many phobias, all of which Dr. Weiss was able to successfully mitigate by helping her access past-life events and traumas.

This patient had an intense fear of water that seemed to originate with her death by drowning in a previous lifetime, and connecting to and transforming that death through hypnosis helped her process it. As Dr. Weiss explained, it seemed she had gone somewhere and relived the experience, bringing her superconsciousness along and knowing that death was but a small part of a continuous experience. As a result, she was spontaneously released from her fear of water and drowning.

My immediate reaction to Dr. Weiss's account of this "regression treatment" was that whatever he was doing had proved very therapeutic, whether or not he had actually succeeded in helping his patient return to past lives as the hidden sources of her fears.

I was energized to find out more about hypnosis, reincarnation, and even clairvoyance (the ability to see things beyond the normal range of human vision).

Two Visits

My next step was to connect with a clairvoyant named Rosemarie. I asked her to contact my father and then listened carefully to the many amazing things he wanted to tell me through her. Though the experience was illuminating, I felt I needed verification that my father had really communicated with me. I asked Rosemarie to ask my father something that only he and my mother could possibly have known—something I would have no way of knowing myself. My father described a gift they had exchanged that was enclosed in multiple boxes, with each box fitted inside another. I was given a very detailed description, and when I related it to my mother, she confirmed everything. It was hard not to believe that the consciousness that had spoken to me was indeed that of my father.

Then I found a hypnotist. Under hypnotic trance, I returned to the day after I was born when my mother took me to see my father, who was dying of cancer. I could see the moment surprisingly clearly. As I had after my visit with the clairvoyant, I asked my mother to confirm what I'd learned. She was startled by the accuracy of the description of what had taken place that day. I was now convinced of the efficacy of hypnotic trance, and I knew that it would be possible to revisit most if not all of the past events of my life, and maybe even previous lives.

A New Path

For twelve years I'd had a chiropractic practice in a small town in central California, but then an injury made it impossible for me to continue working in my chosen field. I tried a few other jobs outside of the health professions, but none were fulfilling. I knew I had to find my way back to doing what I felt I did naturally: working with people who were in need of healing, whether physical or emotional.

I decided to return to college to learn more about the relationship between mind and body and to earn a master's degree in psychology and philosophy. An important aspect of my new direction stemmed from my experiences as a chiropractor: I wanted to understand more about the kinesthetic sense of energy that I felt in my hands while treating patients, and I wanted to develop my intuition. My studies led me on a journey similar to those of shamans and other traditional healers.

Heaven and Dr. Newton

My new path continued to unfold. After I received my master's degree, I began training in homeopathy and hypnotherapy. My most important learning experiences in these areas stemmed from my studies with Dr. Michael Newton, who had written two books, *Journey of Souls* and *Destiny of Souls*.[2]

Dr. Newton facilitated thousands of hypnotic journeys in his practice. He was especially interested in ways to access the events that transpire between lifetimes, between one physical incarnation and another. He wanted to discover what went on in the realm that many religious people call "heaven." Dr. Newton helped me and his patients understand many things about our true human purpose. While many people had looked into their past lives and the stories within those lives, through his between-lives research using hypnotic trance, he found a pot of gold, enabling people to understand the origins of the difficult lessons that they had been wrestling with. With the benefit of this new awareness and perspective, his patients were able to transcend and heal some of their greatest psychological issues.

These sessions were unlike any others I had witnessed in my hypnotherapy training. To begin with, they were three to four hours long, allowing a depth of trance that few other hypnotherapists had achieved. This afforded access to much deeper information, of the kind that the conscious mind locks up and rarely releases.

Let me share with you the five most profound experiences I encountered in my hypnosis practice, and some of the thinking those unusual and fascinating events generated. All but one of the sessions I describe here were structured using Dr. Newton's protocols for determining the nature of the existence of that soul's life between each earthly life.

Dr. Newton's hypnotic procedure for returning a patient to the memories of what happens between each life begins with leading the subject through several stages of gradually deepening hypnotic states, a process that takes between thirty minutes and an hour. The hypnotist guides the patient slowly backward, retracing the subject's present life from adulthood to childhood to infancy, and beyond, to the fetus in the mother's womb.

When the patient is back within the mother, the hypnotist suggests that the unborn baby continue farther back in time and experience a previous life.

In my own practice today, I refine this method some and suggest that the patient return to the most recent previous life, or to a lifetime that seems most significant in relation to the issues the patient seeks to transform. I don't choose this lifetime for the patient, but let the session unfold organically. I have found that the soul has the surest notion of which previous life will be the most therapeutic to revisit.

The Spiral Stairway

A patient had come in to work on issues of loss and abandonment in this life. When she entered deeply into hypnotic trance, I asked her to go back to the previous life that seemed most relevant in addressing her present distress.

She returned to New York City, where she had lived in an earlier existence and where during the 1920s and 1930s she had experienced the most important events of that lifetime. I confess to being pleased that she had lived in the United States, because here there's a chance we can access official records to confirm the patient's recollections while under hypnosis.

In that life in New York, she had also been a woman, married to a prominent man with a garment manufacturing business. My subject had a very clear memory of her husband, her children, and the house where they had lived together, which she was able to describe in detail including the address. The strongest feeling that emerged for her was that the man she had been married to in New York was the same man she was married to in her present life.

Just as she awoke from trance, I asked her to sketch the New York house on paper. That way, if she decided to look for the house to check the accuracy of what she'd seen, she would have a vivid mental picture of it. The patient was reluctant, and I think a little fearful, to discover whether her experience under hypnosis was factual, but in the end the clarity of the images she had retrieved made her curious and she decided to investigate.

The address, she discovered, was correct, and the house was still there, looking much as she had described it to me and drawn on paper. The central entranceway was circular as she remembered, with an impressive set of stairs spiraling upward to the second floor, a vivid feature of the house she had seen when she visited it during trance.

Going There

I have had the experience of traveling between lives myself as well, and I saw, heard, and felt things that I believe are universal, things all souls encounter between earthly lives.

When a classmate placed me in a hypnotic trance and asked me to return to my previous life, I found myself in ancient Egypt, where I was a seer for the reigning pharaoh. I could see in vivid detail the clothes I was wearing, and I could clearly make out my hands and feet. I was unable to see my face, although I knew that I was a man. It was a very peaceful period in history and I felt great joy in the guidance I was able to offer my ruler. I learned that my advice to him was helpful in creating the kingdom's prosperity and maintaining years of stability.

My classmate then guided me forward to the latter days of my life in the land of the pyramids, and then I experienced my death and was transported to an alternate realm—the realm most people call heaven. Over the course of two hours in that trance state, I was asked to describe the events I witnessed in that world between my lives in the physical world.

I experienced a Council of Elders who gave guidance to departed souls just arriving from their earthly existence. One of the elders or souls I saw in this meeting represented that I was part of a specific group whose abilities, makeup, and purpose would be identified by a specific pendant. This elder was also wearing the pendant that indicated we were from the same cluster or group. Other people who have undergone hypnotic regression have described similar pendants or adornments, which signify the activities and attributes of the subject under trance.

This pendant was inscribed with two symbols. One was a curved Middle Eastern sword, a scimitar, the other a multipointed star, like an elaborate mariner's compass. This complex symbol, I was told by the leader of this group, identified me and others like me as souls who possessed intuitive potential. I felt the sword was symbolic of my ties to the Middle East and a passion to push forward. This hypnotic session was much like a very interactive dream state but I knew I wasn't sleeping. In fact, I felt more awake and focused than ever.

Such an experience is an integral part of merging your consciousness back into the between-lives realm. It commonly features the classic white light and being comforted by the souls that are most important to you. I would later find out that we all handpick our Council of Elders, and they know exactly how to support our transition from the previous life to the next. Their entire discussion is about the emotional obstacles and old ways of being that we are to overcome in our next lives.

My elders helped me see all the ways I grew and transformed the energy consciousness of my soul. They also gently showed me where I had missed the mark despite the many opportunities they and I had created to enable me to transform.

There is truth in Shakespeare's lines "All the world's a stage, / And all the men and women merely players." In the play of our soul's evolution, the set and the stage manager are our very own soul and the help of Creation, or God. The Council of Elders is part of that oneness. In that hypnosis session I learned that most of my experiences and the people I would meet in the next life were established in the between-lives world, creating opportunities to evolve and grow. It was in this realm that I began to understand the underlying pliability of our so-called concrete physical world.

I also believe that appearing before a Council of Elders—a common thread in between-lives accounts—explains the age-old religious concepts of a judgment after death. Yet interestingly, the most severe judge of the preceding life is not found among the elders, but is instead ourselves, the departed souls under "inspection." In fact, one of the roles of the Council of Elders is to ease your own self-condemnation.

In my case, I was terribly upset by all the opportunities I had missed by following the same knee-jerk patterns, which created the same poor outcomes: our modern definition of insanity. And in fact, we are creatures of habit, basing much of what we do and how we think on the past. But when we are in a soul state, not tethered to an ego ruled by fears, our evolutionary path shines with clarity.

I have worked with many patients who are so caught up in self-condemnation that they are unwilling or unable to work through problem areas of personality and character. They continue to carry these issues with them, from one lifetime to another, and are continually hampered by them in their present life.

These regression subjects understood that their previous lives had been carefully orchestrated, allowing them repeated opportunities to confront the actions that had caused chronic disharmony in their belief systems or emotional lives. Unfortunately, they turned away from each new opportunity to face their shortcomings and amend their negative ways of being.

The beauty of the hypnosis session is that we can see the underlying belief systems that create our negative actions through the eyes of the soul. This perspective is profoundly helpful in harmonizing this life, and once you gain this knowledge, it cannot be taken away.

The lesson we learn is that so often the fear of being wrong—of receiving and feeling blame, of not being "good enough"—obstructs us and discourages us from beginning, continuing, and completing the work we need to do. This is the mark of the personal ego, a small portion of our greater self, which inherently fears unworthiness and possible retribution, whether it is inflicted by others or by the ego itself. More than anything, the ego is afraid of "not measuring up." It fears being unworthy of love.

The Snowball

My own hypnotic regression to a previous life and an existence between lives has given me invaluable guidance in my present life. This learning is not unique to me. The message I received is universal: the most important things we can do in our current existence are to transcend hatred, refuse to seek vengeance, practice loving-kindness toward others, and reject any feelings of shame and inadequacy and any other negative feelings about ourselves.

The negative thoughts we carry within us, which often manifest as hurtful actions, are self-destructive. But they are not only self-destructive: there's the real possibility that our own self-destruction may harm something much larger than a single failed individual. The more we understand the unity and interconnectedness of consciousness, the better able we are to understand the power of individual action, and that positive actions like "paying it forward" are much more powerful than negative ones. I believe this is how the universe is set up. You can think of a single positive action on your part as a snowflake that falls on a mountaintop. Sprinkle on a few more, and a small snowball will form. Add more helpful actions and then a puff of breeze, and the snowball will begin a journey down the mountain, gathering more snowflakes as it goes, until it becomes an unstoppable force for good in the world.

The Sun and the Satellite

Much of the work of personal growth depends upon recognizing the central place of the ego and its constant needs and demands in the conscious mind. The stronger the ego's grasp on our thoughts, the more difficult it is to access the wiser perspectives of the soul, which underlies the ego and waking consciousness and is the entity that experiences other places and times during hypnosis.

Finding our true selves requires the understanding that the ego is only a narrow and limited aspect of us and the belief that our real identity is vast in comparison and more complete. This effort to displace the ego from its central position in our consciousness is our greatest challenge and demands the most inner work. We need the ego for our day-to-day survival, and we especially call on it in adversarial or difficult situations— an unavoidable part of life. So we are not trying to rid ourselves of ego but rather to identify the belief systems it holds that lead us to act in ways that don't contribute to the transformation of humanity and the creation we are a part of. It requires nothing less than dislodging the ego as the "sun" around which our identity revolves and then, in its place, positioning the deeper soul. The soul then becomes the center of our spiritual solar system and the ego is reduced to an orbiting satellite.

Meeting a Fellow Traveler

I once met a woman who was teaching a class about intuition and in it, I experienced a real-life confirmation of my trance experience in ancient Egypt. While attending a lecture she was giving I noticed that she was wearing a small set of earrings bearing Egyptian symbols. In her talk, she described the mystic schools that flourished in the Egypt of the pharaohs, and afterward I asked her about her experience with that distant time and place.

She told me she felt that she had lived there long ago, in a previous life, and I had my opening: I described the lifetime as a seer and counselor to the pharaoh that I had recalled under hypnotic regression. As I related what I had learned and experienced under trance and came to the pendant I had seen around the neck of one of the elders, she interrupted me. And then she described its design: the curved sword and the complex star. Her description of the symbol I had seen was as detailed as it was perfect, and she explained that it sometimes appeared to her in her dreams.

This encounter was pivotal for me. It bolstered my belief in a soul-directed life: one in which events are arranged so that we meet certain people and have certain experiences in order to revisit and repair past mistakes in present time, to confront old problems and transcend them as we transform ourselves and continue our spiritual evolution. I feel deeply that if we don't recognize and take advantage of these preplanned opportunities, the soul will patiently re-create the same encounters in a new setting until we learn our lessons at last.

This was an experience of recognition. I understood not only that I was supposed to meet this woman who knew all about the ancient pendant, but that she was part of my core group of fellow travelers from life to life: a cadre of time travelers who interact in both positive and negative ways in order to mutually grow and advance. Usually this cast of characters or souls aligns in each earthly existence until recurring problems are transformed and each soul can move on to learn other lessons with other souls in different times and places. This is not to say that new souls don't join in the transformational experience; they do.

As time would show, this teacher and I clearly had important knowledge and experiences to share, and perhaps similar issues that we would work through together.

Souls I Have Known Before

I connected with three other practitioners, each with a unique approach to the work. Together, we formed a healing group for the purpose of helping one another move toward personal, psychological, and spiritual growth.

Our main intention was to identify and analyze the stressful issues and blockages we were encountering in our lives and discover how to address and transcend them. One of the most exciting and unexpected outcomes of these meetings was our increasing power of intuition and access to the wise voice of the soul.

One evening our group conducted a life-between-life (LBL) hypnosis session with our friend Annette, a practicing therapist with a doctorate in psychology. We regressed Annette under trance and asked her about situations from earlier lives that she was now revisiting and transforming in her present life.

As Annette answered our questions, I sensed a different personality speaking. Her speech patterns, vocabulary, and manner of expression had abruptly changed and this new voice wasn't speaking about herself in the first person, but about another woman. I asked her if she could tell me who was speaking.

"You would consider me the soul of Annette," she responded.

I kept my voice calm even as a thrill shot through me, and I changed my line of questioning. I asked Annette's soul about human existence and what lies beyond this world and our human eyes' ability to see. With that dialogue established, we talked for hours about Annette's life, about what she was here on Earth to learn, and about the hidden nature of the universe.

Confirmation

We continued talking with the personality who had taken the place of our friend Annette while I considered ways to verify the information we were getting through her:

"Is it true that all souls are connected?"

"Yes."

"Is it true that we learn as a collective of souls and that we can access the knowledge and experiences of others?"

"Yes."

Then I asked Annette about her sister, who is currently living. "Can you access where your sister is and describe what she is doing now?"

"Yes."

"Is your sister presently with another person?"

"Yes. She's visiting with a friend, in a different city from the city where she lives."

"Can you describe her friend?"

"She's a woman friend, but there's also a man there. He's just arrived to talk with them."

I asked what the three people were talking about, and what the room they were in looked like. I asked if there were any pictures on the walls and what they depicted, information that might be useful in later verifying what the soul of Annette was seeing and hearing while in trance.

After the session ended, I asked Annette if she remembered the information she had given us about her sister. As I went over the details, she confirmed, "Oh yeah. That's right."

Later, we called Annette's sister to ask her where she had been and what she had been doing during Annette's session. She confirmed every detail the speaker who called herself "the soul of Annette" had provided. I found this persuasive proof of clairvoyance, and it gave me confidence during future sessions with Annette—and sometimes with the soul of Annette—that her descriptions of the universe and our purpose in it were accurate.

Annette in Montana

Annette helped me unlock what I believe are secrets of the universe during these hypnotic sessions. On the first occasion, I conducted a session with her at a retreat where we were taking classes in psychological technique in Montana. It was during this session that I began to consider the real possibility that human precognition was a fact. After our therapeutic session she continued to stay in a "waking trance" and was able to walk with me along a dirt road as she spoke about incidents that had previously occurred at the ranch. At one point, she told me that a bear had crossed the road up ahead. One of its paws was injured and she said that I would soon be able to see the print of the bear's hurt foot. The print was there where she said it would be, and reflected an injury.

We came upon a group of horses in a corral and Annette described to me what each horse was thinking. She told me that all of the horses would move away from us as we continued to approach, except for one black-and-white paint that would approach us instead. This, too, unfolded just as she had predicted.

As a result of our numerous talks together while Annette was in trance, I discovered that future events could also be accessed under hypnosis, not just past-life information. At a minimum, a hypnotized subject can see into the near future.

The important question to me was just how far into the future one could see, and whether those future events the subject envisioned were certain to occur. Were they already and forever set in stone? Or were they only probabilities or possibilities, images of things that in due time might or might not appear in concrete, earthly reality?

Destiny, Fate, or Free Will?

I saw two alternative explanations for how someone under trance can correctly predict the future.

On the one hand, each of us over the course of a lifetime makes millions of observations, judgments, and decisions about the events that confront us. From our earliest cognitions we break experiences down into fragments and categorize them. As each new situation unfolds, our mind does its best to find similarities with other experiences, funneling a multitude of scenarios into ones that we have successfully handled in the past. Over time, outcomes become increasingly probable, and this is the model of free will. Using this model it is understandable that we can predict the outcome of current and future based on the past. And as people learn to harmonize their lives, they may also find ways to attract similar experiences into their human classroom. This seems to have the appearance of fate but is in fact free will.

Still in the category of free will are preordained experiences and the people you will meet. The fact that you were set up with the input of your soul is by definition free will, and what you do in these situations will change the direction of your life. Once your direction changes, you will attract a new set of experiences that influence your growth. In this scenario you may be offered a soul who becomes your spouse and he or she may be key in your transformation. You have the free will to reject this person, but there is usually an internal magnet that comes from an inner knowing that makes your meeting feel like fate. When I hear the stories of people meeting in the oddest of circumstances, I know souls are working overtime to set all this up.

Now back to the question of my experience with Annette and the horses in Montana. Annette knew how the horses would behave in advance. Was this fate or the probabilities of free will?

If everything that happened were fated to be, and perhaps everything in time had already occurred, free will would not exist. This makes no sense to me, and based on all I have learned, it's not the way things are. Let us see how the experience of the horses may help us answer this question. Here is how time, or the collection of experiences, influences the solidity of future events. Simply put, the closer you come to an event, the more decisions about it have been made, making the outcome more certain. The further away you are from the event, the more changes can occur in the free will universe, keeping the future flexible. Later, in discussions of life-between-life experiences, we will talk about how souls experience and work with their own past lives. This was unexpected information that is still hard for me to comprehend.

When considering destiny, fate, and free will, it is important to understand that time is very malleable. Let us remember that if we look to the tiny world within us, the quantum world, time is not linear. The closer we get to pure energy, the freer existence or time becomes. I'll have more to say about this in the science chapter.

Mary's Turn

Working with another member of our healing group netted even more illuminating information. Mary was a very contemplative person, a thoughtful medical doctor whose many patients loved her. She was by nature quiet and composed. But during her hypnotic session, like Annette, Mary began to speak in a different voice, using a different vocabulary and rhythm of speech. It was as though an inner, hidden self had been released and all of Mary's usual hesitations, uncertainties, and anxieties had vanished. Suddenly she was exuberant and playful as this new form of Mary invited us all to join hands and accompany her to a heavenly realm of consciousness.

We were surprised and excited, but calmed ourselves in order to open our minds without expectation. We wanted to experience and accept whatever was about to happen as we began the journey with the new Mary as our guide. I calmed myself and opened to the experience.

As Mary spoke, with my eyes closed I saw clusters of illuminated color in a certain shape moving through space. Beyond the shape, the space in the background also shone with various colors, but the two areas felt different and distinct from one another. I was curious about what I was seeing, so I described this to our guide, Mary. She became very excited.

"You're seeing my true essence!" she blurted out. "You've seen the real me!"

Just as we had spoken with the soul of Annette, now we were talking to Mary's soul. As we moved toward this realm, I felt an ecstatic sense of comfort and joy and a certainty that all was and would be all right. I felt sure that our human past and future would always be okay. I felt better than I had ever felt in my life! Later, Annette confirmed that she had felt the same during this session. I believe we moved toward this place only because Annette and I saw ourselves passing through shifting colors.

But even the most wonderful journeys end, and finally Mary announced that we'd come to a place where we had to stop. She had been told that she was unable to take us any further, and it was clear that she was just as disappointed as we were to receive that news.

Connection

As you might imagine, your life changes when you are able to talk with your soul. And Mary had done more than just talk with her soul—she had created a connection. Through this connection, she was able to integrate her soul's consciousness with her conscious mind. It was evident from what her soul had to say that there was now clarity in Mary's conscious mind about the main issues in her life and what she must do to best handle them.

Later, I asked Mary how she had felt when her soul was speaking through her. She told me it was as though the part of her that was her conscious mind had been pushed off to the side. It was still there but had stepped back to listen closely to what her soul was telling all of us. If she had wanted to interrupt her soul, she told me, it would have been very difficult to talk over it. She recognized her soul as the truest part of her, and that she was also part of her soul. The whole experience, she said, felt like coming home and for the first time in her life, being her true self.

A Shift in Wavelength

Why and how the souls of Annette and Mary appeared and spoke under hypnosis called for an explanation. What caused Mary's conscious and ego-dominated mind to step aside and another, seemingly greater, encapsulating part of her to speak up during the LBL session? I wondered if the answer could be found in the nature of the hypnotic experience itself.

The brain activity of subjects in hypnotic or meditative trance undergoes a shift in waveform or wavelength. I believe this shifting of wave shape and frequency allows the subject to perceive and receive information from other, usually unconscious areas of the brain—and perhaps from realms of existence that are normally closed to the conscious, waking mind.

This experience under hypnosis may be like switching a radio from AM to FM. The subject's brain may be undergoing a change in the electrical signals it sends, moving from amplitude modulation, in which waves are farther apart, to a frequency modulation where waves appear in greater numbers at shorter intervals.

Perhaps the souls of Annette and Mary came forward because the hypnotized subjects were now operating on a different, rarely used wavelength. A shift in consciousness had resulted that allowed each subject to access other dimensions in which the soul already existed. The souls of my friends were able to access greater, even unimaginable wisdom and information because their brains had moved to another "channel" that could now receive the souls' messages.

Annette had a similar accounting for why in a trance her consciousness had shifted and her soul had begun to speak. After several sessions during which this merger between levels of consciousness occurred, Annette felt that her conscious mind and her subconscious mind—where the soul may dwell—had become more integrated. A crucial question arises: what separates us from the soul's perspective, and how can we learn to bypass this obstruction to gain greater consciousness?

Young Helper

I will share one final LBL session involving a young boy whose mother was seeking help because he suffered from grand mal seizures. They had tried a number of medications without any resolution. I didn't know what to expect, or whether trance work could improve the boy's condition, but I was willing to try. The boy, whom I'll call "John," had a very unusual case history. Seizures of varying intensity occurred on and off throughout the year, but they were particularly severe and happened with more regularity during major holidays. John had the most severe and frequent seizures during the Christmas season.

My intuitive sense was to start with hypnosis. John instantly went into trance, and very soon I recognized that familiar shift in personality and voice I had observed with other subjects when the deeper soul was making its presence known. John's voice became assertive and his vocabulary expanded well beyond that of a child his age.

I asked John's more sophisticated and mature personality why he "needed" his seizures to occur. He answered that the seizures allowed him to shift more easily into another realm where he could do his work. What I understood him to say was that some part of his consciousness had to leap into a different energetic state that allowed him to travel and do his work in this other place. This, too, was a brain wave shift.

I asked him what that work was. He said that it was his job to find people in conflict and surround them with compassion so they could more easily work through their problems. John went on to say that we all have a purpose in each realm of existence. There are many souls with different work to do, and these individual parts of Creation or individual consciousness take an active role in keeping everyone and everything on Earth properly functioning as parts of the larger whole.

I understood that some energetic aspect of the boy who was John was working to bring peace to humankind. John reported that he worked all over the world, but that he had a special interest in the welfare of his parents.

Working Holidays

When I asked John why he had so many seizures during holidays, he answered that at these times of the year, people suffered much more stress and conflict than usual as they reunited with family patterns, both good and stress inducing, and felt an increased sense of unfulfilled expectations of themselves and their family members. John related that holidays were when his parents had most of their arguments, the worst being right around Christmas.

Finally, I asked John, "If I were to teach this young boy how to practice self-hypnosis, would that allow him to do his work without having to have seizures?"

John's answer was "Yes."

Success and the Unforeseen

I taught John how to place himself in a hypnotic trance and sent him on his way to put the technique to work. In the days that followed, I thought more about the time I'd spent with John's soul consciousness, and new questions presented themselves: questions without obvious or clear solutions.

Two weeks after bringing John to my office, his mother phoned and told me that John's seizures had stopped. A month later I received a concerned call from John's father. He was very pleased to report that John continued to be free of seizures but another situation had arisen. John would self-hypnotize at bedtime but on some nights he wouldn't go to sleep. Instead he would get up, leave his bedroom, sit in one of the big chairs in the living room, and talk to his father. John wasn't sleepwalking; he was "hypnosis walking."

John's father reported listening to someone with wisdom and vocabulary beyond his young son's level of understanding. This was difficult for John's father to comprehend as it felt like the boy who was talking was not the son he knew but someone with a vast understanding of the world. The idea that humans could be multidimensional beings and that there could be multiple aspects or more than one consciousness dwelling in his son's body was hard for the father to understand and come to terms with. Interestingly enough, while the father struggled to come to terms with his son's newfound depth, the mother felt like she had died and gone to heaven. She loved their probing, meaningful talks.

I found it very interesting to think about the internal support system John spoke of. It once again reminded me of our body, with all of its systems that support the whole. We have separated the body into different organs and functions but they are still our unified body. There are layers and layers of healing mechanisms within our body just as there are layers and layers of healing mechanisms within this multidimensional organism that is creation. It was so comforting for me to see evidence of the depth and diversity of souls working on so many different levels or realms to keep the evolution of humanity on track. It also reminded me of the importance of being mindful of our thoughts and actions, as we are not only within but make up the body of Creation. What we think and do in our life has direct consequences for the internal makeup of Creation itself.

3

GOD IN THE EQUATION

During the sessions with Annette and Mary, I couldn't help but ask questions about God. I wanted to be able to picture what God looked like: I was making the same mistake that so many have before me. Both women gave me the same answer, which seemed profound and nearly beyond human comprehension.

They told me that everything is God. There is nothing that is not God. Creation Consciousness, the physical earthly realm, and so many other aspects of creation that you cannot be aware of are intimately entwined and grow simultaneously from each other. I began to realize that we really have no concept of how old this organism is or how many layers, dimensions, or realms it has. I wondered how different the layers of creation were from one another and what each dimension's physical laws might be like. In the world we know we have found that the laws of physics are different on the quantum level than in the perceivable, macro level. How different would they be in a realm that lacked any physicality at all? I wondered if time even applied in these realms. The permutations of possibilities became so big and unknowable that I decided to settle on how what they said applied to our physical earthly realm.

It is an interesting conundrum to be so small and yet be a part of something so unimaginably big. Today most young students go to science class and learn about the electrons, neutrons, and protons of the atom in abstract terms. In the past, students were taught that particles within the atom were solid and the smallest pieces of our universe. It is easy for us to think that with all the knowledge we have amassed through our scientific discovery, we must know a large percentage of what there is to know, but instead we have found the opposite. Each new discovery leads to more unanswered questions. This is the way of knowledge and scientific discovery at its best. I have learned from the many sessions of deep hypnosis with my patients, as well as interviews with people who have briefly died and come back, that we are connected to, if not an integral part of, a grand yet unperceivable organism. In adolescence, many of us asked ourselves whether the stars, planets, solar systems, and galaxies were nothing more than little building blocks of something profoundly big, making us infinitely small. At the same time, we are connected to a oneness that also makes us infinitely large. It is interesting to think that we will never be able to see what God looks like because we would always be inside it and there is no outside of creation to look back from because nothing exists there. We would require space to exist outside this organism that many wish to call God, but from what the souls of these women had to say, if there is such a space, it is still inside creation. As I have learned about the size of the universe and its seemingly infinite solar systems and untold existences, my appreciation for the breadth and intricate balance of *all living creation* is overwhelming.

My interpretation of what I learned through these sessions is that our physical realm is a "collapsed probability," a reality that has taken shape as a result of the past and present, with its fingers in the future. Our very existence occurs in tandem with the creative intention of a Universal Consciousness that includes all consciousness and seems to be structured and maintained by an organizing principle: namely, Creation. In other words, there is connected consciousness and there are experiences within Creation, but some part of Creation has the role of seeing the biggest picture and keeping everything going in its intended direction. In my personal experience, when I hear people talk of this realm of Creation there is a sense of connection, oneness, benevolence, and inner peace—and yet the transformative process is still going on within it.

Some people may find this perspective difficult because there is so much that Creation might be. Through my experiences with hypnotic trance, I have come to see that for many, Creation Consciousness or God is a collection of all experiences that have come from within itself; those experiences create the Body of God, if you will. The outcomes of these past experiences create the physical world and many other realms in which Creation continues to experience all things simultaneously.

The past, present, and future in all the various realms of Creation are entangled. It is a hard concept for us to grasp from our linear belief about time and random future, especially when we are not the pinnacle or central focus of Creation. To understand this concept better we must wrestle with a few foundational concepts. We first need to rid ourselves of our egocentric view and the story it tells: that we are created in God's image or likeness. I think this can be true only if you are open to there being an infinite amount of other likenesses of God. In other words, everything that is living is a likeness of Creation because it is made of Creation. It is important to expand this idea into other realms with other beings and things we may not think of as living.

The picture I have been shown is that the multiverse in which we exist is *living*. All of it, from the biggest thing to the littlest. It is forever living and expanding through its own experience. All the experiences of the living things within Creation are a part of what creates growth for Creation. The metaphor that comes to mind is of the growth rings of a tree. Imagine the experiences that exist inside Creation becoming substance and the building materials for growth. Just as a tree uses the energy of the sun and the carbon dioxide in the air to create the fiber for its own growth rings, Creation uses experiences filled with consciousness and energy to create its own growth rings and expansion. Within the growth rings of Creation is a huge database of experiences, wisdom, and knowledge, just as in the growth rings of a tree there is much we can learn about the weather, rainfall, nutrients, and carbon dioxide content in the atmosphere throughout the tree's life. Just as the conditions and experiences the tree faces shape it, so experiences and conditions shape Creation.

Changing Bodies

Mary and Annette also discussed the physical body in the past, present, and future, explaining that the body you inhabit in an earthly incarnation is only the latest in a vast series of previous and future bodies. Each present bodily form is an evolutionary product of all earlier bodies and, like them, will influence your next physical incarnation and all the ones after that.

For example, the individual bodies that your soul will animate in your next ten lifetimes will take their basic structure from the series of bodies you've inhabited in many previous lifetimes on earth. The body you have in this earthly life doesn't assume its final form until your preceding life is over and your new body is about to be conceived in your mother's womb.

That body, and the experiences that are required for your next spiritual transformations on Earth, are not determined until two tasks have been completed:

You've finished learning the last lessons that presented themselves in your previous life and from your experiences in the heavenly realm between lives. And there is much to do in the heavenly realm to process all the experiences of that life. You will squeeze as many lessons and transformative experiences out of that life as possible before you venture into the next one.

Throughout this entire progression of physical incarnations, the ultimate, perfected body and life situation are simultaneously in the process of creation—from your first existence on Earth and through all your subsequent existences. The selection of your family and friends will create the opportunity for the right souls to intertwine, and you will all come together like the cast of a Broadway show. I can't help but wonder if there are as many loose ends to keep track of before the final animation of the body as there are right before curtain time on Broadway. But just like a brilliantly executed play, things work out in the end. Please now expand the multitude of experiences from the many realms within Creation and imagine how the body of Creation is in a never-ending state of evolution.

Where Is God?

This is another question I asked Mary and Annette. Their answer? Basically, wherever you look. Anything that is, is Creation, also known as God. All of the universes and all of the dimensions, from the infinitely small to the infinitely big, are Creation.

God or Creation is not outside us or separate from us. Rather, we are within Creation. Everyone is a part of it and everyone and everything is participating in Creation's active process of becoming, being, maintaining, and transforming. There is never a dull moment considering the infinite number of experiences that are being catalogued and thrown into a collective consciousness that echoes through Creation. "Creation" is action, not a noun at all but a verb.

Our individual existence in the physical realm depends upon the continual intention of the Universal Consciousness. This constant awareness maintains our lives on Earth and the existence of all beings and physical forms in all of the galaxies of the universe and realms. Without this overarching conscious intent, everything physical would simply revert back to a prephysical form of energy/consciousness that held within it a different intent.

Mary and Annette, as well as other individuals I have hypnotized, repeatedly describe an enveloping spirit of well-being, love, and compassion. This entity or spirit is perfect and reassures them that everything always has been, is, and will be all right. My hypnosis patients always attribute their experience of a benign and eternal unity to the action of a Creation that oversees everything within itself.

THE ESSENCE OF HEAVEN

Annette's and Mary's identical descriptions of Creation bring to mind what is called in science and mathematics a "Venn" or "set" diagram.

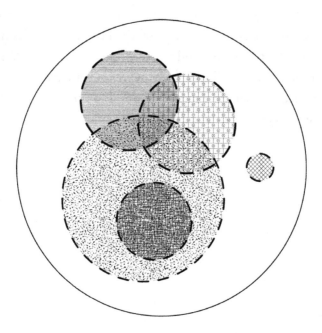

Figure 1.

Figure 1 takes the form of a supercircle that encompasses the circles of all sets—and the component parts within them—that are under consideration. To the subjects' descriptions I would add a web

34

of dotted lines joining everything within the supercircle to indicate the interconnectedness and oneness of all the apparently discrete individual objects. This illustrates a perfect ultimate unity that binds all time and space and individual consciousness.

"As Above So Below" and the Cell

I was already well aware of this concept of parts joined together in a greater whole. My foundational education was in the field of biological research. Human biology and the constituent parts (the suborganelles) inside each single human cell—the nucleus, cell walls, mitochondria, vacuoles, and the other individual living elements—are a perfect example of this. Each of these elements has a unique structure and performs a specific and necessary task. It is only through working together that the special work of the separate cell parts keeps a healthy organism functioning.

As each suborganelle is an indispensable part of its enclosing cell, each cell is a vital and inseparable part of the larger human organism. You could say that the cells of my body are me, as are the suborganelles within all of my single cells. It's not that each of my cells is the same as the collective or summation of the many different parts that make up who I am—or, by extension, that make up all that Creation is. The whole is both the sum of its parts and greater and more complex than that sum.

Remember John's experience. He described each individual consciousness as having a vital task to perform. Each entity was an active, semiautonomous part of Creation, but those separate functions allowed all the parts to form an incredibly complex, overarching unity that was conscious and alive. I enjoy the possibility of being a suborganelle within the body of Creation.

Heaven's Helper

I have a doctor friend who is a wonderful gerontologist. His work often involves helping the terminally ill transition from the present life to what lies beyond. He told me about one woman who was very warm and friendly and always expressed her gratitude and best wishes to my friend and all the nurses on the hospital's special care unit.

But in the course of the woman's hospitalization, it became obvious that her kindness wasn't without an ulterior motive, well intended as her gestures to others certainly were. She was a born-again Christian who spent much of her day proselytizing to those around her. She was struggling with the dying process and what might follow after death, so in preaching to others she was no doubt trying to reassure herself.

Her doctor was a central focus of her attention and concern, and she continually tried to reignite his lapsed Catholicism or get him to accept her own beliefs so that when he died he would receive salvation and go to heaven.

There and Back Again

Ultimately, the woman died. The doctor confirmed that she was clinically dead. But a few minutes after her heart and breathing had stopped, she revived—without any medical intervention. The doctor was present when the deceased woman regained consciousness and began to speak again. She was lucid and very excited. She wanted so much to share with the doctor what she had just experienced as she knew she had died and gone to heaven and discovered that "we are all one."

"Heaven is like nothing I've been told about," she said. "There is no judgment and there is no hell." She kept repeating, with jubilation, "It was nothing like they said it was going to be! But it was *all good!*"

She told the doctor she had seen him in heaven and that his work there was to help people enter it from their earthly existence, guiding the sick and dying to the "other side."

She tried to explain to him that in the other realm we were all made of consciousness. We appear there as vibration and color and move on these vibrations and on our thoughts. Our movements in the world are directed by intention, and we move on vibrations or energy waves, often orchestrated by some aspect of the overseeing principle that is within us and all around us. She no longer worried about death. She only wanted to give others the same sense of grace she had experienced in death and continued to feel having come back to life.

New Information

The woman my friend told me about lived for several more months, sharing with people around her the story of her arrival in heaven and our amazing existence there as colorful vibrations of energy. My friend often relayed to me conversations he had with her as he continued her care, and several of her statements about her post-death experience especially caught my attention.

I was particularly struck that not only is there no hell, but that everyone on Earth is already in the "heavenly" realm. The woman's account taught me that we don't die and go to heaven; we are already there.

As she spoke with my friend, she freely acknowledged that everything about the other world differed radically from what her previous belief system had led her to expect, having been raised as a Christian and, as an adult, "reborn" into the Christian faith. After that rebirth, she had felt that her main job was to convert other people to the teachings of her church so that they would be saved after they died. She had passionately believed this.

I was fascinated that someone who had been on such a mission now deeply believed in an egalitarian heaven where everyone—people of all religions, all believers and unbelievers, all those who had done good and bad during their earthly lives—dwelled together. I found her drastic change of heart and thought inexplicable in terms of a rational, intellectual shift in her religious ideas. Such a reasoned reversal of her earlier beliefs seemed impossible to me. But her new spiritual perceptions of human and post-life existence were charged with the deepest feeling and surety, the emotional certainty that comes only with lived experience.

I believed she truly had experienced what is called *grace.*

Single and Apart

I was also captivated by something else she said: that souls could exist in the heavenly oneness she described but still have their own unique thoughts. This is to say that our souls are in complete oneness and unity but also have the capacity to act somewhat independently—always with a smidge of oversight.

It seemed to me that the enigma of individual consciousness in the realm of ultimate unity mirrored a mystery in our present world of earthly, human existence. We are all a product and a living part of the global ecosystem that is our world, which appears to be a single, if indescribable or unfathomable, multidimensional organism of fantastic size and scope. We speak and think for ourselves as autonomous individuals within this breathing envelope of greater organic being, in which each of us is only one of countless beings.

On Earth, just like the dying woman's experience of heaven, we are each unique and at the same time only a living particle in a vast biological environment, the great web of life on this planet and beyond.

But I was still having difficulty understanding how in either realm we could be semiautonomous *and* one with all the things around us. I returned to my earlier visualization of the Venn diagram, which joins apparently discrete sets and their constituent elements in a greater circle. I then remembered the separate suborganelles that collectively bring life to the cells that make up our bodies and, in a sense, *are* our bodies.

An Analogy

Advancements in nanotechnology—the art of manipulating materials on a very small scale in order to build microscopic machinery—have led medical researchers to discover that each of our cells has a unique "voice" and living identity.

Each cell has a consciousness, with its own special work to do and the free will to function in its specialized task. As we discussed earlier, each suborganelle acts independently as well as cooperatively. This begs to look even smaller again and ask whether the suborganelles also are somewhat autonomous, with their own unique consciousness. Living cells understand and follow an overarching principle of collaboration that has allowed humans and animals to adapt and thrive in changing environments.

Cells contain within themselves separate, freely operating organisms that together make up the greater organism of which they are a part. One thing that makes each individual so much bigger than the summation of its subparts is the power of numbers: all its components with their unique experiences and inputs. It is the combination of unique individuality and inseparable unity that gives us our unsuspected potential.

I began to extend the analogy between the vast cooperation among single, "multi-thinking" cells with their own self-directed inner suborganelles, and the uniqueness within unity of both individual human and heavenly beings or souls. Please also be aware that in both scenarios— the small cells as they relate to our body and we small human beings as we relate to the whole of Creation—there is an organizing principle that keeps all of life functioning correctly and headed toward a positive outcome.

We get up each day and experience ourselves as different and separate beings from our fellow citizens, with our own thoughts and feelings and special objectives and agendas. But when we drive to work, our cars all travel the same highways that interconnect our cities and towns. The network of roads we use to arrive at our individual jobs can be compared to the arterial venous system within our own bodies. We use the same avenues to reach the workplaces where we begin our different tasks that together keep the larger economic entity alive and functioning.

As an exercise in metaphor, I imagined human individuals as the white blood cells that circulate through our bodies, detecting, consuming, and destroying threatening bacteria and viruses.

Our white blood cells break down foreign organisms in our bodies that cause discomfort and disease. They absorb, process, and harmonize the agents of infection so they cannot harm us. The white cells undergo an important "learning experience," allowing them to become stronger and more effective, and perhaps to evolve.

Once white blood cells discover how to disarm and destroy specific bacteria, they remember the experience. This new information is shared energetically through an invisible conduit with all other white blood cells that together act as one united organism. Now the larger organism the white cells protect and serve is no longer vulnerable to damaging effects caused by these negative agents or traits.

You could say that like white blood cells, we're each the guardians, monitors, and maintainers of the existence we all share.

Spiritual Blood Cells

Now, if we expand our metaphor from the physical to the spiritual realm, we can imagine that our special work as "spiritual white blood cells" is to gobble up and harmonize our own portion of the destructive chaos in Creation.

Perhaps the chaos and stress we feel inside ourselves is part of Creation's struggle and chaos: the harmful emotional baggage and inner conflict that cause harmful effects within us and Creation itself. To be successful spiritual infection fighters, we need to identify the imbalances within ourselves and, through our efforts of thought and action, create harmony and spiritual health where there are division and emotional suffering.

In each of the events I've talked about, the only imperative for humanity is to learn a way to let go and harmonize the things that create stress. From my years of work as a counselor and hypnotherapist, I've found that everyone's issues boil down to the fear of not being good enough and the wish to feel connected. You can take any issue—abandonment, betrayal, guilt, shame, and more—and it leads you to this same end point. The opposing end point is the way people feel when they are connected to the energetic or spiritual realm. In our work as human beings we are constantly endeavoring to be more like the soul I have described. Never have I been a party to a postmortem interview or deep hypnotic life-between-life session where our greatest effort was not to transform humanity into something more kind, tolerant, and loving. The other objective that seems to occupy much of our time in the heavenly realm as well as here on Earth is to enjoy the process and play.

A Few Hints

I believe we will have a better chance of approaching the distant goal of even partially understanding Creation, the cosmos, and ourselves if we think on a *much* larger scale. We have and will continue to makes mistakes if we limit our thinking to our human experience and our five senses.

We must not think of ourselves as the main subject of the universe or believe that our present abilities indicate we have reached the highest level of our possible evolution. We will do better.

What I have learned tells me that we will do better if we think of God as a living process and not as a static thing. This is why I have suggested replacing the word God or "Creator" with the words "Creation"—or better yet, the verb form, "Creating."

That said, I believe that humanity is part of the process of the Universe's unfolding, ongoing "becoming," and that our actions are of the utmost importance. We are in relationship with the outcome of humanity and, more importantly, Creation. I have always enjoyed the Jewish concept that we have the power to add lines to God's face or take them off. Keeping with that metaphor, I often wonder if we give Creation a "stomachache" when humankind is at war with itself. This might help me understand the motivation that "the Creating" has to resolve the chaos within itself.

Will Science Still Be an Enemy?

I believe science will someday "prove" the existence of "God." In fact, it may have already. The progressive people in religion have always embraced science as a foundational part of the truth and commonly look for the intersection of science and religion. They might see the seven days of creation as the story of evolution because they are open to learning through metaphor. If a person resonates more with conservative orthodox literal interpretations, there is little space for a happy meeting ground where religion and science coexist. In order for the world to accept proof of God, it will need to talk to science. I truly believe that day is coming, but God will not be a Lord or a white-haired man up on Mount Olympus. The new picture that takes shape will make many people very uncomfortable. It will take generations to internalize this new and hopefully evolving picture of the thing we call God and our place as multidimensional beings. We may not be the center of the universe, with a green light to abuse the planet as we see fit. All of our negative actions may have consequences that we once thought we could escape, as well as positive ones that we will rejoice in.

If and when this time comes, perhaps science and religion will merge in a happy union.

5

SCIENCE—THE EVOLUTION OF CONSCIOUSNESS

Building the Pyramid

Now I'd like to present and review some relevant recent discoveries and insights from the frontiers of modern science to place my experiences, thoughts, and hypotheses in a context of detectable physical phenomena confirmed by cutting-edge researchers in biology and other scientific fields.

A number of exciting advances in scientific knowledge offer important clues concerning:

- The nature and structure of mind and body and their communications with one another
- Evolution and the likely inheritance of acquired characteristics
- Our shared identity with living and inorganic entities
- The entanglement of time and distance
- The similarity of structures and forms throughout the universe and their mutual interactions
- Building the framework for better understanding how Creation can communicate and may help orchestrate our biological and mental functions

Though the research is diverse, our goal remains the same: to examine how the universe functions and evolves so we can catch sight of our human purpose within the cosmos.

In the previous chapter I discussed the main work of humanity as described by all of the people who were able to speak from a soul's perspective or had recently died and come back. I feel strongly that function easily reveals our purpose. In this chapter we will examine our body's evolutionary makeup that helps predict our ultimate function. It is my belief that your form is perhaps the greatest predictor of your function and purpose. To a student of evolution, one thing is very clear: if you don't use it, you'll lose it. The corollary to this is that if something exists, it has a purpose and is being used. The very way in which we are constructed and operate is the best and simplest way to unravel all that we are, why we're here, and perhaps our intrinsic connection to something bigger.

A New Map

We begin with human cells and some of the ways they communicate with one another to maintain the human body.

I learned throughout my science education that cells receive vital communications from the master organ, the brain. Messages are sent to and received by the cells through pathways of neurons, and by the release of neurochemicals and hormones through the glandular system, whose operations are orchestrated by the brain. This scientific model is tidy and compact but does not explain how our body reacts so quickly and efficiently to outside stimuli.

Researchers have discovered that all of the cells of the body seem to react to stimuli almost immediately, before the brain can receive, register, and analyze the new information and then respond with appropriate orders to the affected cells.

The old model of the brain as the master director of the cells via its communication networks can no longer account for nearly instantaneous bodily responses that are too fast to be traceable to a governing source beyond the stimulated cells themselves.

When researchers stimulated motor function at a point in the brain that corresponded to the contraction of the fingers, there was a measurable time delay that made sense: a certain amount of time is needed to conduct information down nerves and jump from the axon of one nerve to the dendrite of another and then continue down this path. However, if you hit your thumb with a hammer, it should take the same measurable amount of time for the central nervous system to interpret what has occurred and quickly create a pain response. A reflex can occur sooner because stimuli such as this only need to go to the spinal cord and back to the muscles of the arm to retract away from pain.

Here's the fun part: there is a simultaneous awareness of and response to the effects of this trauma in the brain and in all other body cells. There is a coordinated effort by the community of cells in your body to help with the healing of this area. All of this awareness and attention to the injured area happens before the old neuron-and-neurochemical system can work. This indicates that another mechanism is occurring, and a system that acts like a simultaneous communication grid might even have additional abilities we had not foreseen.

Thinking Cells

Dr. Candace Pert made a revolutionary discovery years ago that shifted our thinking about neurochemicals. Our tidy model indicating that all thinking was centered in the brain caused us to believe that all neurochemicals also had to be created in brain cells. That's why we named them "neuro" chemicals. This makes sense when you believe that only brain cells have the capacity for thought. I'm not sure if Pert had a gut feeling that all cells of the body can create neurochemicals and therefore can make decisions or if she said, "Hey, let's test what we *don't* think is true just to make sure we are not missing something here"; sometimes it's good to look where you don't want to look because you just might find the truth there. I believe it was her premise that all cells were sentient and could communicate with each other using neurochemicals.

Pert found that certain tissues had more interaction than others. The immune system, for example, has great abilities to communicate with the rest of the body. This makes sense since it's one of the most important systems in the body. I am thankful to her for expanding our understanding through science.

Current research goes even further in explaining how the cells of the body think and respond autonomously. They act both individually and together to receive appropriate signals from the brain and central nervous system.

Fritz-Albert Popp was one of the early pioneers in the research into "thinking cells."[1] His work helps us understand the relationships between cells' individual intelligence and how that collective information is perceived by the overarching unified intelligence and consciousness of the body's larger organism.

Popp studied the light energy emitted by single cells, called biophotonic light. A photon is a little bit of energy that gives off light. Another way to think of it is something like a radio wave that carries light with it. It is energy in the form of a wavelength. Biophotonic light is light energy given off by living things. It's like the radio wave that gives us the quality of light but also carries information within itself. Popp's research showed that this light is dynamic, changing as it mirrors what the single cell experiences, a microsecond at a time. In other words, as the experience of the cell changes, the communication within the biophotonic light changes, which in turn changes the quality of the biophotonic light.

Popp believed that embedded in this biophotonic light was information, a form of communication, theorizing that the biophotonic light was a means of transferring data.

Cells also emit sound, and these "cell sounds" are dynamic, indicating the depth of the "conversation."[2] All of this information going out to the rest of the body echoes the present experience of each individual cell.

Cells' production of their own information through light and sound suggests that the cell may be the body's elemental form or center of consciousness. The differentiated consciousness of each cell becomes a part of a mysterious unity of trillions of thinking and "speaking" single cells that together make up human consciousness.

The Cloud or Unified Field

I think Popp's research helps us visualize the mechanism that allows different cells to simultaneously understand everything occurring in the body and join in a coordinated effort to heal the body through specific targeting and effective treatment of injured cells. This new picture of conscious cells communicating with and aiding one another for mutual protection and survival shows the human body as a cooperative unity made up of countless parts working together for one overarching goal.

Each body cell is apparently in continuous and simultaneous communication with every other cell, processing and integrating millions of bits of information in a charged field of information and knowledge that produces immediate and appropriate responses to identified stimuli.

The cells' ability to immediately signal one another and join in unified actions comes from them experiencing all of the information in "the cloud." This model of information storage is much like the construction of an electron field. An electron is not a thing but a form of energy or a charge that is held around the nucleus. In a sense, electrons are much like the light that emanates from the sun; they are everywhere.

I like to think of this communications network as a quantum field of energy, a cloud of constantly moving and interacting subatomic collections of energy embedded with information producing consciousness. These particles aren't tethered to the macro, earthly dimension of physicality where large objects push and pull and collide with one another, but are relatively unstructured and fluid in their characteristics and movements, like a kind of electrified fog.

I sometimes imagine that all this omnipresent activity of information transfer forms a permeable bubble that surrounds us. Outside stimuli enter this "information aura," what I like to think of as the "original i-Cloud," and are immediately processed. Within this aura, information does not travel at the speed of light but exists everywhere so that it reaches all the cells at the same time. How is that possible?

Many of the boundaries of space we know in our macro world may not exist in the subatomic quantum world, which is wildly different from our "analog" or macro world of here and there, before and after. An i-Cloud or aura may operate like the electrons around the nucleus of an atom, in a subatomic dance of potentials whose location and speed can't be simultaneously determined by observation, and whose future activity remains only a probability.

The underlying concept is that all events within the body are experienced by all of the body's cells simultaneously, in one spontaneous sharing of information. Each cell knows the information at the same time, and there is no hierarchy or precedence, no "waiting line" among the cells for receiving information. All cells are equal recipients in time, regardless of their location or function.

Subtle Messages

Modern physics first described the electron as a defined unit with definite boundaries. It was a "finite particle," like a ball bearing, and at any chosen second had a distinct location and velocity, like a jet on a radarscope.

This stable model of electrons and their activity resembled billiard balls moving across a green felt table. It gave a clear and reassuring diagram that our minds could easily comprehend. The world was concrete, mapped by compass points, and time flowed in only one direction, from the past to the future. It was comforting to believe that electrons behaved as solid objects do in our everyday world. But this portrait wasn't accurate.

Physicists now know that electrons more closely resemble "probability waves" and have the potential to occupy many places at one time. They exist in a kind of ethereal or ghostly state in their relationships to the nucleus of the atom and other particles. The electron can be described as being "everywhere" rather than "somewhere." When we view electrons in this way, it helps us understand or prove how information is processed and instantly shared by all the cells in our body.

Communication for Healing

Knowing this, how can we verify that the cells are communicating with each other? How do we know that the biophotonic light each cell gives off is in fact embedded with information? Fritz Popp described a phenomenon called "photon sucking."[3] His study looked at the transfer of biophotonic light from one cell or group of cells to the cells receiving that light: there was an immediate response in the receiving cells that indicated with a high degree of probability that the light contained information.

Popp did a multitude of experiments where he used information that emanated from living cells from the same organism or from plants and substances that had physiological benefits for the cells being observed. In each of his experiments he was able to see reactions to the information that came to the observed cell via biophotonic light.

He postulated that each cell and its component parts wanted to communicate and act in a simultaneous relationship with all other cells and their cell parts.[4] The cells intrinsically relied upon other cells to maintain their own health and the health of the body as a whole.

Can we extrapolate from this research about cellular information transfer anything about the ways people and animals transfer information nonverbally?

Popp asked this very question. He was curious about how moving schools of fish like herring and anchovies could react and change direction and speed spontaneously, as a single unit that seemingly had a single brain. These animals and others rely on forms of communication based on instinct and intuition, a method that is more intimate than human speech.

Although humans primarily depend on words, we too can quickly gather nonverbal information through the five senses and communicate it without words or rational thought. For example, nonverbal transfers of information may explain how children learn and adapt so much about their parents' thoughts and belief systems very early in life.

Cells in our bodies may communicate in a similar way. If both thought and instinctual knowing are light in the form of the biophotonic light given off by cells, then wordless communication travels at the speed of light or takes place in an omnipresence field that overcomes vast distances and makes the physical separation between sender and receiver insignificant.

The piece of the puzzle we often miss is that consciousness is in the form of energy. Most people realize that the information that is our thoughts certainly does not consist of solid objects or even particles. Thoughts and information are in an energetic form. We now begin to play with the connection between thoughts as emanations of energy, and that this energy may have information as its building blocks. We could go even further and speculate: if the cells' emitted energy didn't contain consciousness, would it exist or would it revert back to nothing? Biophotonic light by definition seems to carry information with it or may simply *be* information.

I believe that light as a byproduct of life is consciousness and that each cell emits its present status continuously into the "cloud." Just as sound waves, mechanical heat, and light are the byproducts of the trunk of a tree cracking and falling in a forest, biophotonic light is given off when we have a thought. The nature or quality of the light may be determined by the information the thought carries, and by our feelings and belief systems attached to that information. It is a universal language that all organic and inorganic things share in common.

For the light to create a unique structure, it must carry within it a unique message. We may someday discover more about this language: how it works and who participates in it. More research will be done in this area now that we believe these possibilities exist. We will need to look at how specific information and attendant emotions and ideas structure the light—the thought's manifestation—and produce the light's individual characteristics. The very structure of the light is the alphabet, symbols, feelings, and potential sounds of the language.

Written in Water

Fritz Popp also wanted to understand how cells communicate so efficiently. He believed that homeopathic remedies and other medicines determine both their usefulness and the speed and scope of their activity.[5] Homeopathic treatments are formulated by adding a substance to water, with the intention of inserting or "downloading" the substance's "information" or its chemical and structural identity into the water. The homeopathic remedy can either be ingested as a liquid or with the liquid infused into a sugar pill.

The key to homeopathic medicinal preparations is water because water is an extremely malleable, special substance. Water has the capacity to store information within it, much like the embedded consciousness that light contains. It can share stored information with other substances and even living organisms. After this, the water continues to emit information until it is infused with new information or consciousness. Water is in a constant state of receiving and integrating information. In this way, water shows us so much about its nature and the nature of all things.

The hallmark of homeopathic theory is that the more dilute the solution, the stronger and more effective it is. Increased strength through dilution, meaning more water and less substance, magnifies the properties of the solution. This notion runs counter to our sense of logic.

We must consider the physics here. The more "elemental" a substance's structure is, the more strength it has. Atomic bombs that break apart subatomic particles within atoms make bigger explosions than chemical bombs that break apart bonds between molecules, which are chains of atoms.

Homeopathic remedies avoid big clumsy groups of physical molecules. Instead, energetic signals from individual molecules are downloaded into the recording mechanism of the water. Information containing the molecules' clearly defined structure and chemical characteristics is carried by the signal and transferred to the water. The solution is very pure and potent. The homeopathic belief is that water changes its structure as a function of the new information carried by the light.

For illustration purposes, imagine the water as a DVD disk, and the biophotonic light is etched in circular lines on the previously blank disk. The lines of recorded light information have a specific stamp, signature, or pattern representing the structure of individual molecules. The surface of the disk now contains the structure of the information etched onto it. That information is converted into sounds and pictures and is then transmitted to a television or computer.

Now imagine that same disk is erased as it simultaneously receives the input of a new recording. To the naked eye that lacks the ability to see the internal structure, the "reprogrammed" disk would look identical to its previous state when it contained different information. To our eyes, water may look like water, but the information it receives is constantly changing and its internal structure follows.

Smaller but Stronger

The homeopathic theory of using something small to produce a large result was studied by Jacques Benveniste and his team.[6] He wanted to show that a substance becomes stronger and more energetically pure when a smaller quantity of it is mixed or downloaded into water. Benveniste used a very dilute solution of immunoglobulin (IgE), a substance the body produces to fight infection. This solution contained one molecule of the immunoglobulin and a huge number of water molecules (10 to the 60th power). Numerically, it looks like this:

1 molecule of the substance to

1,000,000,000,000,000,000,000,000,000,000,000,000,000,00 0, 000,000, 000,000,000,000 molecules of water.

This is achieved by adding the substance to water and shaking (or succussing) the solution. A tenth of that water is taken out and added to nine more parts of pure water and succussed once again. This is done repeatedly until the target dilution is achieved.

Here is how the team's experiment went. The immunoglobulin E activates a basophil, a white blood cell, when they come into contact with each other. But in this experiment only "energetic emanations" of this immunoglobulin E and its collective molecules would be found in the water. It stands to reason that the chances of one molecule of immunoglobulin E measurably affecting the makeup of that much water would be nonexistent. But when this solution containing the energetic signature of the immunoglobulin E was added to living white blood cells or basophils, the cells responded more dramatically than if they had been exposed to large numbers of undiluted intact immunoglobulin molecules.

Research has shown that a molecule's vibration, or sound that has information or an energetic signal embedded in it, is 100 times more powerful than signals produced by the physical substance itself.[7] The potential here is very significant. The first thing that comes to mind for me is that someday we will be taking pills that contain vibratory messages in order to effect change in our bodies. We may be able to achieve the positive effects of pharmaceuticals without the negative effects of those same substances. This may greatly relieve us of the side effects of most pharmaceuticals.

This is also great proof that our cells communicate efficiently through a quantum or energetic conversation within the cloud or field of the body. This opens up the possibility of a mechanism by which we have a sense about the people we meet. Interestingly enough, we use the expression "I picked up their good vibe" (or vibration); maybe we have known this vibrational communication was taking place all along. I will take this one step further into the possibilities we will find in the future. The same mechanism cells use to receive information from substances and from each other gives us a pathway to how our soul and Creation/God communicate to us, feel us, and animate us.

As we go on with this information, I want you to keep in mind that there are mechanisms of communication and connection in the quantum and energetic realm/dimensions. We must also be open to what energy is, how it may come about, what it is made of, and finally how it is made. Much of the point of this chapter is to expand the possibilities of what may be found through advances in science. We are currently unknowing partners in these dimensions, though most of us have a sense that there is something more than we presently know.

Everything Is Talking

Science now presents us with a new picture: every molecule, whether inorganic or a part of a larger organic living thing, is constantly emanating sound that is measured in hertz. This vibration or voice carries information with it. Homeopathy professionals were the first to realize the effects of utilizing the vibrations of plants, minerals, and animals to harmonize the vibrational resonance of their patients. The homeopathic belief system is that humans lose their harmonic resonance through stress, trauma, chemical exposure, and the like, and that the use of synchronizing substances found in nature can bring a patient back into their unique vibrational homeostasis. Knowing that every substance has a vibration and that the pure vibrational message is infinitely more powerful when separated from the large, bulky physical substance, it is only a matter of time before we are using the vibrational signatures of medicines and other substances to treat many more ailments then even homeopaths envisioned.

Scientists are using sophisticated microphones that can hear and record these low-level vibrations. These emanations are quite simple to explain. Everything has electrons and protons; everything therefore has electromagnetic movement and will create an electromagnetic field. Inorganic substances give off a vibration or information that is much more consistent than organic/biological organisms, which are more dynamic. Currently this is where we draw the line between living and nonliving things.

Research into homeopathy shows that nonliving things have an energetic signal that can be recorded, transmitted, and understood by the cells of the body. This receptivity to energetic messages suggests that our body is in constant, nontactile communication with its environment— both living and nonliving sources of energy.

Our cells, bodies, and consequently our consciousness are forever involved in a kind of subatomic dance with the energetic information that is emitted all around us by everything in our immediate environment, and perhaps from energy sources far beyond it. We are active participants in an unending information exchange with all that surrounds us, and are mutating and evolving with these thought energies that are dynamic and fill the world beyond our immediate bodies.

We are not separate from the animate and inanimate intelligences in our surroundings but are in a mutual relationship of co-creation with them. You might even say we in some sense *are* our surroundings and our surroundings are us.

Everyone and everything is an active participant in this system of energy and information exchange that is exceedingly efficient and has a nearly infinite potential for effective and extremely varying intercommunication. This new knowledge of our interconnectedness and intercommunication adds greatly to the hypothesis about how parts of our body supposedly signal and respond to one another.

It's my belief that if we were not active participants in this information system, we would not have adapted to changes in our environment and would not have survived as a species.

Necessary Speed

The old idea that the central nervous system is the command post and transmitter of all communication to and among the cells describes a system that would be too mechanical, slow, and narrow in its range of activities to be sufficiently responsive and effective in meeting sudden environmental challenges.

Just describing the linear process of cell communication sounds clunky and laborious, whether the means of information transfer is electrical or chemical or both. The brain sends out a request for information through nerves to the various cells of the body, where nerve receptors gather information and send it back to the brain, which now analyzes the information, decides on a proper response, and sends "orders" to the cells to begin the proper actions or processes.

We've already considered Candace Pert's revolutionary discovery that body cells have the ability to create, send, and receive neurochemical messages, and that in carrying out their work they make sounds that are important communications to other cells. We've touched on only a very small portion of current research concerning the different structures and modulations of light that cells, proteins, molecules, minerals, and homeopathic medications emit. We've reviewed research suggesting that biophotonic light is information. We now will explore current theories regarding biophotonic light as consciousness.

New World

Scientists who construct theories to describe and explain cellular communications first look for a mechanism through which these communications can conceivably occur. For example, we can understand that the human ear is structured as an organ designed to hear external sounds. Cellular messaging mechanisms, on the other hand, inhabit a universe of infinitesimal scale far different from our physical existence in large human bodies.

As we shift our focus to the supermicroscopic, elemental, undifferentiated world of cellular communications, we must be cautious. We are entering a dimension where discrete mechanical entities performing mechanical tasks are not required, and where cell organelles and their functions aren't needed to explain how communications are formulated, directed, sent, and received. The messaging operations in the quantum world are at a minimum different in appearance and function from those in the macro world but are wildly more efficient and do not need highly differentiated organelles.

The world of quantum mechanics and energy consciousness allows for mechanically generated, linear sequences of communication transfer to be transcended. Strange, nearly magical immediate exchanges of energy and information may occur among particles that change position, speed, and shape yet share aspects of identity with surrounding particles in a shadowy, energized cloud of dynamic relationships.

As the great Irish poet William Butler Yeats wrote, "How can we know the dancer from the dance?" This is a miniscule environment where time can flow in different directions and beginnings and endings, sources and destinations may be difficult if not impossible to disentangle and clearly identify. Cause and effect may become relative. "Triggering events" are perhaps simultaneous, or even subsequent, to their results, so that operations may not be predictable or consistent, and processes may appear evident only after their completion. The quantum world is an existence that has escaped the limitations and confines of its intrinsic chaos.

Consciousness Fields

In biology we observe that undifferentiated forms of life are infinitely more capable of certain unlikely biological functions than are more differentiated and complex organisms. The college biology class dissection of Platyhelminthes worms made a lasting impact on me. No matter how small I cut those worms into pieces, each sliver of flesh grew back into a full worm.

Studies in human physiology note that newborn babies who lose a finger through injury are sometimes able to regrow the finger, because the infants' stem cells still retain an elemental "undifferentiation." Adults are incapable of regrowing lost body parts because their stem cells have become differentiated, turning into specific kinds of cells with specific functions.

These examples are another reminder that elemental structures have a kind of purity and simplicity; their small scale and generic clarity of construction allow potential transformations to exist and become active, possibilities usually denied larger, more complex configurations.

All of these examples from biology remind us that the further we go into the elemental and subatomic world, the more interchangeable and slippery things become, not constrained by our macro world thinking. It is in this world where the rules we are accustomed to no longer exist. It is my hope that all of these examples help our minds consider what *is* instead of obeying the limitations we observe in our well-differentiated macro world. Keeping this all in mind, let's go a little deeper.

Lynne McTaggert, in her book *The Field,* highlights the research of cutting-edge scientists of the last century and concludes that fields of consciousness are responsible for cellular communication.

McTaggert describes the work of Fritz-Albert Popp and other researchers that has contributed to a modern theory of how biophotonic communication works.[8]

Each body cell emits biophotonic light, and each cell has microtubules, intercellular filaments responsible for various kinds of movement within cells. Cell communication scientists concentrated their research on the microtubules of neurons, cells capable of sending electrical and chemical messages, and their dendrites, branchlike projections that propagate these messages. Targeting neurons and dendrites for study indicates that these scientists wanted to delve into the theory that consciousness is centered in the central nervous system.

Microtubules

The microtubules of neurons and dendrites are somewhat akin to the individual pipes of a pipe organ, with each pipe's sound being determined by its length and diameter. But the microtubules are all the same size. This would indicate that a specific sound will be made when the dimensions are all uniform. The water molecules in and around the microtubules are also carefully ordered and sized. There are 10,000 water molecules for every protein in the cell in which the microtubules are found. This proportion of water is very high and alludes to the special function of water in these areas.

The structured relationship of microtubules and water molecules creates coherent emissions of biophotonic light, preventing the messages within the light from deteriorating and allowing for long-distance travel. This protection of embodied information over time and distance recalls the conservative properties of laser light. It is also very important that the light is fed into the field of one's body in the form of coherent light/ information. One's electromagnetic field operates on a quantum level and cannot integrate analog information. It is no different from new television sets that only receive digital signals and can no longer operate on analog information from a simple antenna. The information that is communicated between cells through this process of structuring the information in a coherent form is what can give living organisms much greater potential for healing and effortless communication.

According to cell communication theory, McTaggert writes, the microtubules within neurons and their dendrites may make up a kind of "Internet of the body." Theoretically, every neuron of our brain could "log on" at the same time and simultaneously speak to every other neuron via the quantum process that governs cell communication.

McTaggert describes a study in which "discordant" energy was fed into microtubules. Discordant energy has variations, often in mutual opposition or incongruity.[9] The microtubules were monitored and found to transform the discordant energy into coherent signals. Those signals were then transmitted to the rest of the body, creating a global coherence of information assimilation: a process called "super-radiance." Once coherence was achieved throughout the body, photons could travel at will all along the microtubules, as if these "light pipes" were transparent. This phenomenon, called "self-induced transparency," allowed the photons free, unobstructed passage through the body at the speed of light. This process creates instantaneous "omni-sentience," each of the body's cells having a simultaneous awareness of the same, distinct information.

Photons (alias biophotons) can penetrate the core of the microtubule and communicate with other photons throughout the body, creating a collective cooperation of subatomic particles in the microtubules throughout the brain. If such a superconnected, unified communication system is the body's mechanism for sending and receiving messages, this can account for the unity of thought that is our human consciousness.

As we learn more about this well-designed system uniting each body cell, we find ourselves confronted with new questions:

- Do the functions of super-radiance and self-induced transparency end with communications among our cells?
- Are these observed phenomena that allow for simultaneous messaging and receiving active in events occurring beyond our immediate bodies?
- Is there input from a source greater than us that helps orchestrate the higher functioning of our bodies? We can now see that the mechanisms for such communication are in place.

Super-radiance and transparency give us the potential for a subtle, instant communications system between our individual consciousness and those of other humans and living beings. This also reminds us that there is a pathway of communication through the quantum realm that opens up other possibilities of oversight of our health, high mental and spiritual functioning, and even our own evolution. It may be that there is so much going on that our conscious minds and five senses are incapable of picking it all up. It is possible to explain many biological mysteries if we take this into account. In the next section we will continue to build a pyramid of knowledge that makes all of this discussion even more feasible. Let us look further into the mechanism that may keep us connected to this seemingly magical field of information, oversight, healing, and perhaps even compassion.

SURPRISES REVEALED IN THE CRYSTALLINE MATRIX

Entangled Serpents

Years ago I came upon a book that introduced possible mechanisms of communication between human beings, other animals, and Universal Consciousness. Something about this theory rang true for me. Interestingly enough, more recent research further corroborates this idea. This research into biophotonic energy, consciousness, and super-radiance is still in its infancy, but I am certain these discoveries will be place markers in human understanding of how life sustains itself in our bodies and the communication pathways that exist beyond human senses.

Jeremy Narby, author of *The Cosmic Serpent,* hypothesized that humans could communicate with nature, other human beings, and even a "universal consciousness" through the crystalline matrix of DNA. DNA, deoxyribonucleic acid, is the self-replicating material present in all living things and is the carrier of our genetic information.[1] DNA takes the form of a double helix, which looks like a twisted ladder. Narby interviewed and studied data on shamans: traditional healers from native cultures who utilize an intuitive connection with the forest and Universal Consciousness to combine herbs and plants to heal the sick. He noted that shamans all over the world reported a vision of two snakes coiled about one another just before beginning their intuitive healing work.

These entwined snakes also resemble the caduceus or "herald's staff" carried by Hermes, the messenger of the gods in Greek mythology. The short staff entwined by two facing snakes and sometimes surmounted by wings provides our emblem for medicine. This was the hint for Narby about the connection between DNA and traditional shamans. The idea he put forth was that so-called "junk DNA" that geneticists thought there was no use for was indeed being used for this communication. Nearly all of the animal kingdom shares identical junk DNA. This formation creates a precise matrix much like quartz or any other crystal.

I'd put together a quartz radio as a child, and I remembered how the radio's inner contents were simply wires connected to two sides of a quartz crystal. These wires led to the tuner, amplifier, and then speakers. I was perplexed by the magic of this. When I inquired about this apparent mystery, a teacher informed me that the secret of the radio was the structure or matrix within the stone.

The people we consider shamans and modern-day intuitives are people who may use so-called junk DNA. This may offer a clue as to how humans, and all living beings, could conceivably interface with the echo of information known to mystics and cosmologists as Universal Consciousness and inner wisdom. If the DNA essentially functions like the quartz crystal in the radio, then we are active receivers and senders of information within a vast field of energy and consciousness that permeates the entire universe.

Shamans and intuitives can create a pathway to this information. They have learned to quiet the left brain and the swirling thoughts of the ego, and open up to intuition, which we associate with right-brain functioning. The mechanism for sending and receiving this information may come through this crystalline matrix that we find in DNA and other places in the body. It would be interesting if visions of the intertwined snakes were a clue to help our left brain understand what our right brain has always known.

A living, thinking, and communicating unified universe has been described for thousands of years by nearly all of the world's religions and many philosophers, and it is a model now entertained by some physicists. The underlying message from all of them is that we are all "one" and we are all "entangled." Somehow there have always been connections that make us inseparable.

Who's in Charge?

Bruce Lipton, a gifted microbiologist, wrote about his cloning research in the book *Spontaneous Evolution: Our Positive Future (And a Way to Get There from Here).*[2] Lipton removed the nuclei of cells from cloning fragments and, surprisingly, the cells continued to replicate as before— with no nucleus and no DNA. According to the basic tenets of cell biology, which thinks of the nucleus as the "brain" of the cell, that should be impossible; it would be like a human body functioning normally without its brain. Who or what could possibly be coordinating the necessary operations of a living cell that lacks its control center? Where was the vital information necessary for maintaining life and function coming from and how were communications received and put into action?

Cell Membrane

Lipton discovered that the actual "brain" behind cell function is the *cell membrane* and that our cell membranes fit the magic pattern of a liquid crystalline matrix.

The membrane is covered inside and out with a layer of protein receptors or activators. An insulating, hydrophobic layer of lipid or oily fat is housed between both protein "sheaths" and the membrane. This fatty, hydrophobic protein layer keeps things on the outside of the cell "outside" and things on the inside of the cell "inside."

The receptor proteins on the outside of the membrane receive a myriad of different bits of information about the ambient environment on the outside of the cell. They pass on this information through the fat layer, the cell membrane, and the inner layer of fat to the protein activators/receptors on the inside of the membrane.

The interior protein receptors/activators react and adapt to this information, altering the function, activity, and chemistry inside the cell. This communication between protein receptors on different sides of the membrane allows the cell to constantly adapt to the exterior environment.

The thousands of outer receptor proteins are each tuned to receive a different signal. Each receptor transfers clear messages of information for intelligent, informed reactions and adaptations to reactor proteins on the inside layer of the membrane.

An exterior receptor protein may have a certain shape and electrical charge that exactly matches a substance, be it neurochemical, vitamin, or cofactor, circulating in the bloodstream. That matching substance can attach to the receptor protein like a living key fitting into a living, "fluid" lock. The receptor protein now changes its charge, which changes its shape and sends a signal through the cell membrane to an inner reactor protein that passes the signal onward into the interior of the cell.

An energetic signal that is sent by a substance outside the cell, received by one or more of the protein receptors, and sent on to inner receptor proteins that forward the signal to the cell's interior does not become lost, although its "homing device" remains mysterious. Signals find their way to the proper receptor or activator sites without the need for physical alignment or a sufficiently "attractive" chemical concentration.

These signals may resemble the messages homing pigeons receive, in this case carried and attenuated by the water in the body, or as a probability wave in the body's field of consciousness. The biologist Richard Sheldrake's pigeons always found their home, even when they were blindfolded or the pigeon house was moved after their departure. (Sheldrake believed that "home" was calling to the pigeons.)[3]

I compare this amazing signaling activity to the workings of the Internet, which simultaneously gathers and organizes information from a multitude of sources and relays requested data to countless individual recipients instantaneously, as opposed to the old Pony Express, which passed letters from one galloping rider to the next in a long series before the mail reached its final destination.

Let's back up a little bit now so as not to miss the importance of cell reproduction without a nucleus. Cellular reproduction is one of the greatest miracles for it contemplates the very spark of life: the coordination of duplicating proteins and other suborganelles of the cell, then orchestrating the dance of mitosis, in which the cell must pull itself into two halves and every duplicate part of the new cells needs to know where to go and how to get there. If the nucleus isn't responsible for the exact intricacies that still befuddle modern science, then what is?

What Lipton is putting forth is that the cells can communicate with each other through the matrix that is created by the cell membranes. This very matrix may be what allows us to communicate with other people and perhaps species other than our own. The big piece that few if any wish to talk about is *where* the communication comes from that allows cells to continue their functioning for a prolonged period of time without the nucleus, which contains the DNA and RNA responsible for making new materials for cellular division. It seems that the cells would continue to grow and divide if there were enough proteins within the cell, and this would alleviate the need for the nucleus. So the question returns: what is coordinating the adapting and procreation of life if this function is not embedded inside the cell?

There is of course the possibility that in Lipton's cloning experiments, the cloned cells were somehow communicating back to the cells within the donor body. The other possibility is that the cell membranes are constantly in communication with the "innate" consciousness of the body that orchestrates its good health. This leads us to ask what innate consciousness is. Is it something unique to each individual's body, or is it just another term for the "consciousness of creation"? When I ask this question, the answer I get is that there is an individual aspect of our own innate consciousness that is a part of and gets great input from a farther-reaching, unknowable consciousness of creation. In this scenario we are again given the answer that things are unique and superficially independent but still unified and inseparable.

There are many inconceivably complex interactions that occur in the creation, maintenance, and adaptations of living organisms. The cell membrane can make many of the basal decisions that are programmed into their function. For example, if there are low concentrations of essential amino acids inside the cell and a higher concentration outside it, the cell membrane will actively bring them in. The cell membrane is also very good at managing electrolytes, sugar, hormones, and other substances. The question becomes, does the cell have the ability to take in multitudes of information and come up with new solutions for problems it has no history of solving? Solving problems beyond its own experience is a question of intelligence. I contend the cell has intelligence but not enough to orchestrate complex solutions or oversee the evolution of different species. This means the cell can solve some of its own problems but receives seamless input and oversight from another internal source of greater capacity. For example, Candace Pert found that membrane cells could increase or decrease the number of their neurochemical receptors in response to changing levels of neurochemicals or other drugs in the body. This is well within the capacities of the cells' own innate intelligence.[4]

Acquired Characteristics Survive

Here's the interesting part: Candace Pert discovered that parent cells could pass on the cell membrane's adaptations in receptor quantity to their offspring. When she discovered an increase in receptor sites for neurotransmitters on the cell membrane as a result of a person's thoughts, experiences, and needs, and that those life changes were passed on to their children, this gave us another example of in vitro evolution. The ability to bestow acquired characteristics upon progeny allows for high-speed evolution and adaptability to a rapidly changing environment. In other words, we evolve during our own life because cellular changes are permanent for us as well as our progeny.

This strange phenomenon flies in the face of more than 150 years of accepted scientific law that began with Charles Darwin's theory of evolution and natural selection and Gregor Mendel's discovery of genetics.

One instantly begins to sense the looming shadow of the long-discredited biologist Jean-Baptiste Lamarck, the pre-Darwinian who believed that evolution was based on an interaction between the environment, the body, and the consciousness of the adapting species. His opponents claimed he believed that the intentions and consciousness of the individual played into that evolution. An example was the pre-giraffe that stretched its neck higher and higher to reach uneaten food that was just out of its reach. Its progeny, which wished to gain access to this untouched food source when lower-hanging food was overgrazed, could influence evolution by having a longer neck.

Is it true that DNA can be "consciously" changed and then duplicated in new generations? What proof do we have that the experience and needs of the predecessor are passed on to the next generation?

The work of Candace Pert and others has shown that as living individuals we continually evolve during our own lifetime, and that we can pass on the adaptations that we undergo through sexual reproduction. Our newly formed characteristics are passed on to our offspring.

The crux of Darwin's evolution theory is that random "natural" mutations occur very infrequently and the chance of these very rare mutations being beneficial is very rare. Let's take the bat, for example. This animal hasn't been around for that long. It started as a common rodent but grew skin flaps between its arms and legs. According to Darwin this extra skin in its early phases must still be an evolutionary advantage. It must also extend the long bones in its fingers and arms to hold the new skin rigid. The bones must become more lightweight and the bat must develop sonar for night flight. These changes are examples of the extreme specificity of evolution on our planet. In order to get these few positive mutations, the "pre-bat" would have to go through millions and millions of mutations that went horribly wrong, and its progeny would simply fail. Given the rate of mutation in general and the rate of positive ones, there simply is not enough time for a pre-bat rodent to evolve into extremely diverse, high-functioning bats. Logically, there has to be something more than distant chance driving the evolution of our animal kingdom.

The evolutionary model of Darwin and Wallace has a lot of staying power but science is telling us that something else has input into this system. Perhaps it will not be too long before we are teaching a hybrid of Lamarck, Darwin, and a little Creation Consciousness.

EPIGENETICS AND OUR LIVING EVOLUTION

Oncos Genes

The cell's acknowledged ability to pass on acquired characteristics to other generations of cells has caused the creation of the new field of "epigenetics," a word meaning "above genetics." The appearance of epigenetics suggests that the mechanisms that transmit genetic material still hold many secrets and that sexual reproduction is not the sole or perhaps even the primary conduit of genes from parent to offspring.

When I was receiving my medical training, my classmates and I were introduced to the theory of "oncos" genes: genes that are believed to be predisposed to trigger or turn on specific diseases in response to the body's exposure to certain chemicals in the environment. The existence of these "illness genes" is thought to explain many diseases, including certain forms of cancer that occur in generations of families and appear to be hereditary. The oncos-gene model describes an in vitro, nonsexual reproductive evolution of cells that are susceptible to toxin-stimulated mutations and can reproduce themselves.

Epigenetics doesn't study only those substances or other signals (such as anxiety, worry, and fear) that can provoke detrimental changes in cells. It also examines how positive environmental factors can prevent detrimental change in the body's DNAs. Spontaneous cell evolution can occur in both negative and life-enhancing directions. In both wanted and unwanted experiences that invoke what we would see as positive or negative outcomes, adaptive modifications for that stimulus are occurring.

One of the most startling breakthroughs in the frontier science of epigenetics has been the discovery that severe emotional stress is a much more powerful factor in changing our DNA than toxic chemicals are.

Bad Vibes

The mental stress factor in stimulating gene and cellular mutations is another indication that our thoughts and consciousness, both conscious and subconscious, are important elements in human evolution, perhaps as significant as the transmission of inherited genes via sexual reproduction.

Children adopted into families that have a long, multigenerational history of developing a specific disease sometimes develop that same disease despite sharing no hereditary, genetic link to the family and having been born in other distant environments, including other countries. How might this happen in these unusual cases?[1]

I think there is a logical explanation. Adopted children entering a family encounter chronic family issues. These multigenerational belief systems and other energetic signals are a kind of negative, transgenerational emotional atmosphere that has repeatedly triggered the family's susceptibility to and contracting of the disease. The unrelated child might be especially likely to develop the ailment if she or he is similar in personality type to the family with a history of the disease.

For example, certain families have proclivities toward feelings of shame, guilt, embarrassment, blame, and self-judgment. The tendency toward low self-esteem and the negative projections of these feelings within the family may set up an energized field of unhealthy thoughts, emotions, and actions. The homeopathic term for a general weakness or predisposition to chronic disease that is transmitted down the generational chain is known as a "miasm." The chain can be passed genetically, or more commonly through a psycho-emotional pathway where beliefs and reflexive actions are handed down. These harmful emotions and stimuli are processed in the body in the same way, involving the same organs. This is especially true in family members and DNA that share the same personality type. This emotionally based explanation is in concert with the findings of epigenetics.

Children who are not genetically related to the family are exposed to and become part of the energy field and teachings that surround the entire family, and can potentially catch, carry, and propagate the specific familial disease.

Luckily, when the emotional/energetic factors are at work, individuals within a dysfunctional family can consciously choose to alter and/or eradicate the debilitating stimuli, or at least its unhealthy processing in their own bodies. By changing behavior, emotional response, and thought patterns, people can transform themselves. It is not uncommon for others in a family to transform as one member serves as an example of beneficial change. This can potentially prevent familial ailments from being a foregone conclusion for the next generations.

Twins Studies

There are other indications that in vitro evolution—defined as changes in characteristics that can't be traced to genes inherited from parents through their sexual reproduction—is involved in mutation and the development of new genes, cells, and species.

Identical twins share the same placenta and amniotic environment in utero and have absolutely identical DNA. But after birth, each twin exhibits and develops a distinct personality. This indicates that human personality is not dependent on the current model of the mechanisms of DNA and genetic inheritance; one's personality is not tied to one's DNA.

Each twin experiences a unique set of physical and emotional stresses as well as positive stimuli. Twins look less alike as they grow up, confirming that our physical appearance and structures are at least in part a reflection of the way our individual personalities register and respond to both good and bad experiences.

Epigeneticists have found that as twins age, their identical DNA differentiates, which confirms that humans are constantly evolving and that our DNA is the record keeper of changes triggered by our environment and our experiences within it. Even in identical twins when the DNA is monitored during pregnancy, the DNA of each of the individual twins is expressed differently. Different potentials of the DNA are either up regulated or down regulated based on how that individual experiences events through the filter of its own personality. This research has added to the new reality the greater role to which our nature influences us, the hidden potentials that are imbedded deep in our DNA, and how much emotions play a role in our evolution.

The Missing Link

Harmonious beliefs and unconflicted consciousness can enhance health and increase longevity just as stress and internal conflict can cause disease. My mother once made a needlepoint sampler with a quote by Alfred Tennyson: "I am a part of all whom I have met." I always liked that quote but only now do I recognize the depth and ramifications of its meaning. If our body and DNA are continuously adapting to our experience, then we are a composition constructed by our experience. The DNA we are given by our parents was also woven by the people they had met and the experiences of their lives. Our evolution can no longer be thought of as solely determined by our physical environment.

How is our specific personal evolution, both physical and psychological, coordinated during our lifetime if we change and evolve in response to our experience? The most likely transformer of our changing physical and mental makeup might come as a surprise to most of us, but there is considerable evidence that the mechanism is found in the cell membranes. But how can the cell membrane coordinate these complex permutations in us and in the evolution of our species? Where does the wisdom needed to accomplish that come from?

It seems there must be an organelle that can act as a brain, some cell part that can autonomously store and analyze vital information and quickly generate and send correct and nuanced solutions to complex situations.

Magic Structure

At first review of the available data, we don't find in the cell membrane any obvious mechanism to act as a directing intelligence. We have to look more deeply into its "magic" structure and consider what the existence of a crystalline matrix form suggests about the membrane's potential to communicate with the seat of our consciousness and the wisdom of something greater.

Two differing communication scenarios immediately come to mind. First, the cell membrane may contain within its structure a consciousness with the ability to coordinate complex cellular functions and to direct the in vitro evolution of our DNA. The crystalline matrix within the cell membrane, made from the layers of lipids and protein DNA, etc., would be the likely control center. The individual parts functioning within the greater cell may be constantly sending information to the surrounding membrane, which functions as the switchboard and control center for communications among the cell's component contents as well as with other cells of the body.

This schematic would allow all of the systems and organs of the body, including the brain, to cooperate synergistically. They would contribute individual and unique processes that in combination have a greater efficiency and potency than the simple sum of the contributions of constituent parts.

This cooperative cellular coordination is often found in nature. It is a natural system for many basic parts or pieces to work together to do the necessary complex problem solving for survival, growth, and reproduction. In undergraduate school I learned about the functioning of the heart, lungs, and kidneys separately; it was certainly easier to teach it that way. But in graduate school the physiology of these three organs couldn't be taught separately. Standing alone, none could function correctly—their physiologies are so interrelated that they must be thought of as one system. Together as a team they are capable of sustaining life. If you were to lose the connection between any of them you could not survive.

There are many examples of collaboration in nature that allows all parties to survive when they couldn't survive without each other's help. The lichen is one of my favorite examples: a partnership between an algae and a fungus. Together they are able to live in the hottest, driest conditions with minimal or no nutrients. The algae would simply die under that scenario, and the fungus would die without organic material to break down. But algae grow in sunlight and create organic material to sustain the fungus. Meanwhile, the fungus provides shelter within itself to keep the algae from drying out. Nature seems to be telling us that we can survive better by collaborating than by dominating.

The second possible explanation of how the cell membrane could coordinate and direct messages may at first sound far-fetched, but it is a hypothesis worth examining. Perhaps we are in fact multidimensional beings, and our cell membranes are sending and receiving information to and from the consciousness of our living field of energy, the previously mentioned aura or i-Cloud that surrounds each of us.

The central aspect of this swirling field is the soul, the part of us that exists in a realm that communicates within and outside of ourselves and is a part of the Universal Consciousness. The soul and its link to the Universal Consciousness could orchestrate our body's functioning, growth, and healing by signaling the correct pathways our lives need to follow to properly develop their highest potentials and evolution. This hypothesis would account for the existence and meaningful activity of an intelligence with sensing and communication abilities that appears to transcend the synergistic capacities of our own cells.

If you believe that knowledge stored in our cells has the capacity to solve problems necessary to coordinate sophisticated and pinpoint evolution, then the first scenario is the best explanation. If, on the other hand, you feel that the brilliant decisions that have directed complex evolution on our planet require more wisdom than could come from simple cells' collective knowledge, then the second scenario might be your choice.

There may be one other explanation: that these two processes work together. We are co-created by the personal human collective consciousness of our cells and the coordinating efforts of the bigger collective consciousness. It is my assertion that cell membranes with their little antennae have the capacity to interface with our physical/chemical world as well as the realm of Universal Consciousness or Creation. This realm is energetic in nature—and our thoughts are a part of it.

Limited Views

Once again, these two descriptions of cell membrane function need not be mutually exclusive. Research may miss things when it underestimates the potential abilities of living organisms. I believe that the systems I've described work together in a blended fashion for the transfer of greater quantities and complexities of knowledge. This information is continually being passed back and forth among the consciousness of our cells, our conscious mind, subconscious mind, soul consciousness, and a Universal Mind or Consciousness.

The two prime movers for directing this intelligence are our cells and our soul consciousness, which is connected to Universal Consciousness. Our conscious mind does not experience the actions and events that take place within this network of communication, function, and evolution as specific, articulate thoughts. These activities occur in another dimension of consciousness, on a different level of energy and information exchange, and are beyond the awareness and reach of the conscious mind.

And yet the question remains: *where* is consciousness? We live and work every day in these two realms but the question of where consciousness resides seems so difficult. Consciousness and our thoughts lack weight, length, and width, yet they clearly exist. They are energy and simultaneously inhabit the same space where our physical existence exists. We are superimposed and entangled with the emanations, thoughts, and experiences of our physical world. Our human life is much like the lichen, having two dissimilar forms that are inseparable.

I wonder to what extent we may be "blinded" by our five senses. These are not open portals to all available stimuli, but rather filters that select those bits of information most necessary for our immediate physical survival. From a physical standpoint, we believe that all things must be perceptible to our senses of sight, hearing, touch, taste, and smell. But what if we only had four of these five senses, as many people do? What if we lacked vision and touch? How would we perceive our world? Would we only be able to explain how our universe works through the senses of smell, hearing, and taste? Our understanding would have shortcomings without vision and touch, and in this way we are limited, so we explore and experiment with the energy form of consciousness and the existence of other realms.

Most of our science only tests for the things that our five senses can conceivably register. We will have to imagine a sixth or seventh sense of stimuli reception and create technologies that can test for phenomena that the powers of our five senses can't perceive or allow us to imagine.

Perhaps this "blindness" that we consider our "sight" and our overreliance on our limited perceptual abilities for a definition of our world are what prevent our discovery of other forms of communication. The messages exchanged among our body's collective consciousness of individual cells, and even with that living entity (what I have referred to as our soul consciousness), are waiting to be illuminated.

X Doesn't Mark the Spot

An early American neurophysiologist named Karl Lashley tried to create a brain map to determine where in the brain memory is stored by teaching lab mice different behaviors and then surgically removing parts of their brains. He systematically removed sections of brain and then further reduced in size and capacity those sections that remained.[2]

No matter which section he removed, or how small he made any remaining section, the mice were still able to perform the learned behavior. Lashley concluded that memory must somehow exist in "all" of the cells of the brain, and that the accepted theory of the time—that specific brain functions were limited to specific brain areas—was incorrect. Paul Pietsch, a biology researcher at Indiana University, did further research on the brains of salamanders.[3] He removed the salamanders' brains and, before replacing them into the skull, dissected away certain sections. Pietsch even ground some of the brain into small pieces before reinserting these fragments back into the head. Finally, as if that weren't enough, he reversed the brain's spatial orientation within the skull.

In each of the seven hundred subjects he experimented with, the salamanders with the injured brains returned to normal functioning after a period of recuperation. Pietsch, like Lashley, had discovered that memory was not stored in one section of the brain but evidently throughout the brain, in each of the brain's cells. This is important to us when we are trying to understand where individual consciousness is held. Their research points to the possibility that memory is held differently from how we might think it is. Once again we find ourselves forced to think outside the box.

One continues to ask, where is consciousness and where are memories if they are not solely anchored in the brain tissue?

The Hologram

The results of these and similar studies lead many to hypothesize that memory is holographic. The dictionary tells us that a hologram is "a three-dimensional photographic image of an object, the photographic record of light interference patterns produced by using a photographic plate and laser light." A hologram transforms an image into one that has embedded within it greater information. If memories are spread out throughout the cells of our brain as holographic images, they indeed must have special qualities and capacities that we do not quite understand at this time.

A complete hologram can be reassembled from just one of its parts, which contains an embedded "plan" of the whole. Just so, human memories could be split into an interference pattern and distributed among all the cells of the brain. Each brain cell could store, retrieve, and transmit all registered memories.[4] For many years I have considered the possibility that memory and the seat of consciousness are not centered within the brain. The amount and depth of information stored during an entire lifetime would seem to exceed anything that can fit into our brain.

There seem to be three levels of information. The first one is the storage of our memories and experiences. The second one is our conscious thoughts. The third is the super consciousness or wisdom of our soul. It is easy for me to fathom that there is a Universal Consciousness that exists in an energetic state. This consciousness could indeed exist everywhere. We have discussed the possibility of receiving consciousness via the crystalline matrix found in the cell membranes, DNA, and cell formation of our bodies. This would give the pathway for the superconsciousness or soul to make the profound decisions that are necessary to help us transform ourselves. This possibility would also include a storage place for our experiences and our conscious mind. All of this consciousness would be held in the interstitial aspects of inner space, akin to the i-Cloud or a huge router that connects to a vast and expanding field of energetic consciousness. Interestingly enough, this model would explain how salamanders and mice could remember tasks and function despite the destruction of brain tissue. Different sections of more advanced brains might be attuned to channeling certain functions in certain regions of the brain instead of being responsible for uniquely holding all of the information in one place. There is also the possibility that some or all of the cells of the body have storage capabilities. There exist amazing stories on the transference of memory and skills when people receive organ transplants. The question remains: is memory held in the cells or is it channeled through the cells of those organs?

In geometry, a "fractal" is an extremely irregular line or surface formed of an infinite number of similarly irregular sections. Fractals have fractional dimension: between one and two, or two and three, dimensions. Fractals can represent subtly ordered patterns in apparently chaotic, random, and unorganized structures. The patterns fractals create are patterns found in nature, patterns that become smaller and smaller yet repeat. There is hidden magic in this formation. Scientists have used these patterns to overcome barriers in the fields of electronics, information storage, and sending and receiving communications. In fact, the use of fractal patterns has made wireless communication possible. The consciousness of nature has worked out advanced engineering problems to create the diversity of life that exists, and the more we utilize this knowledge that is intrinsic to nature, the more we see its infinite wisdom. These are all clues that remind us that we are just scratching the surface of what has come before us and what exists now.

The brain may not be the originator of thoughts but a receptor, like a radio that receives ordered, "outside" signals and allows them to stream throughout the millions of brain cells. This seems a likely hypothesis, especially when we remember our body's unified system of communicating and communally cooperating cells, and the idea that each brain cell, as well as all other cells, may store all our memories.

Researching this hypothesis to a satisfying conclusion would be nearly impossible at this time. Is the information being stored within individual cells, or are the cells merely conduits for information transmission? While Lashley and Pietsch proved that certain brain functions were not limited to specific brain structures but occurred throughout the brain, it was not clear from either study whether the remaining brain cells were recalling their own stored memories or receiving and relaying signals from an unidentified source.

Only Time Will Tell

We have added possibilities to many of the big, elusive questions. It's exciting to think about them and consider that many of them may well be revealed as our science probes deeper. There is no doubt that the answers will create new questions and reveal much about the makeup of our universe. We will continue to ask:

- Where does consciousness come from?
- Where are our stores of accumulated knowledge and our memories located?
- How is our consciousness connected to our soul, to other human souls, and to the Creating Force of the universe?
- Do we really need an organelle to hold our consciousness, or is consciousness an inherent, perhaps immaterial part of all created things?
- Do we have within us the capacity to receive adaptive information from our soul or from the Creating Force of the universe?
- Is brain activity consciousness?

The brain experiments mentioned earlier and other studies lend weight to the probability that our cells are designed to communicate within a quantum world of subatomic particles and wave probabilities. Our thoughts, interpretations of experience, and beliefs would appear to arise, exist, and operate via energetic means beyond the capacities of purely physical substances—that is, if there are such things as forms of matter devoid of mind or spirit.

Our modern worldview has been structured by several hundred

years of rapid technological advances that have allowed us to successfully manipulate our outer and inner environments. We are biased against the abstract or apparently immaterial in favor of the physical, concrete reality of interacting bits of unthinking matter.

Despite the revelations from the strange world of quantum physics, most of us still think within an earlier universe of more limited human perception and understanding, where all events can be analyzed on the basis of cause-and-effect, one-on-one relationships between material entities that can, in turn, each be analyzed down to their smallest physical parts.

Our Emotions, Consciousness, and Neurochemicals

Now let's shift the conversation and look at the transformation of our energetic thoughts into physical neurochemicals. When someone is emotionally depressed, many doctors diagnose the problem as a chemical imbalance in the brain and prescribe synthetic chemicals to normalize the body's imbalance. While neurochemical imbalances are indeed a component of depression, I want to suggest that a deeper diagnosis is worth considering.

I would start by asking what *precipitated* the imbalance of brain chemistry that resulted in the depression. There could be many causes but the most likely are an organic dysfunction within the body that interfered with neurochemical production, a lack of the necessary "precursors" that produce neurochemicals, or that the person's thoughts and feelings impacted neurochemical production and imbalance.

This is a bit like the old question "Which came first? The chicken or the egg?" But I contend that our neurochemistry is a direct result of our consciousness. Our thoughts have always created the neurochemistry of our body. While there are some cases of organic dysfunction or lack of proper nutrients for neurochemical synthesis, it is rare that the cells creating the neurochemicals are dysfunctional.

In other words, those cells are doing just as they are told. They create in direct response to consciousness. It is common to say that the neurochemical imbalance and the resulting depression are the result of cellular dysfunction, but taking that approach misses the real and enduring answer to the question. Diagnosing physical malfunctions without determining all the potential causes prevents us from perceiving obvious realities and diverts our attention from more practical, satisfactory, and enlightened paths toward real solutions. Candace Pert calls neurochemicals "chemicals of emotion," and when we are out of emotional balance, our chemicals of emotion will follow. So when a physician finds a neurochemical imbalance, the first question should be "What is going on in your life that causes stress?" not "What pharmacy would you like to use for your prescriptions?" Unfortunately, we do not like to reveal perceived weaknesses—it makes our ego very uncomfortable—and this creates a barrier to humanity's progression toward a kinder and more accepting society. I look forward to a time when discovering the emotional issues of our life is something to celebrate as part of our continued transformation toward inner peace.

As modern, "scientific" humans living in an age of sophisticated science and technology, we tend to seek material causes and effects when we are confronted with any problem. So pointing to a mechanical, physical breakdown as the source of depression comes naturally and seems both logical and reassuring—but it is also highly unscientific.

Believing that for some unknown reason our bodies create the wrong chemicals in the wrong amounts doesn't actually offer any "physical" proof or validation of an organic cause for depression. Our body's cellular functions are very precise and reliable in their operations, not easily prone to spontaneous organic mistakes that can't be attributed to real physical disorders.

The fact is that our thinking processes are fixed upon the material world because we are able to shape that world to our purposes and achieve desired, concrete, and amazing results. Our concept of what's true depends on tangible, tactile, repeatable facts that are easily perceived by our five senses or the technology we've built to expand the scope of those senses. To be convinced that a thing exists, we have to be able to see, touch, hear, taste, or smell it. This is very limiting and has proven to have many shortfalls. We have come to the point where we are developing technology that can reach beyond the narrow view of our five senses.

I believe we are in a defining time for humanity, a time of looking for deeper truths. It is in that search that we will discover our true and vast potential, and we will need to do that in order to overcome the new difficulties created by overpopulation and our inability to comprehend how our actions impact the rest of the world. When we connect to the oneness of all things and see that big picture, we will become incapable of wreaking destruction on the planet for our own short-term gain. This is part of the human journey. It is in the most trying times that we reach our greatest potential and accomplish the most.

The Challenge

Our challenge is to realize that we are emotional beings, each on a journey of discovery and personal evolution. As individuals and as a species, our work is to constructively process the emotional chaos that causes us to create and experience unnecessary and damaging stress and even dis-ease. We must free ourselves from feelings of inferiority, unworthiness, and isolation in order to travel a more positive path of self-realization.

Some of these negative feelings originate from a misperception of or inability to recognize the context and parameters of human life on Earth. We're overly attached to the macro world of our five senses despite being spiritual as well as physical beings. We expect our inner world of thoughts and emotions to be as solid and logical. Yet I often think of emotions as anti-logical. Keeping this in mind sometimes helps us understand and accept our emotional issues and motivations.

This becomes especially true when we realize that many of our emotional belief systems are built by the minds of children. Many of the big stressors in our lives emanate from the emotional belief systems we created between conception and the age of six. As you unravel the belief systems that are responsible for changes in your emotional chemistry, it is important to imagine yourself at a very tender age trying to navigate a world, not only without a handbook, but with a partially developed brain. It is during this time that you adopt both the functional and dysfunctional belief systems and actions of your family. It is during this time that you develop strategies about how life should be and how to get what you want out of life. Some do well with this daunting task and others do not. Changes in neurochemistry, stomachaches, irritable bowel syndrome, increased blood pressure, and a long list of other maladies are often your body's and soul's red flag, signaling for you to pay attention and do the work of a human being.

Harmony

Antidepressants have their value in the treatment of depression, but deep inner emotional work is really the only lasting treatment for creating a normal, balanced neurochemistry. We need to closely examine the role personal beliefs and attitudes play in structuring actions that create stress for us, other individuals, and human beings at large. Harmonizing our inner lives, which ultimately harmonizes our outer lives, is humankind's most important challenge and adventure. I've come to believe that the work of building inner harmony is our central purpose on Earth.

Each cell in our body has a unique consciousness, and collectively these conscious cells work as microprocessors, responding to all of our emotions. This response can be positive and health enhancing or negative and destructive. For healthy and efficient functioning, the systems of our body require us to work through and solve issues that trigger stress.

Dysfunctional emotions cause stress. Almost all of us who have been under stress know that it can manifest physically as pain and dysfunction in organs, muscles, and other structures within our bodies. Many people process their stress in their stomachs, which increases acidity and often leads to ulcers. Others may have headaches, back pain, or even heart problems, depending on where negative emotions register physically.

If we see many of our physical symptoms of stress as the canary in the coal mine, we can learn to make use of those symptoms, even subtle changes such as increases in heart rate or blood pressure, to help identify when the underlying issues and emotions that manifest themselves in localized physical pain are at play.

This is not to say that we shouldn't use medications to help minimize and heal the symptoms of the ailment while we're doing the emotional work; the key is to get away from the medication as soon as you can so you can regain access to all your emotions and continue the true healing work of harmonizing your consciousness. It takes a long time for physical symptoms to manifest, and once they do, it's important to see it as an opportunity. Here's how stress manifests:

When the body responds to stress by producing pain, it is making an urgent announcement that its cells are expending too much of their available energy in processing stuck negative emotions. A failure to transform unhealthy emotions causes the collective cells in the body's affected area to function at less than peak capacity and begin to break down.

As this cellular malfunction occurs, the normal life force and healing intercellular communication created by positively structured water within the cells becomes inoperative, preventing super-radiance and self-transparency. Individual cells become sequestered from one another, and vital communication and healing responses that are necessary for balance and harmony become blocked. There is a health consequence to the cells or organs that are processing the disharmony caused by belief systems and stress, and symptoms of illness emerge.

Homeostasis

Homeostasis occurs when all elements of the mind and body are in a balanced state of harmony that assures physical and mental health. The calmer and more relaxed you feel, the closer your mind and body are to optimum homeostasis. To reach homeostasis, an emotional being must transform destructive patterns of thought and feeling to create a level of harmony that offers the greatest chance of achieving good health in both mind and body.

Early on in my emotional counseling, I often saw examples of where I thought the superconsciousness or soul was trying to draw our attention to the emotional issues we needed to transform in order to heal ourselves and the Whole. I even imagined the soul leveraging the body's health to get our attention: a kind of cosmic two-by-four. Believe me: so much transformation goes on within us when we are struggling with disease and death. This is often our best work; it's when we deeply examine and restructure our belief systems. When seen through the eyes of the soul—which realizes death is only a transitory reality, that our soul never dies, and that we can return to another physical life—disease and even death may not seem like such a big deal. This idea made sense to me and may mean that the most important thing we can do as a living part of creation is heal ourselves internally. A stomachache that results from emotional stress and may even progress to cancer for those who do not actively listen to their bodies may awaken their greatest transformation and healing. Let us remember that denial is self-inflicted: the ultimate consequence of not listening to those emotions and working to harmonize the issues that have kept us from living an amazing life. When you achieve harmony, your body will rest in homeostasis and the simplest things in life will have great sweetness. Heaven on Earth.

Humanity is perhaps the most important piece in manifesting and transforming this world into a better place. We are imbued with the power to do so much. The ability of every cell in our body to communicate and heal the body collectively is a metaphor for what humanity can do for the planet. We'll talk about the power of our consciousness in the next section—and it may just be the tip of the iceberg.

More About Water

In our quest to understand the communication between cells, we return to the "pyramid" of relevant knowledge. The next row of building blocks necessary for understanding these concepts concerns a vital subject: the unique nature of water.

We've already reviewed water's amazing capacity to record and hold information, as demonstrated by Popp's experiment with biophotonic light introduced into water and Benveniste's potent dilute immunoglobulin/water solution.

Water that receives information embedded within biophotonic light or the molecules of an added substance becomes embedded with the structure of the introduced information. Water molecules are constantly recording the information they come in contact with. As they do so, the structure of the water molecules, as individuals and as a collective, shapes how they relate and their very nature. We are still learning so much about the relationship between the embedded information and the subatomic structure of the atoms within these molecules. The key is that something dramatically changes. This line of questioning takes us deeper into understanding what we are made of, and this shifts our attention to the contents of empty space.

We owe so much to the many magical properties of water. Without it, life as we know it would not exist on this planet. For example, consider the unique polarity of water molecules, with the electrons from two hydrogen atoms pulled toward the oxygen atom. This electron transfer results in the hydrogen molecules having a positive charge and the oxygen molecule a negative one. Like attracting magnets, the molecules begin to stack themselves in an orderly fashion, creating a liquid matrix.

When a nonrandom, ordered matrix occurs in nature, new potentialities become available, as we discussed concerning the quartz crystal used in radios. Another great example is the matrix of the ruby that allows us to extrude all of the wavelengths in natural light into one coherent light source that creates the laser.

Science and medicine are finding many applications for "cold lasers" in the healing of living organisms. The effectiveness and healing properties of these lasers may best be attributed to the coherence of the light source. Coherent light is very much the same as the light cells use in intercommunication, so the use of this light as a healing modality may be to amplify this communication. I think of healing lasers as a way to supercharge the information and reduce any blockages to healing that may be in place. In any case, the clinical use of cold lasers is developing much empirical evidence concerning the unusual therapeutic properties of coherently structured light.

We are just beginning to discover and examine the liquid and solid crystal matrices found throughout the human body and to understand the relationship between their designs and functions and our untapped potentials.

Wonderful Water

Water is the main substance found in living organisms, an essential ingredient for life on our planet. Let's take a moment to consider just one of water's wonderful and strange qualities that allows us to live on Earth. Two parts hydrogen gas and one part oxygen gas together make a liquid that at 32 degrees Fahrenheit starts becoming a solid. Water molecules react much differently from other liquids when they freeze. Usually, the colder most molecules become, the slower their motions; they no longer bump into each other as much. As they settle, they get closer or compressed. Water is unique and different. As water reaches its freezing point it actually expands because of the interactions of molecular polarity. This is important because frozen water is less dense than liquid water. This means ice floats, preventing Earth's oceans and lakes from gradually turning to solid ice, from bottom to top. Thus fish and other aquatic species are able to live through the winter, even in the coldest latitudes. This design or nature of water is one of its great miracles.

Earlier I alluded to water's ability to record or take on the information around it. Next we'll look at some of the research that best demonstrates how this act of internalizing or embedding this information affects the water. We will also look at the efficiency with which water can absorb human consciousness versus information from inorganic sources. Dr. Emoto Masaru has described this phenomenon in his book *Messages from Water*.[5]

Structured Water

Dr. Emoto's work has been revolutionary in helping us understand how information, human thoughts, and belief systems can be downloaded into a water molecule, causing the water to restructure itself in different formations.

In his initial research, Dr. Emoto gathered and examined water from a number of different cities. He flash-froze the water samples in an effort to correlate the structure of the water crystals with the source of the water and the water's quality, its level of purity. Water from different sources crystallized in unique formations; water from the countryside, for example, was not the same as water from denser urban areas. Yet this was not a hard and fast rule. Cities that were more upbeat seemed to have better water quality according to crystallization criteria. Dr. Emoto questioned what variables caused positive or negative crystallization. He wondered if water might crystallize differently when exposed to different kinds of music.

He discovered that classical music caused freezing water to form beautiful and complex crystalline structures, while heavy metal rock music produced less intricate, nearly globular formations. Dr. Emoto hypothesized that this disparity in water-crystal form and symmetry suggested that the heavy metal sound waves were more chaotic or had a negative impact on the water's structure.

I question whether the researcher had any bias toward one type of music or the other and if so, how this bias impacted the outcome of the study. As we know from experiments in modern physics, the very act of observation changes the activity of the particles observed. I believe that water lacks the ability to act as a discerning music critic and determine what kind of music is bad or good. Perhaps the researcher's opinion was that heavy metal music is chaotic and cacophonous, while classical music is more harmonious and therefore aesthetically pleasing.

Could Dr. Emoto and his team have such a bias, and could their positive and negative thoughts about different styles of music permeate and become embedded in the water? Could this cause the extreme difference in crystal formation? Could their thoughts about the music, rather than the music itself, be what was reflected in the structure of the ice? I have no direct knowledge of Dr. Emoto's personal musical tastes, but I would be interested in the results of a replication of this water-music experiment conducted by a researcher who loves heavy metal music and loathes the classics.

The next question I ask is why water from natural areas always creates beautiful crystalline structures. Some scientists theorize that moving water that has crosscurrents is structured by the currents flowing at an angle to the water's primary direction. I think these scientists find it hard to believe that not only human consciousness can positively or negatively structure water. Streams of this kind are typically found in the mountains, in natural settings where there is abundant life. The consciousness of the plants and animals, from the smallest to the most magnificent megaspecimens of flora and fauna, are recorded by the water as it traverses a harmonious and largely pristine setting. As we look into the power of consciousness, I believe we will find that water receives and mirrors its environment and its inhabitants, with the power of living things having more impact than the nonliving.

Exploring with Dr. Emoto

Dr. Emoto conducted another experiment in which he spoke directly to water using such statements as "I love you" and "I hate you." He also conducted trials speaking the names of famous people such as Mother Teresa and Adolf Hitler. The crystalline structure of the water mirrored Dr. Emoto's spoken expressions of love and hate. The crystal formations in the vials of water receiving expressions of love were ordered, symmetrical, and beautiful. The same result occurred for vials of water labeled with the names of benevolent people. The other vials were just the opposite.[6]

Dr. Emoto wished to further his research on the powers of consciousness and intention, and he set up an experiment utilizing rice soaked in water and left to ferment. He found what he expected when he studied the resulting rice water: samples exposed to the positive thoughts led to textbook fermentation with a pleasant odor, and those exposed to negative thoughts turned black and decayed and had a distasteful odor. He also used a control sample of rice water that received no input of any kind. The isolated control sample turned black and showed some signs of decay with less odor. It seems that the more we take care of or love things, the better they turn out. Perhaps this is something we all know but sometimes forget.

I brought this concept close to home as a learning experience for my son, who was intrigued by this information years ago. For his sixth grade science project he grew small plants, some of them getting water that he had infused with good words and thoughts, and another group receiving water he embedded with negative words and thoughts.

We repeated the same process, this time directing our attention to the plants themselves and their present and future health and growth. Sometimes he used words and other times he just used his thoughts directed at the plants, as he had done with the water. The plants that grew in positively embedded water and were given a little more love grew much faster and flourished more than the plants that received negative stimuli and grew in negatively embedded water.

There is a growing body of research literature filled with similar experiments, including the study where a researcher soaked seeds in saltwater and then gave some of the seeds to a group of healers. The seeds receiving positive healing messages grew normally, while the "untreated" seeds failed to thrive.[7]

There may be numerous ramifications of these experiments:

- Positively structured water has a positive effect on the growth and health of living things.
- The thoughts and intentions of human beings are very powerful. The consciousness of living organisms is demonstrably stronger than the information contained in inorganic materials.
- The structures of nature hold many secrets that can greatly aid in the healing of living organisms. Cells communicate with a coherent light form we call biophotonic light. This intercommunication is essential to healthy living beings.
- Both conscious and subconscious thoughts and emotions are constantly influencing and altering the world around us. At a minimum, our consciousness influences the health and quality of water, the most abundant and necessary molecule of life.
- We have the ability to create a healthy ecosystem for life to exist or an unhealthy one, inside and outside of our bodies. The extent of our ability has not fully been realized. We are only now beginning to acknowledge our potential for shaping our physical surroundings. As with anything else, the more you feed it the more it grows.

And let me pose this final question: what could we accomplish with a unified field of human consciousness focused on repairing the damage that has occurred on Earth?

Giving Thanks

When we look at the history of consciousness and intention, we can see that their importance and power were understood and utilized long before our modern research in the form of giving thanks. The blessing of food began in the tribal and agrarian culture of Judaism and is the foundation for gratitude practice in Christianity and Islam. In Native American hunter-gatherer societies, hunters blessed the spirits of the animals they hoped to kill for food. After the successful hunt, they prayed for the animal's easy passage into the spirit world. Native Americans' conscious, active sense of relationship with the entire environment—with the animals and plants and water they depended on for survival—permeated their world and was both detailed and intimate.

One of my favorite stories exemplifying this relationship comes from the chronicles of Lewis and Clark. The expedition stopped at Fort Mandan, and both the natives and whites had run out of meat. The buffalo had been nowhere to be found for months. The whites had sent out long-distance hunting parties but to no avail. What Lewis and Clark witnessed next they related back to President Jefferson. A group of local tribesmen left the fort and began a dialogue, asking Brother Buffalo to come and sustain them. The people had practiced this kind of communication with the animals and the land for tens of thousands of years. They stayed out for three days and nights, much to the bewilderment of the whites. After those three days of prayer, the buffalo appeared. The tribe took only what it needed and could store, and then made a great ceremony of gratitude to Brother Buffalo in addition to other spiritual ceremonies.

The whites did not adopt this amazing teaching, as our destructive history with the buffalo shows. The native peoples were able to survive in concert with the earth because of their connection to intention, and perhaps because they listened to the wisdom within that connection to the Creator.

European cultures were structured with hierarchies designed for the domination of people and the natural world. Native American tribes, on the other hand, lived with a sense of mutuality and cooperation. I once listened to a lecture by an anthropologist who believed the communal organization of indigenous American societies may account for longer life expectancies than people in the modern industrialized world. What might explain this possibility?

Native Americans also did not experience the severe illnesses and widespread plagues that Europeans suffered from. Perhaps the lack of communicable and/or environmentally caused disease reflects the physical and mental health practices and belief systems of a culture living in correct relationship with the living Earth.

In this chapter we have created the building blocks of knowledge to begin our journey into understanding consciousness. Though thoughts and beliefs have seemed to lack substance, they are the building blocks and foundation of the physical world. In the field of epigenetics we have learned that our emotional experience is much more important to the preservation of our DNA and our overall health than we ever expected. Consciousness is energy, and information traveling as energy is more powerful than things that assume a physical form. In other words, if you can distill the energetic information of a medication, it will be more powerful than the pill itself. Information structured within energy seems to be much easier to assimilate and integrate into the physical world than physical things themselves are. It is this reality that links epigenetics, messages from water, energetic communication through the crystalline matrices of our body, gratitude, and the creation of homeostasis through harmonizing our emotional issues.

We know from science that all of physicality is made of energy. This means that underneath our physical nature is pure energy. The next step may be to realize that the most powerful building block, whether positive or negative, is energy embedded with consciousness. We have often heard a corollary to this: our physical nature is a reflection of our thoughts. Research gives us evidence that information is constantly being assimilated by water and all living things that have water within them. This may show how our thoughts and intentions are embedded in the energy of consciousness and how it influences us and all living things around us. This makes me wonder whether energy can exist without information within it. Does energy always have consciousness? Is energy by definition consciousness? We know the inverse—that thoughts are electrical and therefore energetic. Can energy even exist without the creative force of thoughts and consciousness? These are all good questions that we will examine as our technology allows us to look beyond the five senses.

In either case, our belief systems about the makeup of our world are changing. We used to see the world solely as something we could sense and describe through our five senses, as a place made of things that were physical and observable, not invisible or imaginary. If we could not see, smell, touch, hear, or feel it, it did not exist. How could the tangible be made of something intangible? This view has certainly inhibited the growth of our scientific knowledge. We must realize that the physical is fundamentally *energetic* and that communication is constant, instantaneous, and *wireless*. We are also just beginning to understand our abilities and potentials. I believe one of the most salient principles we can derive from epigenetics is that the most powerful tool we have for healing ourselves is reducing the stress we feel in reaction to our life experience. The bigger the stress, the more harmful it is to our DNA. Changes in our DNA ultimately can lead to disease. The happier our lives are, the more stable our health and the longer we may live. This place of joy within us will never come from outside; it can only come from the reduction of our internal chaos. This new way of seeing our most important work and humanity's direction brings even more clarity to our purpose.

CONSCIOUSNESS—THE BRIDGE BETWEEN ENERGY AND PHYSICALITY

Mental/Physical

Is there research available to help us understand the interplay between conscious thought and its manifestation in our physical world? The question we will try to address in this chapter is where energy and consciousness stops, the building blocks of the physical world, and the more solid physical realm appears. In later chapters we will discuss modern theories of how this process occurs.

We start with Albert Einstein, who spent twenty years of his life trying to discern whether atomic and subatomic particles were physical entities that behaved like objects in our macro physical world, or were instead potentialities of pure energy waiting to unfold. Einstein and others found that subatomic particles have characteristics of both the physical and the energetic world: they are able to act like both particles and waves. A particle implies something solid, stable, and unchanging. These, however, are not the characteristics of subatomic particles. In the subatomic world, being a particle is only a temporary state or a transitory physical manifestation of energy. The most relevant, and most perplexing, questions concerning subatomic particles/waves have to do with the particle's ability to change and what prompts the transformation. One possibility is the duality of particles: that they exist in two realms simultaneously, where they operate with great freedom if not free will.

Think for a moment about subatomic particles/waves as "potentials." Imagine that subatomic potentials can be anything they want to be as they emerge from the super-small and nearly invisible subatomic world. Think of these potentials as being very agreeable and ready to work with all forms of consciousness.

Now let's go one step further. Imagine that these potentials of energy are pieces of malleable consciousness, that they are thoughts in motion or receptive carriers of active information that is transforming these potentials into something else. These ideas might sound a little wild, but work with me for a moment longer. Once these subatomic potentials are asked or signaled to come forward, they collapse into a specific form. They begin to change and evolve in a process. Once the probabilities have collapsed, it's harder for them to revert to their earlier energy state. The more specialized the potentials become, the more committed they become to their path of ongoing change and the less flexibility they have in taking on other forms or behaviors.

This scenario could be extended from the transformation of subatomic potentials to describe the dynamic world of subatomic functions, processes, properties, or acts of creation.

Consciousness can be a catalyst for this change.

Thomas Young

Now let's turn to an experiment that was conducted at the beginning of the nineteenth century. It is important to the history of science and our inquiry because its results provided physicists with one of their first perceptions about how what I've called "subatomic potentials" might dwell in two realms.

The work of Thomas Young opened a door, allowing a new frame of reference for what had appeared to be a solid, largely mundane world, predictable in its forms and properties. Entities that had seemed separate, intact, and unchanging might in actuality be highly malleable—and in a very elemental way, alive.

The world that had looked "real"—stationary in form and always subject to the strict rules of the macro world—might in fact be something completely different, made up of potentials that could change their states, movement, and locations like something alive, perhaps with a consciousness and the ability to intend and carry out intention.

It would take only one step further along Young's line of investigation to arrive at the idea that everything that exists is made up of the same "stuff."

In the early 1800s, Thomas Young designed an experiment to determine the properties of light. He first directed light at a barrier that was cut with a single slit. He then directed light at a barrier cut with two separate slits. He noted the patterns and the intensity of the light that appeared on a back wall after passing through the two different barriers.

The accepted scientific belief of the day was that light was made up of discrete particles, not unlike pellets or BBs. The stream of light particles should have illuminated the wall in patterns matching the shape of the slits in the barriers: one uniform pattern of light from one barrier, two uniform patterns of light from the other barrier.

However, if light traveled like a wave instead of like a particle, it would move forward not in a single straight line but in a crescent pattern, striking each barrier with a backward-curving edge.

Imagine dropping a rock into water and watching a wave spread out in a ring toward a half-submerged tree trunk. The leading arc of the ring reaches and strikes the trunk, the ring's foremost edge like the rounded "prow" of a tugboat. The center of the prow makes the first and most forceful contact with the tree trunk, while its more backward-curving sides make less direct and powerful contact.

A crescent-shaped light wave's main force—the leading edge of its prow—would push through the barrier's single slit, the light wave's greatest intensity at the middle of its arc, and with decreasing intensity at its descending edges. The pattern of light projected on the wall behind the barrier would be brighter at its center and dimmer at its periphery.

Light waves passing through the barrier with the double slits would "add and subtract," creating a striped interference pattern, with the greatest intensity in the middle and less intensity at the outer edges.

And that is just what happened. The light patterns on the wall behind the slitted barriers proved that within light there was a wave function.

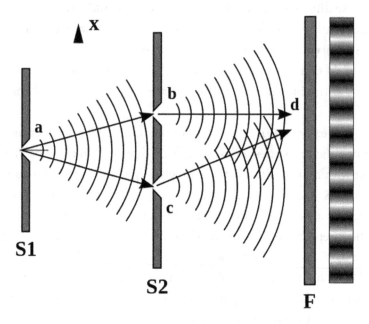

Figure 2: The unobserved photons acting as a wave form when it is not observed or entangled with the experimenter's thoughts.

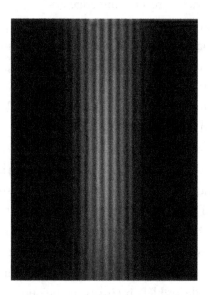

Figure 3: This is the pattern that would be seen on the back wall F.

Since Thomas's discovery there have been many variations on his experiment and some of them revolutionized our thinking concerning the nature of subatomic potentials.

1961

In 1961, Claus Jönsson of the University of Tübingen repeated Thomas's experiment, using electrons (electron "potentials") rather than beams of light. Scientists were now able to "shoot" electrons one at a time toward a barrier cut with two slits. Something highly unusual was observed when Jönsson altered the experiment after obtaining his initial, expected results.

First, electrons were shot toward the two-slitted barrier, at a target area directly between the two slits. An interference pattern appeared on the detector wall behind the barrier, just as was expected and confirming again that electrons have a wave function, just as Thomas had discovered about light more than a hundred years earlier.

Next, Jönsson and his team decided to shift their attention from the pattern on the wall behind the barrier. Now they closely observed how the electrons passed through the barrier; again, the target area was the solid space between the two slits.

The shift in the experimenters' focus of attention resulted in a transformed pattern on the detector wall. The wall displayed a pattern that was made by particles, not waves.

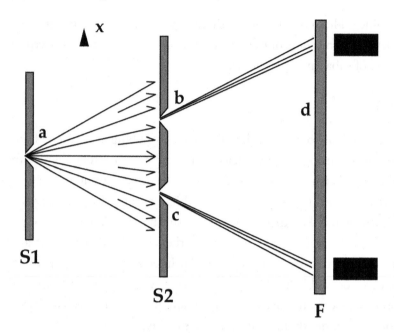

Figure 4: This diagram represents the experimenter observing or entangling with the photons as they pass through the double slits. Here they act as a particle, with the darkened rectangles as the areas where the particle-like photons hit wall F.

The discovery that electrons could shift suddenly in form from waves to particles was revolutionary. The physicists' changed focus of observation—from the electrons' projected pattern on the wall, to the electrons passing through the barrier—showed that each electron existed somewhere between a wave and a particle—and could assume either form in an instant!

The electron was no longer a certain, identifiable "thing" but a potentiality that, once started through observation on the path of specialization, could evolve into a solidified particle or particle state. The increased focus of human consciousness on the electrons triggered their transformation from wave to physical form.

It appears that human consciousness is involved in the change in an electron's potential state: the more human attention it receives, the greater the likelihood the electron will collapse into physical being.

Sensitive Potentials

Other experimenters set out to "trick" the electron potentials, to prevent the particles/waves from "knowing" when they were under human observation. The goal of these experiments was to determine whether electron potentials changed in response to being watched; physicists were trying to outsmart the subatomic entities and register their unobserved behavior.

The most noteworthy experiments were conducted by John Archibald Wheeler in 1978 and by Yoon-Ho Kim and his team of Kulik, Shih, and Scully in 1999. Let me summarize Kim and his associates' work as straightforwardly and as briefly as I can.[1] (See figure 5.)

Two photons—each a "quantum," the smallest discrete quantity of visible light—were shot from two different laser light sources. Both photons passed through a special prism-like material that split the two laser-driven photons into halves. A photon split in this manner divides into halves that are "entangled," remaining intimately connected in behavior although now physically separate entities. The halves of the original but now split photon continue to act in the same manner, each mirroring the behavior of the other, or rather acting simultaneously in identical ways.

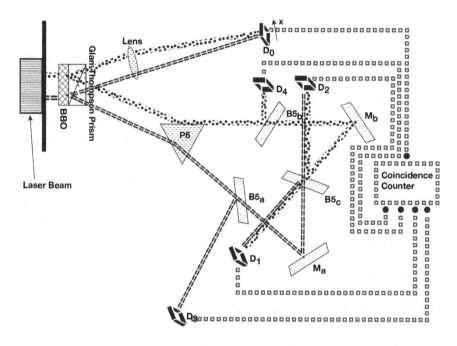

Figure 5.

"A," the first beamed photon, passed through material that divided it into halves and sent each half on a different journey through space. One half-photon was directed toward a coincidence counter, but on its path it first had to pass through Detector X. The other half-photon was sent on a different path and was refracted by mirrors and other materials toward Detectors 4, 1, and 2.

Then "B," the second beamed photon, was sent, as was A, through the splitting material. Half of the B photon was sent off to Detector X, while the other half was bounced among photons traveling toward Detectors 3, 1, and 2.

Still, both halves of photons A and B arrived at Detectors X, 1, and 2.

In other words, the photon halves—or photon potentials—"knew" that the observing physicists couldn't determine which half of either photon was registered by Detectors X, 1, and 2. The light patterns that appeared after the four photon halves passed through the slits in a barrier were the classic wave interference patterns.

The monitoring device for the A photons was Detector 4 and the monitor for B photons was Detector 3. Using these two detectors, the experimenters knew which photon half was which and where it was coming from. On these two detectors, the produced patterns indicated that the photon halves were particle-like in structure. So the electrons somehow knew when they were being watched and when they were not.

In John Archibald Wheeler's experiment, which had been conducted twenty-one years earlier, astronomical light was studied, the photons originating from stars in distant galaxies where the light was split by celestial bodies having great mass. The experiment's results describing "photon intelligence" matched those that Kim's team later noted in their experiment with photons from laser light. The photons from deep outer space and those fired from a laser on Earth showed the same mysterious, intelligent behavior.

The different photons from two ends of space were not only "smart," but behaved in the same way, which isn't surprising if we remember that all particles/waves have a common source, and thus a resulting symmetrical and entangled relationship.

That source, like ours, is the original Big Bang.

Other Oddities

There are two strange and interesting research discoveries that I find especially relevant in considering the subatomic quantum world where electrons change back and forth between particles and waves, entangled photons mirror each other's behavior, and micro-entities operate with an awareness of their surroundings and a sense of when they are being observed by human consciousness.

In an experiment designed to observe electron probabilities (particle/wave states), physicists directed energy at an atom to "excite" it and observe the resulting behavior of its electrons. The infusion of energy caused the atom's electrons to move outward from a small "shell" or orbit to a larger shell. The experimenters expected to observe this movement of electrons. However, they discovered that electrons don't "move" from small to larger shells through space and time. Instead, the electron ceases to exist in the small shell and simultaneously appears in the larger shell. The electron moves through a realm or dimension with different rules (or no rules?) of time and distance, a world that we cannot currently investigate with the scientific tools we have.[2]

An experiment known as "Josephson's Junction" and "quantum tunneling" offers another window onto the strange space-time world that electrons inhabit. The general design of the experiment involved a wave generator that created a wave probability inside a box. The walls of the box had detectors that sensed when electrons hit or attempted to pass through the walls. The electrons were each probabilities, and together had probabilities in terms of the pattern they would form inside the "inescapable box."

What the researchers found was that the electrons' probabilities projected both inside and outside the box as intended. They also found that these probabilities were influenced by the observer. The most interesting part was that the electrons that were generated inside the box found their way to the other side of the barrier without passing through it. The electron probability or potentiality apparently "created itself" on the other side as if the impenetrable barrier of the box's wall wasn't there.[3]

The experiment demonstrated that electron potentials are created in some unknown fashion that doesn't follow our expected rules of energy and matter, time and space. The electrons appeared to simply "pop out" from another realm of existence behind or underneath or superimposed on the "normal" realm that we live in and believe we fully understand.

The electrons' sudden appearances resemble mini–Big Bangs of creation. "Something" is not "coming from nothing" but from a realm of existence we can't yet perceive.

Small World/Big World

Studying the bizarre subatomic world where particles/waves disappear and simultaneously appear elsewhere makes us wonder whether similar or identical phenomena may be occurring and affecting us in our macro world.

The day-to-day big world in which we live is much more dedicated to specialization, to determined paths and forms, than the quantum world is. The electron can easily change its identity and structure but large organisms can't. The ability of our consciousness to manifest choices and intentions, from a mental to a physical plane, is a little more limited.

The best opportunity to bring thoughts into concrete existence in the macro physical realm occurs at the moment of creation, when specialization hasn't yet taken hold and evolving structures haven't started along a path that is more difficult to influence. Once you have become an elephant, you would find it difficult to re-create yourself as a jellyfish. The "jump" would be too far, the critical decision to become an elephant too long ago in the line of now irreversible development to make such a sudden, significant change.

Databank

Now let's imagine a more realistic situation, where our thoughts may produce crucial physical results. I'd like to introduce you to John, who might be any of us.

John is a worrier. Every time John gets stressed out, he can feel discomfort in his large intestine.

Over the years, John develops irritable bowel syndrome, which causes chronic inflammation in the lining of his intestine. The inflammation triggers cellular changes in the intestine and detrimental alterations in John's DNA.

For decades, John avoids any effort to resolve his constant state of worry and deal positively with his feelings of stress. He also ignores all the warning signs his body has been sending him in the form of symptoms of irritable bowel syndrome.

One day, much to John's surprise, he learns from his doctor that cells in his intestine have become cancer-like.

John's case is an example of how epigenetics works: how our emotional responses to stimuli become physical responses and then embedded physical structures whose codes are registered in our DNA. These acquired or evolved structures become part of us and our genetic identity, and can be passed down to our offspring at the moment of conception. This is a common example of consciousness changing physicality.

The fact is that our bodies are involved in a constant, swift activity that in some ways resembles the speed and flexibility of electrons. The cells of our bodies are re-creating themselves all of the time. Some of our tissues can change very rapidly. For example, the tissues of your mouth and eyes can re-create themselves in one or two days. All of the body's organs are in a perpetual, dynamic state of re-creation.

Our "solid" bodies are in reality an ongoing process of change and transformation. Because our bodies aren't static but evolving, we have the opportunity to manifest dramatic physical alterations, to use our consciousness—our thoughts, emotions, and intentions—to determine the structure of our tissues and cells.

For a moment, let's trace a possible path, from one mental state to another, toward a possible ultimate source that also may be a possible goal.

We all know that we have conscious thoughts, and most of us realize that we have subconscious thoughts. We have always seen that the conscious mind is the home to the ego and the subconscious mind is the place where our greater wisdom or perhaps soul dwells. Imagine these different levels of consciousness existing in a realm that is much larger than our individual brain. Imagine that in another world we each have a very sophisticated and powerful databank for registering, analyzing, sorting, storing, and sending information.

Flexibility

Now let's return to the day John learns from his doctor about the cancerous activity in his intestine.

What if John interprets this information as a message from a source within and the doctor is simply verifying this information?

What if John decides that the cancerous cells are a last-ditch effort at communication from his caring conscious/subconscious/soul consciousness databank?

The databank is alerting John that he needs to immediately wake up and transform the belief system that has allowed and fed his constant state of worry—worry that progressively irritated the tissues of his intestine, and finally resulted in very serious harm to his body.

John understands the message and its ultimate source. When he worries incessantly, his body experiences every imagined worst-case scenario as if it were actually happening. His constant efforts to control the world, whose uncertainties caused him so much worry, have worn down his body and made it sick. He now chooses not to worry about what might go wrong, and begins to work on altering his anxious patterns of thinking and behavior. He decides to accept the world as it is and take things as they come.

By changing his response to present stimuli and not fearing the specter of future events, John is beginning to undo the negative history that led to his present ill health. These changes in thought and feeling shut off the continuous barrage of negative neurochemicals, consciousness/energy, and negative cellular activity in the intestine. The cells in the affected tissue no longer need the receptor sites they've created to receive toxic neurochemicals. The evolution of the cells reverses, positive structuring occurs, and normal life force and intercellular communication return.

The cellular structures continue to work toward re-creating their initial healthy state and their efficient, normal functioning that preceded John's growing tendency toward worried thoughts and emotions. The tissues undo and repair the effects of his anxious response to stress, which began the cells' negative evolution that on the physical plane mirrored his negative mental state.

One of the many amazing qualities of all living things is their ability to constantly re-create themselves in positive ways, to maintain their good health and vibrancy. Although we are much larger than an electron, we have almost infinitely more flexibility than we might first imagine.

We usually assume that we aren't constantly changing. We wake up each morning apparently the same person who went to sleep the night before. When we look at ourselves in the bathroom mirror, don't we closely—if not identically—resemble the person who lay down and turned off the light eight hours ago?

But we wildly mislead ourselves. Our picture of the same, unchanged person rising in the morning couldn't be further from a true picture of reality.

We are each an evolutionary process, constantly responding to and creating interior and exterior stimuli. Our responses are both mental and physical. Their causes and effects are very visible when we look at them over longer periods of time.

I think it's important to remember that good health reflects positive thoughts, but healthy thoughts are not the denial of negative thoughts. Instead, they are a transformation of negative thoughts into positive signals that our subconscious mind registers and cycles back in harmonious patterns to our conscious mind—and to the cells of our body that re-create and sustain our evolving physical being in well-organized ways that produce good health. The sooner we are aware of the negative patterns through the symptoms of our body, the greater ability we have to change them.

There are a few things to remember from this chapter. One, the subatomic world that makes up our body and all things around us is very amenable to the wishes of our consciousness. Two, the wise consciousness or soul within has a strong self-interest in keeping its human side alive. Three, don't ever think you can outsmart a subatomic particle. Their thoughts may be a part of something much bigger than you knew.

9

DIMENSIONS VERSUS REALMS

A Question

Years ago, I taught science to upper elementary children. At the start of the year, the students arrived to meet their teachers and one of the fifth graders, a boy named Bryce, approached me.

He said, "I have a question for you that no other teacher has been able to explain. If we live in a four-dimensional universe, made of up and down, side to side, forward and backward, and time, and you take away one of the nontime dimensions, won't all of the dimensions collapse?"

Bryce's question was an interesting one about how space works, and it was especially so because he used the word "dimensions." I asked Bryce if he ever remembered any of his dreams and he told me he did. To be more specific, I asked him if he remembered a dream in which he had been running, and again Bryce said he had. Then I asked him how far he'd run in his dream.

"Maybe hundreds of feet," he answered.

I asked, "How far did you really run?"

The insightful boy realized what I was suggesting. According to his sensory awareness within the dream, and in his later memory of running in the dream, Bryce had traveled hundreds of feet. But when he returned to full waking reality in our physical realm, he knew that he was in his bed and hadn't taken a single step. No distance had been traveled, at least in the physical realm we know as waking reality.

105

I told Bryce that within our consciousness, the experiences we have in dreams, under hypnotic trance, and in waking reality are perceived as being equally real and true, equally "solid." Our mind registers events that occur in different states of awareness in the same way, without differentiating between the various physical or mental realms in which these events take place. In our total consciousness, experiences in dreams and under hypnosis bear the same reality as events we encounter when we are wide awake in our physical bodies.

I asked Bryce to consider space as a dimension that is not hard and fast, but rather a setting or environment that allows us to experience different actions and thoughts, in the same way a stage allows actors to realistically perform their play. Space, our sense of location and physical direction, is a crucial part of our experience, but space and distance alone don't define the complete structure of our four-"dimensional" world. I saw the wheels begin to turn and asked Bryce, "How can we be sure we are truly traveling in space in our waking reality?" I told him that I felt that was an even better question.

I suggested that Bryce might use the word "realm" instead of "dimension." I added that there was a possibility that our sense of distance is tied to the laws and parameters of perception that operate in each realm. I added that there is a possibility that each realm, waking or sleeping, is a projection of energy or consciousness, a Creation Consciousness. I told him that we would be discussing concepts of space, nonspace, and the many possibilities that might exist in an entangled universe where time and space from several realms might be internally folded upon one another. We would explore all of this in greater detail when our class studied quantum mechanics.

Bryce ended our conversation by saying that this was the first time he had received a likely or perhaps correct answer to his question. That morning's exchange made me wonder how long before his first day as a fifth grader Bryce had been asking teachers his question.

You may have entertained the possibility that "we are multidimensional beings." I would rephrase that statement as "we are beings who dwell in several realms, each of which has its own unique experiences and laws of physics."

The idea that there might be different realms of human existence may be verified in the not-too-distant future. Scientists are currently developing instrumentation to detect the potential existence of other realms in which we are conscious and involved.

A Third Realm

We have previously considered the possibility that there are at least two different realms of human existence: the physical realm that we perceive through our five senses, and the energetic realm of unified consciousness, which some people call "heaven." Dr. Newton labels this second realm "unified consciousness," "life between lives," or "LBL." I have related the experiences of subjects under hypnosis that suggest the realm of unified consciousness is a place we always inhabit, not just in the time between one physical life and reincarnation into another.

Are there really other dimensions, what I prefer to call "realms"?

I believe other realms exist because of the answers I've received during hypnotic sessions when subjects under trance spoke with what they called their "soul voice." Interviews with patients who have died and then returned to life also point to another realm of consciousness.

I have also used the muscle-testing technique I described earlier, which can access the soul within the physical body, to investigate the reality of "heaven." Subjects during these tests described three to six different realms in which humans can simultaneously exist. Interestingly, I have never tested anyone who mentioned fewer than three realms or more than six.

Certainly everyone is familiar with the physical realm that we all know as life here on Earth. I am going to enumerate that one as the third realm just so this discussion will make a little better sense. The next realm is a place of pure potential creation and oneness. I'll call this the energetic realm or realm number one. From what I have learned, there is another realm that lies between the two that has been described as a "creator realm." I believe this is a dimension where transitions take place and we encounter a process-oriented existence. This realm is a unique one where existence is stable; however, it is part of a stepwise process in which energy becomes matter, a "place" in the sequence of consciousness becoming physicality. Most people would call it the heavenly realm, part of the stream where energy, intention, and consciousness manifest a unique "intermediary existence." And it is tied into what we identify as process string theory and creation.

In other words, imagine that there are many transformative steps between pure consciousness energy and physicality, much like a chain of steps or processes, in a continuum between the realm of consciousness and our physical life on Earth, where the process stops and stabilizes. This indicates to me that there is a collective of experiences here that do not occur in the other steps of transformation. The other steps are too transitory to be considered a realm.

Also, from my interviews with subjects under hypnosis or during muscle testing, I have learned that all organisms that have ever lived on Earth—and all organisms that may live on Earth sometime in the future—exist in this creator realm. Any organism that has lived has a blueprint or template or matrix, some aspect of itself, in that dimension. All animals and plants that became extinct still exist there. They are, however, conscious in an ongoing "living" existence in some capacity. As long as this creator realm exists, so do those once-living beings that may now be extinct. It is a master library of experiences.

The most important function I've learned about this realm (#2) is that our souls are more individuated from the collective there, which allows greater freedom to create our physical existence. The spark of the Divine or Creation that exists in the energetic realm (#1) is completely merged as one with the whole, and the experience of that realm is one of unified and inseparable oneness. This is a central hub of congruence where the bridge of the creator realm allows the expansion of experience and purpose to grow. It is here (#2) that our souls have free will and individual oversight to help orchestrate our lives as individuals in the physical realm.

When we think of the soul as a unique entity, we are thinking of that consciousness in this intermediary realm, where the soul is semiautonomous. Here is an analogy: The identity of your soul in the intermediary creator realm would be an ice cube in a vast sea of ice cubes. Finding your soul in the energetic realm of creation, where all things are merged, would be like looking for one melted ice cube in a sea full of them. The physical world we experience is like a rocky island in the middle of the vast ocean of ice cubes you can't see or feel with your five senses.

All of these realms are superimposed. There is intimate communication between the creator realm and the energetic realm, and similarly there is great communication between the creator and physical realms, whether you are open to hearing it or not. Your life is much more orchestrated by this realm than you might think. The experiences you will traverse and the important people you will meet are coordinated from the consciousness that dwells here. The creator realm is the hub of activity and coordination. It is quite entangled with all the other realms that human consciousness can play and exist in. It is like an octopus with many arms of coordination. The interactions between the realms are quantum-like. There is a constant interchange of information that, by all accounts, is instantaneous. This means that Creator/Soul Consciousness in each of the realms is aware of much the same information at the same time. There are, however, certain limitations or capacities to each realm. This is a minimal point but needs to be mentioned. This is very beneficial to help guide the experience toward the best outcome for creation.

There is more information going out from the realm than comes in, despite all the input. This is an existence that is very curious to me, and I will ask many more questions when I have the opportunity to meet the next messenger.

What I have learned is that all things have consciousness there, and that this other realm may occupy the same "space" that our physical Earth does, though it exists "out of phase" with our Earth and remains invisible. One can think of this in several different ways. One way would be similar to how we see the colors of a flower compared to how a bee sees them. I always found the difference amazing: our sensory organs seek different light. Yet this does not completely explain how two realms can exist in the same space, overlapping each other. The word that describes this is "superimposition." If we remember that the building material of every physical thing is energy or fields of energy, we begin to understand how this can occur. Things feel physical because the charges around subatomic particles like electrons and protons give off electromagnetic force fields. In fact, when you walk on the ground, you never really touch the ground. The nuclear forces or force fields between molecules create a space between the bottoms of your feet and the earth; it feels solid but it is far from it. This is one of the great illusions that trick us into thinking our realm is physical. If the force fields created by the building blocks of our realm do not interact with the force fields and building blocks of another realm, they can exist in the same space. If these building blocks from another realm are out of sync with ours, then what we see as light reflecting off these bundles of energy/building blocks would also be different from the ones we see in our realm. This is how two realms can be superimposed and entangled with each other but not perceived from either.

I acknowledge that it is a challenge to understand how consciousness and a transitional creator realm might exist outside our grasp, but scientists have continued to ask these big questions and have worked to discover more about other realms.

Stumbling onto Other Realms and Dark Matter

More than two decades ago scientists began to add up the mass of the known universe. At the same time, they knew what the mass of the universe needed to be in order for the forces of gravity to hold it together. Without gravity the intricate orbits of our solar system, the Milky Way, and the rest of the universe would not exist and everything would fly apart. Our universe has become much less chaotic than it was in its earlier years. Unexpectedly, when all of the sums were in, approximately 95 percent of the mass needed to hold everything together was missing.

This startling discovery sparked a search for other kinds of matter. Under the laws that scientists knew governed the physical realm, there simply wasn't enough mass to keep the universe from fragmenting and wandering off in trillions of separate pieces. It wasn't even close.

Yet the universe did hold together. The absent mass had to exist, in some form, somewhere, and exert gravitational force. And so the concept of "dark matter" was born. The name "dark matter" communicated the idea that though it surely existed, we were presently unable to see it.

I find it staggering to imagine that only 5 percent of the mass of the universe is visible. The other 95 percent, almost all of the mass created by the Big Bang, or the theoretical start of our universe, is beyond human sight or current means of detection. We must acknowledge that the human eye can only see a thousandth of the visible light spectrum. This miniscule perception of visible light, as well as our inability to perceive possible light emissions from other possible realms, may be hiding many things from our awareness.

Scientists know dark matter exists even though they can't "find" it. They postulate it must either emit a kind of light apart from any light spectrum we know of, or simply not emit or reflect any light that interacts with the physical realm. Physicists and astronomers are searching for the "stuff" or "matter" that is apparently "out of phase" with our realm of physicality.

It is theorized that the forces of gravity may be active or can spill back and forth between our physical realm and other realms. This suggests that what would be considered matter in other realms could be counted in the mass of the universe. The force of gravity could interact with all the realms that contain things with mass, and that could account for the missing 95 percent. There is only one natural force active from realm to realm and from dimension to dimension. Scientists have mapped out those areas of our universe where large expanses of dark matter should and most likely do exist. They have identified these locations by observing anomalies in the path of light and the orbital motion of celestial bodies, which can't be accounted for by the influence of any visible, known mass or force.

Superimposition

Imagine a universe like our own, one that is filled with infinite numbers of galaxies—Milky Way after Milky Way. Imagine suns thousands of times more massive than our sun scattered throughout those galaxies.

Now imagine another universe whose space is nearly filled with dark matter. The theoretical "shapes" of dark matter aren't necessarily round and may not resemble our planets. Scientists have mapped and described areas of dark matter looking like massive, irregular pieces of a jigsaw puzzle. A universe made up of dark matter would have unimaginable mass and therefore a gravitational pull so strong that it could provide the "glue" to hold our universe together.

Our two imagined distinct universes, one made up of galaxies of stars and orbiting planets and one made up of dark matter, each contain unimaginable numbers of massive celestial bodies, like huge spinning mobiles moving through the fabric of space.

Now superimpose one universe directly onto the other, so the universes are like the transparencies animators use, or visualize two different movies projected on a single screen at the same time. Because the two universes remain distinct entities, they are "out of phase" with one other. Instead of colliding, they simply glide through the same space with minimal interaction. The only weak interaction we see comes from the force of gravity.

At this very moment, dark matter from that other realm or universe is probably passing through our bodies and we don't even know it. The fact that we don't feel or see or otherwise sense the presence or passage of dark matter reflects a property of superimposition, of two worlds somehow sharing the same "space" but occupying different realms. Scientists hope to discover and measure some of the minimal interactions that might exist between our universe and a superimposed universe of dark matter. This would be the proof of another realm that would contain some or all of the missing 95 percent.

In Minnesota, a vast research laboratory has been built deep underground.[1] Extremely sensitive screens have been installed that can register the passage of miniscule amounts of mass and energy. The screens must be located deep in the crust of the earth, so they are shielded from other forms of energy that are active on the earth's surface. In this laboratory an increase in heat or energy emission picked up by the sensing screens might indicate the presence of dark matter. Scientists are trying to detect a particle, or even an entire "planet" of dark matter passing through a screen, so they can determine just what dark matter is and how it behaves. This is always our struggle when we're trying to figuring out a way to detect matter that is different from our own and that we know so little about. This is why research is slow to come from this realm.

Dark Energy

Along with dark matter, there is another mysterious aspect of our universe called dark energy. Dark energy is a powerful force that causes the universe to expand, acting as a counterforce to gravity. The massive gravitational effects of visible and dark matter pull our universe inward, holding it together by decelerating its expansion that began with the Big Bang and is furthered by the propagation of dark energy.

Dark energy apparently occupies all of space that science once considered completely empty, is inherently expansive, and in our realm is responsible for creating space and time.

Planets and stars give off colors depending on whether they are moving toward us or away from us. Astronomers have recently found that the vast majority of planets and stars are moving away from us. The only ones that are moving toward us are those that have an orbital pattern that moves them closer to us despite the expansion of space. The distance between all celestial bodies is constantly becoming greater.

Imagine for a moment a triangle with a planet on each of the three corners (see figure 6). If you make the triangle or the space within the triangle bigger, from the perspective of each of the corners or anywhere within the triangle, all the planets will be moving away each other.

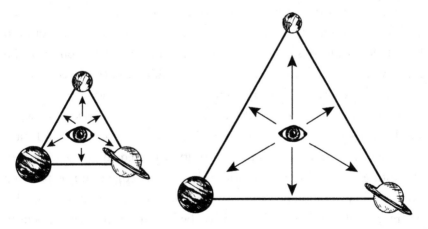

Figure 6.

Now let's go to the next step. Imagine two triangles side by side, both with planets on each of their corners. If space is expanding at a similar rate within the triangles and outside them, from any perspective in space or on any of those planets, the corners of the triangles will be moving farther apart from each other.

In this way the "push" of dark energy causes all of the planets and stars to move outward and as they do, space continues to grow larger.

The current, accepted scientific belief, arrived at by mathematical calculations and precise astronomical measurements of light in our universe, is that our universe is infinite in its reach through space. Space evidently goes on forever and never ends, always expanding outward because of the force of dark energy, although the celestial bodies in the universe are not moving outward at the same speed. The far edges of the universe are expanding much faster than the universe's theoretical center. This makes sense if you think of concentric rings, much like a bull's-eye target, in space. Locate the center of space smack dab in the center of the bull's eye. Imagine that the first ring is expanding at five miles an hour. Imagine that the next two rings are each expanding at five miles an hour. The outside edge of the third ring would be expanding at fifteen miles per hour. The same phenomenon is occurring in space. The outer edges of the universe are continuously picking up speed as the metaphorical rings of space are added. We live in an infinite universe without boundaries, a universe continually creating new space as its expansion accelerates to incredible speeds, pushing its seemingly limitless perimeter onward into infinity. The rate of this expansion has or will exceed the speed of light. The larger the universe becomes, the faster it will expand.

You can see that the word "infinite" becomes a relative term when we don't have the capacity to comprehend or visualize what "infinite" really means or what infinity times infinity would equal. It would be very interesting to visualize this mystical place at the edge of our expanding universe. The question becomes, what is just on the other side of that edge where space does not exist? I would also be curious to see what happens to planets being pushed beyond the speed of light relative to the center of the universe. According to our theories of relativity, going the speed of light is a pretty tricky deal. It involves infinite mass, or perhaps a point where things don't make sense to us. I have wondered if this margin would be a place where the rules change much like when you superheat subatomic particles and they become completely interchangeable. Neutrons can become protons, protons neutrons, and electrons can make miraculous metamorphosis. Perhaps as physical planets exceed the speed of light, they too undergo metamorphosis or even revert back to energy. Maybe the planets' speed is only relative to the space they exist in, exempt from the additive speed from accumulated space. This is indeed all theoretical but these are the questions that lead us to understand what we are made of and how we might contribute to the process.

Along with theories of relativity, Albert Einstein coined the term "space-time." This term refers to the fact that space and time are intimately connected and cannot exist separately. The existence of space allows for the experience of time.

The more capable we are of investigating these unforeseen territories and new horizons, the more we understand that we are just scratching the surface of what exists. It was not very long ago in our history that a member of the scientific community put forth the belief that we had discovered all that needed to be or could be discovered. The greater truth is that the more we know, the more we realize how little we know. The exciting part of this for me is that our box of knowledge has no limits and is forever expanding. No one has all the answers, and the truth continually evolves. This is a scary concept for those who do not like ambiguity or admitting they don't have the answer. Part of the exploration into dark matter and dark energy is to shake up what you think you know and allow a dynamic truth to stay on the path of evolution.

Let us look a little deeper into the hidden and mystical potentials of dark energy.

Inner Space: Home Sweet Home

To study dark energy, perhaps we should focus on the infinitely small instead of looking outward toward the infinitely expanding universe. Scientists tell us that dark energy exists everywhere, filling the utter emptiness of space between the celestial bodies of our galaxy. It also fills the great expanses of what we once thought was the "nothingness" within atoms, the space between the nucleus and its orbiting electrons' potentials.

To illustrate this further, visualize the nucleus of an atom to be a ball four inches in diameter. The atom's outer electron shell would be approximately five miles in diameter. Dark energy exists everywhere throughout that vast empty space within the atom.

Now let's look into the neutron of an atom itself. The neutron operates according to the principles of mass, but the inner world of the neutron is made up of even smaller subatomic particles—quarks, gluons, and more—that lack the same characteristics of physicality. This is where we see a transition point at which energy turns into what we think of as physical. If we now look inside these bundles of energy, we can also find dark energy.

We realize how entangled space and dark energy are when we see them as an inseparable entity. Whether we are in outer space, above the atmosphere in a vacuum lacking gas molecules to fill that space, in the tiny spaces between electrons and the nucleus of an atom, or in the bundles of energy that make up neutrons and protons of an atom, they are all made of space. All of those spaces have in a sense been created by dark energy. Space is a defining condition for our physical existence. It is certainly something we take for granted. It's one of those things that are everywhere, and we lose sight of its importance. Space may be infinite but it is infinitely filled with dark energy.

The World Is No Longer Flat

We can take this description of dark energy one step further. I attended a university scientific symposium where many of the mysteries of physics that we've been considering were discussed. A scientist from South Africa gave an hour-long lecture on dark energy and what it truly is. The information he offered was revolutionary, but I felt he was holding back an even more obvious answer. He was supporting the belief of himself and his team that there was information within dark energy. He talked about dark energy as a place where information was stored. He was reluctant to say if it was consciousness.

Later, I saw the lecturer walking across the university campus and approached him. I wanted to ask him a vital question concerning the crucial issue that I felt was missing from his presentation. I asked him why he didn't just come out and say that there was consciousness within dark energy or that dark energy was actually consciousness.

He remembered me and the other questions I had asked during the lecture. After a little more conversation, he told me that he and his colleagues did feel that what we are now calling dark energy was consciousness and that consciousness in and of itself was conscious.

He reminded me that it would take time and repetition for people to feel safe and accept new beliefs as significant as this one. He knew others would come to the same conclusions as time went on, but currently he and his team had no proof, only indications. There were currently no means to directly or indirectly extract or test the hypothesis that information or consciousness was inside or constituted dark energy.

It could be that some researchers within the scientific community don't want to be the next Copernicus or Galileo, an outrider presenting strange new ideas that would expose them to ridicule and jeopardize their professional standing. After all, scientific knowledge is built step by step on a stairway of proven facts and repeatable experiments and calculations toward the verified discovery of a new law of nature.

Scientists may believe something is true, but until they can confirm its physical existence they are hesitant to voice their intuitions and hypotheses. And yet, as I discussed at the beginning of this book, doesn't scientific discovery occur in this exact way? We start with an idea that may or may not be true and set about trying to discover the answer.

There may not be any technological avenues for tying dark energy to information at this time. Maybe the idea of information-bearing dark energy hasn't yet achieved substantial force and scientific support to fast-track further research, but this does not mean it isn't true. And if it is true . . . what are the implications?

The Body of God

As time went by, I thought about what the scientist had said. I continued to consider the likely possibility that dark energy somehow was information. One thought led to another, in a chain:

- Certainly, consciousness is energy.
- Dark energy could represent a collective consciousness.
- Dark energy is a self-propagating energy.
- This consciousness is sentient, aware of itself and its surroundings.
- Does experience expand in the same way space expands?
- Whose experiences—organic, inorganic, or from other realms—feed into this collective consciousness?
- Where would a Universal Consciousness or a Creator of all things reside in the universe, if such an entity were to take on a physical presence?
- A Universal Consciousness would have to be in all things, just as dark energy both creates all space and fills all or is all space.
- Dark energy is in all space and God or a creative source for the universe would be everywhere. Everywhere would be the Creation or God itself.

If this line of logic is true, we are returning to what shamans, mystics, and many ancient religions tell us. We are inside the Creation of God and therefore inside God/Creation itself. This, I believe, is the same as saying God is inside us and we are an aspect of this Creation. As you know, I use the words God, Creation, Nature, and Unknowable interchangeably. Please use the one that suits you best. Seeing the interchangeability of all these names has helped me get over my phobia of the word God. I know that the later religions of our world see God and all other living things, including humans, as separate from God, but I believe physics is returning us to the older belief. If all things are a part of God, then all of the experiences feed into this collective consciousness. The far-reaching reality of this is even greater. We will return to this in the latter chapters concerning religion.

Quantum Mechanics

The physical world has been closely observed by scientists over many centuries and we have reliable laws that explain its behavior. Mathematics can repeatedly predict the movements through space and time of the tangible things that we perceive in daily life through our five senses. Newtonian physics and the principles of space-time set out in Einstein's Theory of General Relativity allow us to correctly calculate the present and future speeds, directions, and other operations of macro-world entities. We can understand the mechanics of both an apple falling from a tree and of a distant planet orbiting a star.

We have also achieved a greater capacity to look into the subatomic world. The particles and energies within atoms exist in a realm where reality is more chaotic and uncertain and tiny entities can exercise the freedom to change their identities and behaviors at will. A whole new set of principles and physical laws was needed to describe, understand, and predict the operations of mass and energy in this infinitely small world. The effort to discover the rules and structures of this strange realm within the atom and its subatomic contents is called "quantum mechanics."

Quantum mechanics constructed many concepts to describe and explain observed events inside the atom. On the subatomic scale of existence, time can flow backward or forward with equal probability. The phenomenon of superimposition proves that multiple things or realms can occupy the same space at the same time. The concept of entanglement describes a vast connection and cooperation, even a "oneness," among subatomic entities. Their actions are in direct opposition to the behavior of objects in the physical macro world, where we constantly perceive the separation between things without a dynamic interrelationship and shared identity.

Is it possible that our macro world, whose building blocks are made from components of the subatomic world, reacts more like the quantum world? We will learn more about who we are and an inherent flexibility that lies within us waiting to be tapped, as well as the role of consciousness in this creation process. Some important terms help us understand the way the quantum world works.

Entanglement

Entanglement is a term that reveals the unseen connection that is within us and reaches out to all things that exist. We believe the birth of all things in our universe, seen and unseen, occurred in the singular event known as the Big Bang. Every piece of matter and energy that was created at that time might best be seen as one massive expanding organism. This means that everything within that "organism" *is* that "organism." Everything is connected or entangled and existing as *one* thing. Native American cultures knew this deeper truth of the universe when they referred to the animal kingdom as their brothers and sisters and the earth as their mother.

Here is how scientists reveal our seemingly invisible relationship. There is a large body of scientific work around splitting single photons into "twins." The process of creating the twins involves sending a photon through a certain medium that splits the light much like a prism, sending the two identical aspects of the original photon in two separate directions.

In one experiment, scientists sent each half of a photon a far distance down a photo-optical wire, until the photon halves were widely separated in space.[2] The researchers then manipulated one of the photon twins, only to discover that the other twin had changed in the same way, instantly, without manipulation. The separated halves of the single photon were evidently "entangled" in some sort of extremely fast communication with one another.

The next step was to determine how long it took for this reaction to happen. It was assumed that the sent information would have to have traveled at a very high speed, perhaps even the speed of light. Surprisingly, what they found was that the twins changed *simultaneously*. The obvious problem was to explain how this simultaneous transformation took place.

Two possible explanations are immediately apparent. The first is that the information exchange between the twins exceeded the speed of light. But that is supposed to be impossible under the rules of Einstein's General Relativity Theory. The second explanation is that space may lack the linear and additive components of distance in the subatomic world. Space could also be a holographic construct. Many have pondered the idea of our reality being a *projection* of consciousness while everything is occurring inside a living consciousness—or, metaphorically speaking, inside the projector. I'm sure there are other possible explanations for this experiment, but the bottom line for me is that space has much more flexibility if you are a subatomic particle living in the quantum world.

Space-Time Out

Modern science remains uncertain about many aspects of what we call "space." We are still in an early pioneering stage in our understanding of dark energy, which as we've discussed fills, creates, and structures space.

You could say that we are presently using the term "dark energy" as a kind of place holder until we have a clearer idea of just what it is and whether, in reality, it is the prime agent behind the existence of space. We need to remember that quantum mechanics also contemplates the possibility of "infinite potentials" capable of creating an infinite multi-universe. Some scientists postulate that anything that can happen is currently happening, or will occur, in at least one of the vast number of different universes that may exist or are even now in the process of creation.

The deeper you delve into the world of quantum mechanics, the more unfamiliar our universe appears. The quantum world may be one of infinite chaos, infinite potential, and infinite freedom. It may be a realm that comes into being in the first instant that any act of material or energetic creation occurs. Most physicists agree that there is much more to be discovered.

I mentioned "string theory" as one of several ideas that attempt to account for our universe and the subatomic realm that underpins it. String theory is an appealing hypothesis because it proposes an explanation for the process of creation in our universe and how the universe functions. It has been a frontrunner among intriguing theories of creation. Its history is an interesting one, and it isn't over yet.

String Theory

We currently recognize four forces in nature that govern our world: gravity, electromagnetics, and weak and strong nuclear forces. Each of these forces has its own equation that describes its behavior, but physicists have been searching for one grand equation that will bring these four forces into a coherent mathematical relationship. This elusive equation could be called the "theory of everything." A viable equation must be able to predict outcomes and provide solutions that make sense when other values are inserted into it. This simply means that at the conclusion of the calculation, the numbers on either side of the equal sign must be the same; i.e., seven must equal seven.

When a complex equation works mathematically and explains an observed phenomenon, theoretical physicists can examine the equation and search it for meaning and usefulness, gaining at least some intuitive sense of what natural relationships the equation describes or can potentially describe.

A physicist named Leonard Susskind was working with an old equation used to explain the actions of electromagnetic forces. The more he worked with the equation, the more strongly he came to believe that he had found such an equation, connecting the four forces of nature. He called his equation "string theory."

String theory, like most new ideas, gained momentum only slowly. Over time, increasing numbers of theoretical physicists were drawn to Susskind's equation that alluded to a specific universal mechanism or process.

The equation suggested the possibility that there might be an infinite number of different "strings" whose special vibrations transformed raw energy into the four forces of nature and bound them together. The existence of these strings and their vibrations might be the basic building blocks of the macro world we live in. Perhaps the size, shape, tension, and other qualities of the strings were responsible for all the various aspects of physical nature.

String Music

The more I learned about string theory, the more attracted to it I became. It "felt right" and it seemed that it might be capable of explaining the existence and functioning of the entire universe and defining the unified forces that created it.

One feature of this theory that especially interested me was that it suggested a process that could collapse undifferentiated energy into the specific forces that were capable of creating our physical realm. String theory proposes that a string creates a vibration, a pattern, or perhaps a standing wave that holds energy in a specific form and function.

Susskind presented a lucid way of describing the forces that he perceived were acting in the infinitely small quantum world. What those processes are and how exactly they function are still unknown. The better we understand the process at the moment of metamorphosis, the closer we will come to understanding how we as humans come into being.

The Great Mystery

As you can imagine, the great mystery that had always presented itself to religion, philosophy, and science swiftly appeared again. If there are vibrating strings that underlay our universe, who or what is plucking the strings in such a way that a universe had been created and continues its structure and current path of evolution?

It seems science is now talking about a universal life force/consciousness that is actively creating reality through the way that it strums the strings. That is to say, a sentient creative force (God) is plucking the strings of intention.

In trying to understand the human mind and body and their functioning, we look for an organelle or some other organ of reproduction to account for cell creation and communication. Somewhere within individual and cooperating cells, within the brain, or within an i-Cloud surrounding the body, shouldn't information, knowledge, and our essence be stored?

Metaphor and Science

When we contemplate the existence of a multidimensional universe, we wonder where to look for an entity resembling some incredibly complex and powerful cell organelle, responsible for the processes that create space, time, planets, and human and all other forms of life.

Whatever the creating force of the universe is, we must remember it is not a white-haired, punishing, egotistical man who lives in a distant place, whether on Mt. Olympus or elsewhere.

Of course, many people have imagined God as a man, their picture of the divine intelligence based on the writings of a priest that are found in the Jewish Bible and repeated in the Elder Testament of the Christian Bible. Genesis 1:27 reads "and God created man in his own image."

From a literal, paternalistic, ethnocentric perspective, we could take this description to mean that God has the same body and appearance as a human male. However, it is important to consider the actual Hebrew of this biblical passage. Genesis 1:27 is literally translated as "And God created the human in His image; in the image of God, He created him; male and female, He created them." The Hebrew word for God used here is Elohim, a plural name for God. This fluidity between singular and plural and masculine and feminine is important when we try to define what humans being created in the image of God means. Hebrew is inherently a gendered language but the name for God here is plural.[3]

The actual Hebrew text leaves much room for fluidity and interpretation. We can even understand that all things are created in the likeness of God, because all things are God, no matter how they appear. We as humans are not the only image. Everything that exists has God Consciousness within it, and in this way everything resembles God, because it is an aspect of God, a self-creation of God.

Genesis 2:7 can literally be translated as "And the Lord God formed the human of dust from the Earth, and He breathed into his nostrils the soul of life, and the human became a living soul." We are told in the same scripture that creation comes from the breath of God. God's breath—the thoughts and words of God—creates humanity as well as the physical universe. It is also interesting to think how we as souls need to be as we are animated into a physical existence. How can you create a body of flesh that can hold a soul while being made purely of consciousness or energy?

Proverbs 20:27 says "the light of God is the soul of a human being." Here is another ancient message that may bare profound truth. In the previous verse we see the importance of focused intention of consciousness in creation. In this proverb we could interpret the light of God as being the energy of creation and that this light, a piece of energy, can individuate itself as a human soul. Simply stated, a human soul is made of God's energy and so might be humanity. This again supports the idea that we are not only made of God but within It. Let's return to science and the description of the process within string theory and its history.

Perceptions and Equations

The string theorists continued to seek the cause of the vibrating strings or bundles of energy, and questions inevitably arose as to whether Susskind's equation was really the one and only formula that expressed "the theory of everything." Mathematicians and physicists created derivatives of the equation, and five different functional equations for string theory took the place of Susskind's single unifying equation that everyone had been so excited about.

The different equations together suggested that if string theory were true, there would have to be, at a minimum, ten different realms or dimensions. The repercussions of this made the scientific community very nervous until one physicist explained that each of the equations was correct. The multiple equations each described a perspective or a separate realm that had its own unique parameters and laws of physics and required its own explanatory equation. This led to the creation of M theory.

"M" or Super String Theory

The brilliant physicist Dr. Edward Witten looked at all of these equations and saw them as different perspectives. He then extrapolated one additional equation that brought everything together. This equation alluded to an eleventh dimension that had an appearance of a "membrane" or "brane." All of the strings of creation had to be connected to or internalized in this membrane or series of membranes. A name was given to this membrane aspect of string theory—"M theory." There is an inescapable comparison to our very own cell membranes, where the protein filaments are analogous to the strings attached to the dimensional membrane. As discussed in the theory, the protein filaments retrieve and orchestrate changes inside the cell from the messages it receives from the physical world and from Universal Consciousness.

The theory that vibrating strings produced and continued to sustain all of creation and its ongoing evolution became "thicker" and more complicated, with many more elements to take into account. The eleventh dimension, the theorized membrane, was referred to as the "bulk." This name gave substance, depth, and even space to the term. The bulk was believed to contain all of the various and nearly innumerable strings, the mechanisms for their operation, and perhaps a consciousness.

Bread, Wishing Wells, and Holodecks

The M theory membrane has often been compared to bread dough with all of its ingredients mixed and kneaded together and ready for the oven. Imagine what would happen if you kneaded space-time into itself, folding space over and over again until all parts of the "bulk" had space equally mixed within itself and everything was unified and entangled.

All of space would be in all aspects of space, much like a hologram that has the big picture of everything in the smallest part of itself. This would not only entangle all time on itself, but would superimpose all time and space on itself. There seems to be no perimeter or boundary of space-time that would keep it from mixing into itself.

As an avid baker, I like the bread analogy because I have experienced mixing different grains into a well-mixed dough. The bread's integrated mixture always reminds me of what inner space might be like with all its discrete but interrelated and well-organized bits of energized information internally folded so well that everything is in communication with everything else. I also enjoy the mechanism of yeast making bread expand as it bakes, just as dark energy is believed to be the mechanism for expansion of the universe.

Physicists have theorized that the membrane in string theory's eleventh dimension is a unified entity made of a series of smaller, microscopic membranes, each with its own edges or boundaries. Energized membranes organized within a larger energized membrane could create an infinite-potential field, much like a wishing well where intentions can come true. All of the building blocks for everything in the universe could be waiting in a state of potentiality for manifestation in physical form. The change from potential into concrete form would only require an effort of intention put forth by consciousness. Once the intention that holds the energy in physical form is halted or altered, the physical form would revert back to energy or change into the new intended form.

You can see how an infinite-potential field might resemble the simulated reality on the Holodeck of the Starship USS *Enterprise* in the *Star Trek* TV series and movies. On the Holodeck, crewmembers could choose a destination and then travel in virtual reality across time and space, anywhere they wished to visit. All they had to do was program in a desired destination or learning, and they would instantly find themselves in another realm. Could the infinite-potential field be Creation itself, and could the soul direct the program for the Holodeck of life? It is all part of the great mystery. The more energetic in nature the dimension, the easier this transformation would be. This is why it is easier to transform things in the quantum realm and why the creator realm would need to be maintained in an energy state.

These analogies of the bread, cell membranes, the wishing well, and the Holodeck are meant to help visualize an infinite-potential field, and to emphasize that physicality requires the architect and construction crew of consciousness to create and hold physical things together.

I want to return for just a moment to the "Josephson's Junction" experiment I described earlier, in which a wave generator was placed in a sealed box and the movement of an electron was tracked. The electron emanating from within the contained area of the box (with walls the electron could not penetrate) was found not inside but outside the box, although the scientists knew that the electron hadn't penetrated any of the walls.

What exact mechanism or quality allowed the electron to pass from its initial location to another location without apparently crossing the space between the two locations?

The first explanation is that the electron "heard the call" of a human observer, whose consciousness pulled the electron from the box's containment field. The electron "jumped over" into the energetic realm, which I have called the infinite-potential field, traveling through a realm where space is not the same as in our world, and then popped up again in our earthly/physical realm. This suggests that the electron that fired inside the box was the same electron that popped up outside the box. To perform this feat, the electron would have to be semiautonomous.

In the second explanation, the fired electron was resorbed into the infinite-potential field and a different electron manifested outside the box, in response to the observing consciousness that expected to find it there. This suggests that the infinite-potential field is a single entity and that the electron that was resorbed into the field did not retain its unique identity during its journey beyond the box's wall.

These two theories might take advantage of the possibility of space being entangled and superimposed as mentioned before. The ability to mark the fired electron and determine its identity would help us better understand the nature of the energetic realm of the infinite-potential field.

Whatever electron appeared outside the box, and however it traveled or appeared there, the central message of the experiment remains the same: human beings and everything else are a part of one Creation. Human consciousness is capable of creating as a part of the Universal Consciousness. One might expect that all "living beings" contribute to the creation of our universe. Defining what is living if all things physical are created from living consciousness might be difficult. This is another good question contemporary science has yet to answer but that will become self-evident once we develop the technology to explore the quantum world.

Cell Membranes and M Theory

I believe there is a fascinating analogy between the cell membranes of our body and the membranes of M theory. M theory's membrane of creation contains an infinite number of integrated strings. These strings provide a sensory-process interface between energetic realms and our physical realm where the wishes or needs in one realm are transformed into physicality in another. This is identical to the function of our cell membranes. Remember how the protein receptors of the cell membrane pick up information outside the cell and relay the information inside, where physical changes such as creating new proteins occur? The cell adapts to changes just as realms might adapt to changes in Universal Consciousness. We must also remember that these strings of protein and strings in the quantum membranes do their best work when they are receiving energetic messages. In both cases these seem to be the antennae that receive ambient information and, I believe, coordinating information from Creation Consciousness or God. The cell membrane does more than oversee the internal functioning and changing needs of the cell. The exterior information gathered by the membrane also guides necessary alterations in the cell's DNA, allowing the cell to evolve and continue to thrive as the world outside the cell changes. Sometimes negative adaptations result from big dramatic events and harmful chemicals. Other times, as we have discussed, pinpoint and positive alterations to the DNA occur to help different species adapt in a positive way. This is where I see Creation Consciousness communicating with or through the cell membrane to create the larger genetic shifts that are responsible for the beneficial nonrandom changes to DNA that have occurred for humans and all the animals and plants of Earth today.

It stands to reason that many of these changes in the physical world in cell membranes have also come about as a result of the same oversight and intentions toward the strings that make up the M-branes. All this information would not be carried by substances but by energy consciousness. It is in the purity of thought that the strongest information can be relayed. We can reconnect to the science that shows us how things in an energetic form, such as consciousness, are much more powerful in creating our physical world.

This information is very exciting to me because it speaks to who we are. Form indicates function and helps us understand our purpose, how we are made, and what we are made of.

The Take-Home

The idea that I am putting forth is that energy plus consciousness results in physicality. Even better, energy consciousness is the same as conscious energy. Energy and consciousness may be a single, self-propagating entity, much like our mind and body. It is conscious energy that makes physicality. When we get down to the elemental pieces of the brick and mortar of our physical world, the illusion is revealed. Everything is energy, conscious energy. One cannot exist without the other when they are one and the same. The two rely on each other, and we are now beginning to understand the depth of what this may mean and the potential that comes with it. What the frontier scientists in physics are outlining in string theory, quantum mechanics, and other theories is the process of this conversion of conscious energy into physicality. If our minds can conceive of this for a moment, it will answer so many of our biggest questions and perhaps open the door to our potentials.

Using this model, let's outline how the physical world is created. We start with the process in which conscious energy is willingly focused and consolidated by an overseeing aspect of the same Creation Consciousness. Here energy is transformed into the forces of nature that can make up the subatomic particles and the illusion of physicality, the main forces being gravity, electromagnetics, and both strong and weak nuclear forces. Now energy interacts with attractive and repulsive forces much like magnets and force fields. These subatomic particles collapse into atomic particles and on up into the molecules through the fusion process of a hot and chaotic universe. This physical process creates the tiny elements of our world all the way up to the celestial bodies of our universe. After a few billion years of this recombinant process and cooling, there exist planets such as Earth where organic life can prosper. It is here where all the minerals such as nitrogen for amino acids that will make proteins and carbon, hydrogen, and oxygen come together to form lipids or the fatty layer of cell membranes. We now ask, how do these amino acids and lipids become sentient to form even simple life? In this model it's much easier to give clues to this answer because everything is already made of life, if not sentient life. The root of all things is living conscious energy. In this model, inherent in all things is an organizing principle for life and its expansion. Sure, the early forms of life were not complex nor did they have existential thoughts, but in that simplistic and elemental state of primordial life there were flow and freedom of conscious information. This is the very thing that might have been needed for greater communication and input to make the jump to a simple form of what we call life. If we integrate some of our fundamental lessons from physics, that there is great potential in the pure or primordial forms of energy, we understand that it is only in this elemental, pure state that the magic of quantum reality and infinite potential could exist. This would allow a collaboration of molecules into compounds and compounds into simple organisms. A few hundred million years later, much more complex living beings, including us, would come about from this continued expansion of life. Every one of our cells is in communication with that collaborative voice of life and evolution.

So Why Is This Important?

Perhaps there is a potential for communication with Creation? For some this may be easy to comprehend while others see it as far-fetched. Many of us have experienced thinking about someone who shortly thereafter calls on the telephone. Much of humanity spends much of their day in prayer or meditation to connect with this very source. It is perhaps one of our greatest wishes to connect, communicate, and be in an intimate relationship with this consciousness. Shamans and healers for thousands of years have practiced ways of calming the mind and stepping away from the ego to listen to the healing subtle voice of wisdom. This connection has allowed them to mix complex combinations of herbs from the forest to cure many of their tribes' illnesses. They are accessing information beyond their knowledge. In one of the forms of Taoist meditation, one sets the intention to tear away at reality and go into the void. This void is the very place of creation from energy to physicality. Taoists believe this is where the blueprint for our pure creation exists. It is here that they seek wisdom and a way to reboot their physical form and health in concert with its younger state. They have realized the power of this elemental primordial energy state.

What Is Our Potential and Our Purpose?

If one really understands a soul-directed universe where our souls work in the energetic realm to set up our experiences so we can transcend unharmonious belief systems, then our opportunities for transformative work become a bit easier to engage. The one issue I see in common with all people is a sense of not being good enough. We all wish to be in relationships that require us to feel lovable and have some sense of worth.

We see the symptoms of this in our wish for control, power, and material wealth and issues such as abandonment, betrayal, grief, loss, and so on. In most of the philosophies and religions I have studied, there is a spiritual call to *return*. This raises the question of who we really are and who we are returning to be. I find clues in humanity's greatest pain and struggle: our feeling of separateness in this realm. In the act of taking on our physical form, our senses and our reality shift away from our experience of being a soul and an integral piece of an unfathomable community in which there is a sense of grace. Embedded in each of us is the wish to return to that community and, even more important, to create it here in the earthly realm. When we see people performing great acts of kindness or giving up their own needs in order to help others, they become our heroes. These are all clues to what we really wish and inwardly feel must be done in order for us to find happiness, and to become aware of the connection that already exists but feels out of reach.

If we see earthly existence as a place to confront our challenges and grow, the lessons we need to learn will always be easier for us. Most commonly these lessons are self-created and the consequence of our disconnected actions. Another way of putting it is that these actions come about when we forget that we are all connected and that what affects one will affect everything: i.e., "oneness."

I will never forget a biology teacher I had who said that we are no different from yeast in a petri dish. He was referring to an experiment in which scientists gave yeast an unlimited amount of food in a closed system. The yeast feasted and reproduced until their own waste material become so toxic that it killed all of them. The greater lesson for humanity to learn is that we are nothing more than a big petri dish and the signs that our waste products are beginning to kill us are increasingly present, yet we choose to remain on our present course. The consequences of our ego-based reality will create the very lesson that is paramount for our greatest self-discovery and transformation. So what are we up against?

Our human "ego state" drives us to consume, be selfish, and fight to dominate others, resulting in wars. In order to support humans' ever-expanding needs and population, we have had to eliminate other species of plants and animals that do not directly support our need for water and food. There will come a time when the fabric of interwoven relationships between the earth's species becomes so weak that it tears. The effects of our out-of-balance population choosing not to see our impact on the rest of the world is the creation of toxicity in our environment, climate change, detrimental effects to the ozone layer, and increased cancer rates, to name a few. This outcome is nearly guaranteed by those people who live in denial and espouse a self-serving belief that no matter how much you destroy, there will be no impact. The only way intelligent beings who can see all the signs can stay on this course is by giving priority to the needs of the ego. Dwelling in the consciousness of our "left brain" that believes in survival of the fittest, that we are all individuals completely disconnected, we believe safety can only be attained by utter domination of others and the environment and the continual strategy of putting others down mentally and physically while lifting ourselves up. This part of us is selfish and narcissistic and is the reaction of living in the fearful state of not being good enough.

Here we are with our self-created lesson unfolding before our very eyes. This is a problem that we cannot run away from. There are no new continents or planets within our reach to run to. To save ourselves we must put the needs of our earth and its remaining inhabitants before our own and our wish to increase our numbers. The beautiful part of this story is that if we take care of one salient issue, I believe we will uncover the tools to accomplish more than we have ever conceived. Humanity is at its best when it is faced with the most difficult problems. It just may be that everything is right on schedule for us to receive our greatest lessons on how to be spiritual beings in physical form.

The Path

If you are ever wondering what to do when the path you're on isn't working for you, nine times out of ten the correct path is to do the very opposite of what you have done in the past. Our modern society has been ruled much more by our ego than by our soul. It is the separation of our thinking mind from our knowing mind; it's the difference between having information and having wisdom that has caused everything from poverty to pollution.

Imagine the possibility of hooking into Creation Consciousness much like the cell membranes do. Imagine a fluent conversation with this consciousness. If humanity were able to be a bigger part of creating positive changes on a subatomic level, doing that would reflect all the way up into our lives. This has the potential of writing most diseases out of our lives as well as healing the planet of all the things we have caused. In order to get to this point, we would no longer see ourselves as separate from the creation of all other things. This, by all accounts, is how our souls see reality. The ego could no longer shut us out from this knowledge, nor would we ever want to leave the connection that we would create. How we live with the living Earth, and the number of people we think is appropriate for a healthy Earth, would change.

In my studies and experiences I have learned that there are only two ways to access this wisdom. One is to die or come close to dying and then come back into your body. People who have had this experience have great insights and seem to be speaking from the soul's point of view. They are very different after the experience. It is, however, hard for them to hang on to this divine connection. The other way takes longer but is more sustainable. It is a two-pronged approach. One part is a practice of meditation and learning to free the mind of your conscious thoughts and even some of your subconscious thoughts and fears. This helps you get rid of the noisy ego that is always demanding attention. This path allows you to hear and interact with the wisdom your body receives. The second part of this approach is to heal all of your wounds and find the motivation for every one of your actions. If they are ego based, you must do transformative work to change your beliefs and actions. I think the easiest way to sum up the direction to move toward is to increase your "divine humanity."

I put these words together in the belief that we can become more like each other. I use the word *divine* because most of us have an archetypal belief of the divine as a benevolent entity, without the need for revenge, and the word *humanity* because that's what we bring to the table. Our journey is to become more humane. These two words together remind us of the relationship that exists between the two. What affects one affects the other, both good and bad.

In hard times we go to the spiritual side to find answers and teachings about our most painful events. Life becomes less logical and more of the great mystery. It is these struggles that will force us to make the changes necessary to adapt. I have given you many examples of how consciousness creates reality and how our brain and body can cooperate to create great healings that we have written off as placebo. It is placebo that reminds us how consciousness might be able to transform our most severe diseases, though we have dismissed this internal power because we don't understand how it can be. As science progresses, it seems destined to prove what mystics and traditional healers have said for thousands of years: *we are one.* Our thoughts create reality. Everything is energy. Miracles or miraculous things can happen. It may be in humanity's greatest struggles and losses that we access a greater communication, lose the beliefs of the ego, and realize our potential for simultaneously healing ourselves and the planet. The second act is complete and the stage is set for the struggle that will reveal us.

In the next chapters we turn from science to the religions and philosophies of the world to learn more about our possible potentials and gain insights into our purpose.

NOW EVERYTHING CHANGES

The View from Here

We have now reached the apex of our pyramid of current scientific knowledge: Creation, or God Consciousness, lives in everything, because it is everything.

Although we currently lack the technical instrumentation to physically confirm that a directing consciousness permeates the entire cosmos, theoretical physics offers increasing evidence for a conscious universe rather than one made up of blind, undirected matter and energy.

I hope that as science grows, society will quickly grow with this new knowledge and entertain the possibility of an awake, sentient, evolving Creation that we are a part of. My guess is that as science proves this connection, it will radically accelerate this process and we will incorporate it as self-evident and proof enough. Science will then turn its attention to the new questions it found along the way.

Who Am I, Religiously?

I am often asked what my religion is. I regularly hear people say that they are Christian, Jew, or Buddhist. I have always found this language particularly interesting. It denotes a particular attachment when someone says, "I am a (fill in the blank)" as if it were genetic. My interest in the statement already tells you something about me. My mother raised me within her own humanistic, moral, atheistic philosophy, although she grew up as an Episcopalian and didn't leave the church until she was a young woman, shortly after my birth. My father's family was Lutheran but also of Jewish heritage.

Growing up on the plains in South Dakota, my mother began to dislike the actions of organized Christianity because she believed whites and their Christian churches had destroyed Native American culture by assimilation and the threat of hell. The message of the conquering Europeans was to submit or be destroyed. Most of us know this history, but she was there witnessing the final part of this conquest and its long-term effects.

The final blow to her Christian belief was the deaths of those she most loved, within two months, beginning when I was eight months old. My father died, and then her father, and finally even her beloved dog. Prior to their deaths she had made a pact with her Christian God. She had vowed to continue her Christian ways but with more fervor. She would do God's work and always pray. But after three tragedies, my mother's grief and sense of loss were overwhelming. She later told me that it was during that heartbreaking period that she felt betrayed and questioned the existence of God.

If God were all-powerful and benevolent, why would God allow her loved ones to so unjustly suffer and die and leave her in such loneliness and pain, with a baby to care for by herself?

My mother left the church and followed the direction of a strong moral compass, a gift she had received from her father, a highly ethical and loving man, an esteemed attorney, and president of his state's bar association. She raised me with the values she had learned from him: the importance of treating others with compassion, respect, and a sense of equality. My mother was a social and political activist who spent much of her life helping the downtrodden, those falsely accused, and those who lived with bigotry. One of her final acts, along with helping set up educational programs in cinema on Pine Ridge Reservation, was to create a monument to our First Amendment rights at the University of Southern California. This monument was to remind us of the horrible atrocities that occurred during the McCarthy era. The walk around the monument is filled with statements from the blacklisted twelve in the motion picture industry whose lives were destroyed by accusations of communism. She hoped

137

we would always be aware of how certain groups use fear to manipulate humanity into alignment with their political agenda. That was my mother, Christian or not.

So when I'm asked who I am, Christian, Buddhist, Jew, or something else, I say that I am an Earthling and that I don't limit myself to any single religious doctrine. I approach all sacred scriptures not as literal history but as parables and metaphors that teach important truths about humanity and our relationship to God. I have studied with friends from many faiths and find divine wisdom in all the holy books. I am also aware of the historical, societal, and political experiences that put things in context and shape each religion's sense of the sacred.

My sincere respect for and interest in religious beliefs and practices may seem strange in someone with my family background. But since my atheistic youth I have had many important experiences that have caused my thoughts and feelings to radically change and evolve. I continue to learn about the extraordinary and mysterious universe that awaits our further discovery and greater understanding. I was never indoctrinated into any one belief, and instead have lived with an openness to helpful divine wisdom from all over the world. At the same time, I'm capable of seeing our human failings and our ego-driven need for control, often in the very same scriptures where I find divine wisdom.

Outer or Inner Space?

I think many or even most followers of organized religion feel that God is separate from us, that He or She exists up in the heavens and orchestrates our life from that vantage. Numerous sacred stories suggest that God is far above and humankind far below, the Creator far removed from the created.

Throughout history, many teachers and scholars of the sacred have interpreted the holy texts as a map of heaven and earth that sets out the almost unbridgeable distance between the human and the divine. From that reading of the texts, it would seem that to find God we would need a powerful mystical telescope to search the highest reaches of the farthest sky. But what if the lens through which we look for God were replaced by a mirror or microscope? Or what if we altered the direction in which we pointed our gaze by, say, 180 degrees?

Our relationship to God would certainly change with this different view. Now imagine if we internalized the ancient holy stories, reading them as if the actions and thoughts of God or Creation were taking place inside us, not outside.

Wrestling Match

I recall stories from the Elder Testament in which there is a vivid interplay between the Unknowable God, beyond all forms and descriptions, and the human characters.

I think of Jacob, waiting at his camp, perhaps by a fire outside his tent. He has sent all of his worldly possessions as offerings to his brother Esau, to ask pardon for stealing Esau's birthright. Jacob and his mother, Rebecca, tricked Isaac into believing that Jacob was the firstborn and therefore deserving of the oldest son's traditional privileges.

The night before he meets Esau, Jacob wrestles with an angel. In the Elder Testament angels are not only messengers but sometimes even aspects of God. Though his hip is injured in the struggle, Jacob holds down the angel and won't release him until Jacob receives the angel's blessing.

Jacob is blessed and renamed "Israel," meaning "one who wrestles with God."

If we understand this story as symbolic, as a description of an inner rather than an outer struggle, the meaning of the battle and the identities of the contestants deepen and expand. One way to read this story is that Jacob wrestles all night with his own conscience or soul about the decision he has made to try to reunite with the brother he has wronged. Jacob is giving up all he has in order to meet his brother and ask for his forgiveness.

The next day, after the long night's internal wrestling match, Jacob is ready, and when Esau forgives him and tries to refuse Jacob's offering, Jacob insists. Jacob's wrestling with the angel, the messenger of the Unnamable, has been an inner confrontation with a divine aspect within himself. There are a number of lessons within this story that are profound, revolutionary, and transformational.

First, the story tells us that we can discover our own aspect of divinity through acts of humanity requiring us to abandon the personal ego. People can overcome even an angel of God if they are on the path to self-discovery and resolute in their wish to make things right. This is the process of restructuring and harmonizing your life.

Second, we learn that displacing the ego requires acknowledging the equal humanity, and even divinity, of the other person: in this case, Jacob's brother Esau.

Third, and perhaps most striking, the story is about the unfolding and perfecting of the universe. In surmounting his purely personal (and selfish) needs, in an act of self-admonition and an expression of love for his brother, Jacob has challenged and joined forces with "the God within," the Creator or Creation, in an act of co-evolution. Jacob and the internal God, which is an aspect of the Creator of the Universe, have both been changed—and with them the very nature of the universe.

Revisiting the Scene

The famous story of Sodom and Gomorrah is a uniquely Jewish story. To understand it correctly, one must see it through a Jewish lens. Many see it as a story about the evils of homosexuality. This could not be further from the truth. The great sin in this story according to Jewish teaching is that Sodom is a city filled with inhospitable, greedy people. Jews are taught to welcome the stranger, and inhospitality is one of the greatest sins.

Homosexuality is about a loving relationship between two people of the same sex. This story does not tell of the people of Sodom wishing to "know" the visitors in the biblical sense of carnal knowledge. The story tells of heterosexual men plotting to rape other heterosexual men. This violation and need to dominate another person is part and parcel of the inhospitality, not homosexuality.

The three visitors in the story look like men but are referred to as angels later in the story. They are received with kindness and hospitality into the tent of Abraham and his wife, Sarah. In the presence of the three disguised angels, God reveals to Abraham that He is going to destroy the prosperous cities of Sodom and Gomorrah because "their sin of inhospitality is very grievous."

Abraham asks the Unnamable God if He plans to kill both the guilty and the innocent. "What if there are fifty innocent people there?" he asks.

The Holy Voice answers. "I will not kill any, neither the innocent nor the guilty, if you can find fifty righteous souls." In his humanity, Abraham begins to negotiate with God, asking about forty-five innocent souls, then forty, then thirty, then twenty, and finally whether ten good people would be sufficient to save Sodom and Gomorrah. Each time, God agrees.

Ten good people among the inhabitants will save all the rest. Surely ten fine people can be found in two very large and powerful cities. Now two of the visiting angels travel to Sodom and meet Lot, Abraham's nephew, who convinces them to lodge in his house and share a meal with his family.

The biblical text tells us that Lot's house is surrounded by the men of Sodom. They demand to have forced intercourse with the two visitors. To protect his guests, Lot offers his innocent daughters instead, but the unruly crowd refuses and starts to break down the door.

The angelic visitors rescue Lot, strike all the would-be attackers blind, and announce that they must destroy Sodom because not even ten of its inhabitants are righteous. Lot and his wife and his two daughters would logically make four, six short of the required number. Like Abraham and Sarah, Lot's family will be saved, although Lot's wife ignores an angel's warning to not look back at the burning city and turns into a pillar of salt.

What does the ugly scene of attempted sexual assault, of violent rape unconnected with sexual preference or human love, symbolically allude to? Or Lot's offering of his virgin daughters in place of the angels?

The people of Sodom were guilty of economic crimes, blasphemy, and violence. One rabbinic tradition identifies the sins of Sodom as greed, disrespect for others' property, and lack of compassion and hospitality. The Sodomites believed "What is mine is mine, and what is yours is mine" rather than "What is mine is offered to you in respect, love, and generosity as a fellow human being, my brother or sister, and a child of God." This story is a timeless reflection of those who are driven beyond their humanity to attain wealth. They wish to violate those outside their coveted community of affluence. And they never reach out a welcoming hand to the weary traveler or to those whose lives have taken a turn for the worse. They wish only to take and keep taking and never give back to the system that created them. For the ego driven, there can never be enough. One can easily see this in our world today with the separation of wealth: all lessons of what not to do. This biblical text uses a particular name for God. It is the Hebrew word made up of four letters: Yud-Hay-Vav-Hay (YHVH). As there are no vowels in the Torah scroll, this word cannot be pronounced. God is referred to by many names in the Torah but this is the holy name of God that represents God as "The Unnamable" and "Unknowable": a strong reminder that we will never completely comprehend "the Great Mystery" and that when we put limitations on its description we will never *know* or move beyond that limited view.

In the story I am struck by the fact that the Unnamable God is willing to throw the baby out with the bathwater. His penalties are swift, incredibly violent, and all inclusive. The two cities are destroyed all the way down to the last man, woman, and child. Only Abraham, a mere human, is able to postpone the catastrophe for a while by bargaining with God. It is the humanity of Abraham that persuades God to soften, if only temporarily, and have greater compassion and understanding for God's imperfect and evolving creation, or perhaps the acceptance of one's imperfect self.

As in Jacob's story, we sense that the divine and the human share a relationship of mutual evolution. God and humankind are inseparable. Each desperately needs the other in order to become something greater than either is alone. This is a deeper teaching from this parable.

My Friends, Cain and Abel

Holy books are full of parables, symbolic stories whose meanings the individual listener or reader must search his or her own heart to interpret. The same mystical story can amplify different teachings for different times in your life. You have to look inward, awakening another aspect of the self, to delve below the day-to-day world of waking reason and find a deeper truth that must be personally experienced. The final "lesson" may ultimately exist beyond all words and human rationality and require the understanding of the divine that resides in each person beyond the shadow of the ego.

I was listening to a conversation between two of my friends, one

Christian and the other Jewish. Both are quite conservative, nearly fundamentalist, in their faith and their interpretations of the Bible. They were discussing the story of Cain and Abel, and each friend voiced his religion's usual, traditional interpretation of the deadly conflict between the two sons of Adam and Eve.

The surface plot of the story is fairly clear cut. Cain is the firstborn son of his parents, the first human child born on Earth. He will come to earn his living as a farmer. Abel, the second born, becomes a shepherd. Both present gifts to God representative of their work. God favors the gifts from Abel, and in a jealous rage Cain kills his own brother.

My friends' interpretations were different and each friend claimed that his understanding was the story's "one truth."

All Cain's Children

As the two men debated the meaning of the ancient homicide, I reflected that the Bible story could represent that followers of one religion are willing to kill followers of another religion, in some strange effort to win the favor of God.

It is almost ridiculous to think that God would ever sanction one person killing another to gain God's goodwill. God's most important Utterance (or Commandment as it is commonly mistranslated) is "Do not kill." How can breaking God's greatest taboo ever achieve humankind's greatest desire—God's love?

The end result of the Cain and Abel story is that Cain is banished from his home to wander in isolation from others. In killing his brother, he has unknowingly murdered something in himself that binds him to both the human and divine—and to his own best, truest nature, which is a union of the two.

We all know the very bloody history of the Middle East. Jews, Christians, and Muslims have each in turn, as a gesture of their devotion to God, attacked those different from themselves who worshipped a supposedly foreign or evil deity. The three religions share a common heritage, are all "People of the Book," whether it be the Torah, the Bible, or the Koran. The three faiths have a common root in Abraham, who is the father of Isaac and Ishmael, and their holy texts share similar stories and similar ethical and moral lessons.

And yet here I was, in the twenty-first century, listening to my two friends, one Christian and one Jewish, debating the "true" meaning of the Cain and Abel story, taught to them as children in their respective religions. My two friends might have *been* Cain and Abel, arguing over which of them was truer to and most beloved by God. Neither of my friends thought to mention that we are all descendants of Cain, the murderer, and in need of redemption—as perhaps also is God, who in choosing one brother before another displayed a human selfishness and failure of self-awareness.

This is an invaluable story that tells us what not to do. The well-written script casts God sharing some of the traits we think of as human, or perhaps giving early humanity opportunities that reveal where we need to do our work. One teaching of this story certainly foreshadows our human struggle with a God who we fear will show favor, and that we will even murder our own family to feel that God is on our side.

These stories from the Torah or Jewish Bible have the amazing capacity to give us valuable guidelines and lessons in life. Oftentimes the parables are difficult to read because they reveal the truth about humanity and our human view of God. I can just imagine tribal people thousands of years ago, sitting around a fire under the stars telling these rich stories, sometimes showing us a wiser path to take but more often relating horrifying examples of wrongdoing. The storytellers and writers of these stories knew there was often greater impact in teaching *what not to do.*

Asha and Druj

My mother was a screenwriter and documentary filmmaker. When I was eighteen, we traveled to Iran to make documentary films about Iranian history and culture. It was there where I first learned in detail about the ancient visionary prophet Zarathustra (in Greek, "Zoroaster," meaning "golden splendor").

The Zoroastrian faith emerged in the eastern Persian Empire sometime in the seventh century BCE and later influenced the development of Christianity and Islam. After a profound mystical experience, Zoroaster clarified a previous larger pantheon of deities and placed special emphasis on one god, on a central moral purpose of creation, and on the ultimate conversion of all darkness into light.

Zoroastrianism is a dualistic, monotheistic religion whose roots reach back to between 1500 and 1200 BCE and that perceives the universe as a battleground where the forces of light fight the forces of darkness. Spenta Mainyu (progressive mentality) and Angra Mainyu (destructive mentality) combat one another under the eye of a benign but unmanifested (immaterial) Creator of the Universe, Ahura Mazda (illuminating wisdom).

From Zoroastrian priests and devotees, I learned of their belief that creating human happiness and the internal harmony of the universe are one and the same. This is the single goal of both humankind and God, who are joined together in an effort to create ultimate universal unity. When I asked people who followed the Zoroastrian faith their main tenet, they told me the teachings of their faith were to find joy in every day, laugh, smile, and remove anything within them that kept them from deeply enjoying the day. The message was simple and pure while the work was deep and lifelong.

There is a struggle between good and evil both in the heavens and within each person. Everyone is a warrior whose most important tasks are to nurture goodness within and to perform good deeds in the service of others. Individual human acts and thoughts of goodness reduce the chaos in the world and the universe. They assist the forces of light in their struggle to overcome the destructiveness of darkness.

Order (Asha) is in opposition to chaos (Druj). Both humans and animals, as created mortal beings, are intimately involved in this conflict. I enjoy this because this philosophy does not include a hierarchy that degrades or allows the destruction of the animal kingdom. The first duty of sentient beings is to further order within the universe, which would dissolve without their moral efforts.

Ethical deeds are critically important and asceticism, an avoidance of earthly experience, is discouraged. In fact, the purpose of a soul's incarnation on Earth is to collect mortal experience. The avoidance of both life's pleasures and life's challenges is seen as a failure of duty to one's self and family and the wider community, as well as the benign elements of cosmic evolution. I saw this result in the common get-togethers and parties of Zoroastrians. These were times when they treasured and focused on friends, family, and happiness

Zoroastrianism places special weight on moral choice. One furthers either asha or druj, order or disorder, and men and women are responsible for their individual and group actions. Success and failure, happiness and grief, are the results of how people conduct themselves.

The Zoroastrian sacred book is the Avesta, in which the key to right conduct is clearly and simply set out in the phrase "good thoughts, good words, good deeds" (Humata, Hukhta, Hvarshta). Through good, asha is strengthened. Through good, druj is kept from growing and spreading, and is finally extinguished.

After death, the individual soul is led by angels across a very narrow bridge. The good will cross into paradise, into a world of light, but those who have followed "The Lie" (Angra Mainyu—destructive mentality) will fall from the bridge into darkness.

Eventually, at the end of time, the light will prevail, darkness will be destroyed, and in a Last Judgment the dead will be resurrected after the arrival of a savior.

This fascinating ancient belief system teaches that the ethical pursuit of joy and happiness and even laughter is our primary purpose and duty. Love and compassion are the paramount virtues, and the universe is constantly creating itself, through human and divine consciousness, toward greater harmony and integration. This is the purpose of an ongoing cosmic evolution.

Sometimes Ahura Mazda is depicted as Ohrmazd, a created Light God who fights against the Lord of Darkness, Ahriman (Angra Mainyu: The Evil One), and we can easily identify the precursors of the Christian God and His adversary, Satan. Across the centuries, we've received from the Zoroastrians the image of a little devil on one shoulder, an angel on the other, both whispering in our ears.

This is indeed the human struggle. It is the Jacob archetype wrestling with the divine within us. We must learn to distinguish between our actions that come from an ego state, the place where all of our insecurities dwell, and the wisdom that comes from the divine that is embedded in the makeup of each cell in our body. The more quickly we learn this lesson, the faster we will find inner peace. The more we live in an ego state, the more separate we are from the moral compass that tells us what is right and wrong and that empowers us to look out for others, to give a helping hand to the downtrodden. The alternative, the ego state, is familiar to all of us. This is where we are constantly comparing ourselves to others, trying to put them down while lifting ourselves up. This is a place of judgment and righteousness gone wrong.

Some would like to believe that there is an actual entity that takes control of us and makes us do wrong things. This would be the work of Satan. This, however, removes responsibility for our actions and slows our work as humanity. Judaism describes Satan differently. Satan is called haSatan, meaning the Adversary or Accuser. The Adversary/Accuser is not a red creature with horns and a pitchfork. Rather, the Adversary is part of our nature, our evolutionary process. The Adversary/Accuser is embedded within the process of creation to urge us toward facing and harmonizing the challenging parts within. As you walk through life you will find the Accuser often in the people you relate to throughout the day. These are the people who use the technique of blaming or accusing others of wrongdoing as they try to gain the power position. This often puts the other person on their heels as they try to explain why the accusation is not true. It is a great technique for the ego.

Knowing this, look around and listen for those who are the Accuser, and tell them that you can see them continually accusing people and that you will not respond to these words. The more aware you are of how some accuse others, the more you will be aware of any accusing that you might do of others—or even of yourself. This will help you get rid of your Satan.

These are the teachings that remind you of the importance of walking in the feet of your soul and listening to the wisdom you are telling yourself. The next time you feel insecure or in need of revenge, remember that you are wrestling with these two opposing forces within yourself. I hope for you and humanity that the choice you make is the same one Jacob made: the path of the soul.

11

My Evolution of Evolution

Another Look

We've previously considered cellular changes that occur in living organisms in response to environmental changes and emotional events, and how these acquired characteristics are passed on to new generations. This contradicts Charles Darwin's theory of evolution, which clearly asserts that species can change only through mutations of newborn individuals, who later pass on their mutated genes via sexual reproduction to their offspring.

Now I'd like to return to the subject of evolution, but from a slightly different angle. In this section we'll look at the interplay between physical and emotional experiences, all working in concert with input and oversight from Creation Consciousness. It's time to explore *the evolution of theories of evolution* to see which ones have worked and which still fall short of explaining the specificity and speed with which life on our planet has evolved.

In a new model of unified creation, all plants, animals, and the Creator interact with one another and with the environment in a dynamic interplay of myriad forms of conscious matter and energy that are all linked and guided by Creation Consciousness.

Creation can then be seen as a single conscious organism developing within itself toward a single, further evolution. Taking this holistic view of evolution, we can perhaps reconcile two views of evolutionary change that are once again in conflict after the recent reconsideration of Lamarck's old theory.

Lamarck maintained that offspring can inherit the acquired characteristics that result from their parents' intentions and interactions with the environment. About fifty years later, Darwin's work was published, for the most part invalidating this idea. Darwin's supporters triumphed over Lamarck's, and for at least 150 years, the idea of inheritance of acquired characteristics has languished in the dustbin of science.

Now, as we discussed in earlier chapters, interest in the crystalline matrix, the development of epigenetics, and further work with oncogenes have reignited this old and apparently settled debate.

Darwin and Wallace

At approximately the same time in the nineteenth century, Charles Darwin and Alfred Russel Wallace conceived similar theories of the evolution of species. As the backstory goes, Wallace was not a man of high standing and could not get his treatise on evolution published, so he gave it to the more respected Darwin and asked him to publish his paper. Darwin's own theory apparently had some holes in it, and he plugged them by integrating some of Wallace's information. Darwin's grand theory of evolution was born, and Darwin did indeed publish Wallace's papers after his own. It was a collaboration that as I mentioned carried the day—perhaps until now.

Let's turn back to Lamarck now and continue to look at evolution through his eyes. Lamarck believed that early humans had an intimate relationship with their environment, an integrated experience and understanding of their immediate world and their place in it that allowed them to sense the best direction for their own evolutionary changes on some level, whether conscious or subconscious.

Lamarck proposed that the intentions or needs for survival of an animal in a constant state of evolution were factors in directing changes in its physical form. The classic model of this view is of a short-necked "pre-giraffe," under stress due to dwindling food sources. The pre-giraffe becomes the giraffe as day in and day out it stretches its neck to reach the leaves and fruit of trees in higher and higher branches. Reaching that untapped food source is vital to its survival. Somehow the animal's internal knowledge of its needs and of the potentially available food and the chemical interplay of the cell membranes throughout its body "co-create" its longer neck in the next generation.

Both the supporters of Darwin and Wallace on one hand and Lamarck's supporters on the other believed that evolution occurred in response to environmental changes, but it was Lamarck who sensed that humans and other living things had such a close, visceral relationship with the environment that their innate experience and knowledge could identify and produce needed evolutionary adjustments.

This sense of humankind deeply enfolded in surrounding nature incorporates the concept of a co-creation. Our living consciousness, the consciousness of our very cells, and perhaps the consciousness of an overarching but also indwelling Creation embarked together on a collaborative evolutionary journey.

My First Debate

Years ago, I went on a fishing trip to Mexico with several executives from Golden State Mutual Life Insurance Company, the largest black-owned insurance company in the western United States. One of the executives was a close family friend—actually my legal guardian should anything happen to my mother before I turned twenty-one. I met an especially admirable and accomplished man on that trip, a Rhodes scholar at Oxford in England and a prominent attorney in Los Angeles.

There was a lot of time for conversation on the journey down to San Felipe from Los Angeles. The topic of evolution came up and I quickly jumped on the Darwin bandwagon. My new friend, the attorney, sided with Lamarck. We argued back and forth, and after our pleasant but serious and even heated debate, the attorney asked me to prove my hypothesis. I began researching when I returned home to California. That research led me to two firm conclusions.

First, my faith in Darwin's presentation of the evidence was secure and I felt that I wouldn't again feel the need to defend his theory of the evolution of species, or try to persuade someone else to accept it. It was just a scientific fact, whether you chose to believe it or not.

Second, after my research into evolution, I understood Lamarck's belief system, the points he made, and the reasoning behind his theorizing. His view was attractive, even admirable, but seemed to lack a basis in material, scientific evidence.

My abiding belief was that evolution had happened just as Darwin suggested, and over the years that belief remained unchanged. I am a student of evolution and have taken many zoology and physiology courses that carefully trace the nearly innumerable small changes in physical form that have occurred over millions of years to bring about the animal kingdom's present state.

Math and a Change of Heart

Then my beliefs were tested. The more I learned about evolution, the more I saw faults in Darwin's hypothesis. His theory that evolution was completely random, a matter only of blind chance, began to ring false. Lamarck's idea of intention on the part of humans and other living things and each species' role in a co-evolution with the environment began to make sense, especially when considering the mathematical calculations involved.

Only so many "positive," survival-enhancing mutations will appear in individuals and in their immediate breeding group within a certain period of time. Millions of mutations can occur, but 99.9 percent of them will not lead to an evolutionary advantage. Only .1 percent of mutations present changes that will increase the survival skills of that species.

For a mutated gene to successfully enter a gene pool, to reproduce itself and have a noticeable effect on a species, one individual with the mutated gene must mate with another individual who has the same mutation, or at least a double recessive trait for that mutation, so the mutation can appear in offspring.

I finally realized that if over a relatively long period of time a species produced a hundred minor mutations, most of them with only an infinitesimal chance of being beneficial, Darwin and Wallace's

151

hypothesis could not account for the masterful mutations that have apparently occurred so rapidly in the millions of species that inhabit the earth. There simply aren't enough mutations in any generation of any animal population to allow for the needed adaptations that were apparently rather speedily put in place, at least in the sense of the long expanse of geologic time. Living creatures somehow changed themselves in response to environmental trends that could be drastic, sudden, and potentially catastrophic to continued survival.

I decided that there had to be another powerful force, beyond random mutation, that was responsible for the amazing, perhaps conscious "self-selecting" in a co-creating process of evolution. I turned to Lamarck's belief that within all living things there was a mechanism or organ of adaptation that was always interacting with the environment and when necessary fashioning needed changes.

After Napoleon was driven from power in the early nineteenth century, the Catholic Church in Europe regained its influence and Lamarck was ridiculed for his ideas about animals—and especially about humankind—co-creating themselves with the environment instead of being formed by God. And then Darwin and Wallace's theory discredited Lamarck among scientists.

Think of an animal such as a rodent that will someday fly and be called a bat, and the random chance that this rodent will develop skin flaps from its feet to its fingertips and elongate and minimalize the weight of its bones. There are millions of evolutionary possibilities: bigger bones, shorter bones, losing or gaining hair, head size, more teeth, longer tail, and increased brain size among them. I think you get the point that there might be a few gene mutations that are passed on to surviving progeny, but there are millions if not billions of possibilities. How is it that once these adaptations occur—for example, the rodent gets a little skin flap on its side—evolution continues in this direction with pinpoint specificity to favor the selection? Sure, there are a few experiments in the fossil record that didn't last long, but most of our fossil record shows evolution to be expeditious way beyond chance. If the rate of normal mutation was known back in Darwin's time, his theory would never have made it off the ground.

Even modern knowledge of hypermutation that occurs when a population is being stressed cannot account for the specificity or velocity of evolution.

People who believe in the creation story of Genesis as literal truth have seized on the "time problem" in Darwin's theory, arguing that evolutionary changes couldn't have kept pace with challenges to survival presented by sudden environmental events. Human beings, then, must have been created in the form they now have and have always had, from the time when God made them.

Interestingly, these anti-Darwinian arguments based on the Bible have focused on the story of Adam and Eve, humankind's parents, and have referred less frequently to the other story of creation that is also presented in Genesis: the evolution story whereby God created all things in a stepwise fashion—the earth, the oceans, plants and animals, and then human beings—all alone, in six days. Incidentally, I believe that timeline has less to do with the actual timeline of creation and relates more to the creation or maintenance of a workweek, the calendar that was set up with lunar cycles, and creating a seventh day devoted to rest, family time, and spiritual work.

I understand the need for humanity to put itself at the center, with the universe rotating around this central focus of God. Choosing this story as the literal explanation for how humans came about and why we have complete dominion over all the animals and plants of the earth serves our need to feel powerful. But it does not serve us or the inhabitants of the planet in any way.

As we continue to explore how our universe works, physicists are revisiting Lamarck's theories and are focusing closely on the quantum process of transition, in which energy consciousness is transformed and structured into physicality. Einstein believed that "the particle is determined by the nature of the field." Stephen Hawking has said that the universe is created by the observer. Lamarck's theories are now being supported.

With opposition from Camp Darwin and the very powerful church, Lamarck's conclusions about evolution were about two hundred years ahead of his time, ahead of the nineteenth and most of the twentieth centuries.

Personal Evolution

Can we draw any conclusions from this discussion about the evolution of our soul? I continue to be fascinated by the capacity and abilities of the human soul, which experiences and adapts to the nearly countless events that occur in multiple lifetimes, life after life, yet still remains unified. An individual soul uniquely encounters each new event in the soul's present bodily existence.

Simultaneously, this "private" soul is taking part in a collective experience, joined in collective consciousness with other humans and all of nature, and with the Creator or Creation whose consciousness permeates all things and spans all time.

That's a lot of data to store and manage! One would think that each human soul, to function at all, must be semiautonomous. It's as if the soul would have to necessarily be enclosed by something like an energetic cell wall that filters stimuli, letting through news of only the most important events occurring beyond the soul.

A "soul envelope" would seem to be required to limit the input of the consciousness and life experiences from previous individual existences, the collective consciousness, the experiences of our species, and the rest of nature. Otherwise, the individual soul would seem to be vulnerable to a wild influx of both new signals and stored memories from all of time and space, overpowering its ability to respond to the immediate environment and its requirements.

And yet, the soul can "tune in" to important, relevant information collected over millions of years and stored for future reference and use. The human soul is both a room of its own and a door to collective co-creation.

Thought Problem

Imagine that a soul is actively and consciously participating in all the experiences of that soul's present existence. Imagine that this soul is arranging encounters with just the right people at just the right moments and choosing to have other specific experiences for the purpose of taking advantage of the greatest potentialities for its positive evolution, to harmonize both the chaos within itself and within Creation.

Remember that as each human personality has different experiences, the body's DNA changes in response to those experiences, as we've learned from our discussion of epigenetics. The "mental" changes that an individual undergoes in the course of a lifetime are not just emotional and ideological shifts, but are registered physically in DNA.

Physicality is therefore a reflection of consciousness. The role of the mental factor in determining physical form is one way in which the soul and an indwelling spark of a divine creative consciousness participate together in the co-evolution of the individual and the larger cosmos.

Past, Present, Future

I once heard a Native American elder say that the decisions we make now must consider the effects those decisions will have on seven succeeding generations. Only then, seven lifetimes in the future, could a decision be judged to have been good or bad, constructive or destructive. This forward projection of the facts has its place in how future bodies for a soul are created.

As I said earlier, I have put subjects into hypnotic trance that allowed them to return to previous lives. They have described their experiences in general as well as specific terms and commonly report that the next body and life they will choose has been in the process of creation over many previous lifetimes.

I have not asked how far into the future this ongoing formation of bodies and life experiences extends, but I expect that the future must include many incarnations and that the generation of future bodies and life events is presently occurring far in advance of the next bodily existence. What I have been told is that the life choices we make (baby, family, etc.) are the result of every life experience we have had. The creation of all future bodies and lives has been in play since the first human experience, if not the first experience of creation. This means that the body and life you choose now began its creation many, many lifetimes ago. The experiences you need for the issues you will be wrestling with come from your collective experiences. The body you are in now is something like a pyramid, each row leading to the end product at the apex. The probabilities and options narrow with the experiences we have until a final choice must be made.

These reports while in hypnotic trance provide a clue about an evolutionary system that is both planned and spontaneous. This system operates over vast time periods, composed of individual moments of evolutionary transformation. Time appears to be both long and short, preplanned and elastic—our concepts of free will, destiny, and chance become entangled and are not easily separated or identified.

If the body we choose in a future existence has been in the process of generation over at least seven previous lifetimes, time really is elastic and should extend at least seven lifetimes into the future from the present moment, in order to keep the process of preparation on schedule. I use the number seven because of its connection to Native American thought. In actuality, the number of future lifetimes spent in preparation may be much greater.

The important point is that time is expanding beyond itself, into future times, as moment by present moment any number of probabilities are collapsing into physical form, from energy to matter, while other possibilities remain dormant. The future is dependent on the past, on free will in the present, and on the overarching needs of Creation.

Subjects under trance relate that when they select a body to inhabit for the next lifetime, there are usually at least two and sometimes three bodies to choose from. All of these bodies "on display" are physical, collapsed probabilities, accomplished material facts, yet with choices or free will, we may move somewhat individually as we choose what we wish to work on and the family that serves us best.

It is an amazing universe in which we live, in which we experience life, evolve, and transform. In our lives we often feel alone, unsupported singular entities in a sea of humanity, never realizing that we are a part of something so large that we are never alone and are helped in everything we do. In order for humanity to have free will and do the work that transforms us and all that we are a part of, we must wear blinders and be more autonomous. We could never make the hard choices and truly transform ourselves if we knew who we really were, yet even with this in mind, we must find a balance. What makes our individuality stable is our ego, yet too much of its direction leads us to ruin. What restores balance is the call from our soul to *return* to the reality of who we really are, energetic spiritual beings *co-evolving* and harmonizing Creation through the physical realm. We will always have one foot in the physical earthly realm and the other in the energetic realms.

12

FEAR AND AWE

I n the balancing act between the perspectives of ego and soul, we find my favorite Hebrew word from the Torah: "yirah." It describes which of these perspectives you dwell in most, and has two opposite meanings— fear and awe.

Some people primarily think, feel, and act fearfully while some of us confront life with a sustained sense of awe, of the miraculous, of the unworldly. Most people alternate between these two opposing points as they experience life's day-to-day challenges.

The Effects of Fear

We know that fear is harmful. Research in epigenetics tells us that our emotional state affects our own physical health and the well-being of those around us. If a pregnant mother feels her environment is unsafe and fear inducing, the child in the womb will register the same neurochemical and emotional-energetic signals she does, which will affect its own developing body and brain.

The fetus within a fearful mother physically and emotionally experiences a conflict between safety and threat, nurture and danger. This negative and fear-based sense of its environment causes hypertrophy to the areas of the body that help the fetus survive in these perceived conditions. This increases function to the motor centers of the brain as well as performance in the arms and legs. All of this will help the fetus cope with a harsh, fear-based environment.[1]

After birth, the effects linger. The child will tend to be reactive instead of looking for solutions to the problems it faces. The child will react to uncertain stimuli, perceive them as potential threats to survival, and employ either a flight or fight response. Fear-centered individuals create a fear-centered humanity, a world that runs on fear and has only two choices in confronting each new challenge: escape or combat.

The Effects of Awe

A humanity that experiences life with a sense of awe will be more creative, insightful, tolerant, and likely to perceive the miracle that it is a part of. Fear-influenced people are suited for war and battle, whereas those who are nurtured with the sense of awe have a greater frontal brain capacity for thinking complex thoughts.

These thoughts, which are the result of an environment suffused with awe, genetically modify humankind and influence the evolution of creation in a positive and unifying direction, just as fearful thoughts and actions influence our evolution—and that of the cosmos—toward reflexive actions of conflict and toward chaos and disunity.

The soul is relieved to find itself a conscious being enclosed in such a grand and amazing cosmos, while the ego operates from a place of fear. We realize that, small as we are, we're also huge, sharing an intimate identity with all of creation, and that somehow our own destiny is the destiny of the universe.

Future Humans

Parents who raise a child in an environment of unconditional love, directing their attention toward positivity in the world, give the child a sense of awe and connection with all Creation. Within its genetic makeup, the child will have the ability to pass along this way of being to its own offspring, furthering the positive development of human evolution. Imagine a lineage of such children extending into the far future and what life in a world of awe-centered humanity might be like.

Scientists who study humankind's evolutionary past and our chain of adaptations to changing environments across human prehistory sometimes imagine the structure and abilities of future humans. Most of their distant predictions suggest that we'll resemble those advanced extraterrestrial visitors often described as tall and slender with larger skulls to contain a larger brain with increased capacities.

The greater brain case size would allow for improved nonverbal communication. There may be an improved connection between the conscious mind and soul consciousness, allowing for a greater connection to other humans, to the earth, and to the universe. It's my guess such future humans would be passive, creative, and seekers of holistic ways to solve complex problems.

In contrast, if our offspring and their descendants are surrounded by fear, threats to their survival, skepticism, narrow-mindedness, and lifestyles based on the needs and fears of the ego, we can expect human beings to develop quite differently. They will evolve into frightful warriors battling with one another with ever more powerful weapons. This will lead to eventual self-destruction and destruction of all life on Earth.

World Genetics

American society is currently very polarized politically. Because men and women of like mind and background often marry, we may be unknowingly producing a genetic narrowing of future generations, a society sharply divided between the fear centered on one side and the awe centered on the other.

This phenomenon is not unique to the United States. It can be seen around the globe, where old tribal ways are in conflict with new ways of being that value personal freedom; resist sexism, racism, and sectarianism; oppose armed conflict; desire a fairer and more equitable distribution of the world's wealth and resources; and are concerned with the ecology of the earth and the survival of both its human and nonhuman inhabitants.

Just as an individual body is created from its own thoughts, the earth's increasing billions of human beings may be in the process of creating a "split" species, with half of humanity chained to the fight-or-flight response and the remaining half awe inspired, with a natural gravitation toward cooperation, sharing, nonviolence, evolved education, and spiritual experience and knowledge that are the source of unity and not conflict.

Resolving this confrontation between an old consciousness and a new one in a humane manner is perhaps our greatest challenge, a struggle that, as we all know, begins within our individual selves.

Actions and Consequences

My mother always emphasized the world of consequences. All of our actions, as individuals and communally, have consequences. For example, my thoughts, and the words and actions that spring from my thoughts, directly connect me to consequences that benefit or do not benefit me and others. This is the nature of our minutely interconnected world. I am part of the earth as well as being a part of each of its human and nonhuman citizens, with whom by my very existence I am "entangled." This is just as every particle in the universe is entangled, from the moment of the Big Bang and onward toward some ultimate future, where all chaos will be transformed into the ordered unity to which it belongs.

I understand that I am affected by all consequences, whether I or someone else sets the actions in motion that produce the consequences. It helps me remember that my actions affect others and that my effect on others is simultaneously affecting me.

Lessons from Native Americans

As I wrote earlier, there is a Native American teaching that each decision should take into account its effect on seven generations beyond one's own. In reality, this could be a metaphor for planning as far as a hundred generations ahead. It is with this level of care and foresight that we must make our decisions and choose our actions, as they will affect not only ourselves and our contemporaries but many future inhabitants of Earth.

The intention behind this teaching is to remind us of our oneness with Earth and all of its past, present, and future beings, both human and nonhuman. Taking this long perspective dampens our left brain's tendency toward greed and immediate gratification from our actions. The two negative habits arise from a sense of separateness from others and from

161

our environment. The long view encourages a positive inertia to curb snap judgments that fail to consider ultimate consequences.

Native Americans see all the animals and plants of Earth as their brothers and sisters. Everything in their environment has a "medicine," an individual power and an influence. This is critically important to the health of the community. This truly holistic view of humankind's relationship to Earth allowed millions of Native Americans to successfully inhabit the Americas for at least 20,000 years without degradation of the land and water or extinction of other animals or themselves, as has occurred during the post-European settlement of the Americas.

I also mentioned earlier that the lifespan the Native Americans was believed to be significantly longer than that of Europeans. Logically, decisions made that keep in mind the future and that stem from a general belief about the relations between all living things could have made a healthier continent. So the two paths of fear and awe are very different. These opposing and emotionally charged worldviews produce different levels of health, people, and lifestyles.

Another Way

The far-reaching effects of displacing the ego from its central position in the human psyche will profoundly affect society in innumerable ways.

Individuals who have broken the yoke of the ego and placed the soul at the center of their consciousness will no longer feel the compulsion to compare themselves with others. They will become free of negative feelings of low self-worth, envy, or a need to compete when in the company of those who have more money, power, beauty, or strength. People will be motivated to do well in their work, not because of the money or power it brings, but because of the joy and satisfaction it offers.

As we move into the next section of the book that explores religion and discuss the inner meanings of some of the sacred scriptures, we will see that many of them give us great guidelines for identifying and averting the needs of the fear-based ego and turning toward our connection to who we really are, seeing the world through the eyes of *awe*.

13

PERSPECTIVE AND RELIGION

Two Hemispheres

E very day each of us is changing, becoming someone different as we move along the path of personal evolution. The road we travel has potholes, bumps, and detours, and at the same time unfolds many exciting adventures. Our evolution is never ending, self-perpetuated by the joys of growth and liberation. Religions and philosophies can help us find the best ways to navigate the way to our truer and most unified selves.

In studying the major religions of the world, it became clear to me that lessons in personal evolution had to address the needs and challenges of both right- and left-brained individuals. There are people who rely on their five senses and logic and those who rely on intuition and knowings from beyond the five senses. And there are people who integrate both hemispheres of the brain. Each perspective is seen as the absolute truth. Recognizing this will help everyone understand why some writings resonate with some people and opposing writings appeal to others. It also tells much about which side of the brain the authors are coming from, and this reveals their beliefs and the filters through which they view their experiences. Please also note that we say "right and left brain" to express well-known differences in how the two sides of the brain perceive the world around them. And while both right- and left-brained people integrate both sides of the brain in their thinking, they place different priorities on which side to use.

Left Brain

As a rule, left-brained people are categorized as logical individuals who perceive life through the five senses. They are attracted to concrete, literal, and well-defined concepts. They value traditional ways of thinking and behavior, resist changes to accepted ways of being, and feel most comfortable with clearly articulated rules of behavior. They identify with right-and-wrong and yes-and-no sets of precepts, allowing them to make correct decisions with a minimum of uncertainty and remorse.

These people feel closest to God when they consciously follow the moral rules and deeds of their religion; in doing this they feel they can best honor and respect their God. Commonly, individuals with left-brained orientation see man in the image of a God who resembles a traditional patriarch, and they accept and try to abide by God's laws without question. Along the same lines, they are faith based and willing to surrender to a higher power. They have a greater sense of hierarchy, believing in a chain of command along with laws that need to be followed to prevent chaos.

Left-brained individuals would probably interpret the Hebrew word "yirah" as "fear" or "God-fearing" rather than "awe." For them, one of the most important aspects of God is enforcement, striking wrongdoers with the swift hand of justice. The left-brained religious believer can fairly be placed on the conservative and even fundamentalist side of the spectrum of religious beliefs and practices.

Right Brain

A generalized profile of right-brained religious individuals would include their tendency to read sacred writings as metaphor, as symbols that embody deeper, nonliteral meanings that can be found "underneath" the words and stories of religious texts. Symbols, by their very nature, simultaneously represent different levels of meaning and unify apparent contradictions into a greater whole, requiring that the reader delve below the literal meanings of human language, which can never fully express the mysteries of Creation.

Right-brained people are usually intuitive, hence gathering the lesser part of their information from exterior stimuli. In the purest form they don't rely heavily on logic and do base their decisions largely on feelings.

The spiritual path for the right-brained is directed inward, seeking an increased connection with the Creator through introspection, meditation, and private prayer. Right-brained people are drawn to an egalitarian view of humanity, and their perceptions and experiences of God are closer to awe than to fear. Typically, they do not see God primarily in the image of a human being but as a mysterious, energetic form of consciousness—a cosmic creative force or power of Creation that both includes and transcends the human. They are attracted to the idea of "oneness" and attempt to think and act in a manner that reflects and furthers the experience of "union": among people, with God, and with all living things.

The right-brained religious perspective is largely "gnostic," the Greek word that means "to know through experience." This approach places special emphasis on immediate, firsthand spiritual experience as a necessary prerequisite for belief and the acceptance of traditional religious precepts. The inward sense of the Divine or the Universal Consciousness is reached through personal intuition rather than by the calculations of logic.

As individuals, right-brained people are independent in their thinking and not overly impressed by the authority of ancient religious texts—or by the vast numbers of believers who have accepted and followed the doctrines of organized religion over the course of millennia. They are apt to see the texts as subject to interpretation. This mystical view is used to find meaning for new events in their lives.

The enduring nature of a specific religion would tend to impress the left-brained practitioner, who through logic might perceive a belief system's vibrant longevity as evidence of its truth. The right-brained individual will see truth by experiencing it.

Though both the left- and right-brained often find a strengthened connection with God amid the pristine outdoors, the right-brained religious personality is especially drawn to nature and seeks lessons about life and the way to inner peace through time spent away from the works of man. Those with a right-brain perspective are usually considered liberal or progressive in their political and social views and are open to expanding or changing their religious and philosophical ideas. There is of course a large percentage of people who find themselves with views from both sides of the brain, which creates a blend of beliefs.

Tradition and Change

As we all know from watching the daily news or studying the history of human civilization, religious conflict is as old as humankind. These disagreements, which have often resulted in horrific clashes, usually involve those who wish to maintain a unified, traditional religion and its teachings and those who want to expand and further develop certain aspects of the same religion.

In viewing both contemporary and historical religious controversies, it is important to understand the opposing perspectives and keep in mind that each individual believer is drawn to those religious teachings that bring meaning to life and provide a direction that he or she believes will lead to God or the Creator. The fact is that religious preference may largely depend on the way each brain operates and perceives the human and the divine.

If we could all accept that there are various paths to God, both within our own religion and in other religions, we could avoid breaking so many of the important rules that our own religion and all others hold dear.

One of the most important gifts offered by the multitude of organized religions is the opportunity for each person to develop a sense of tolerance and acceptance. This is in the service of avoiding violent conflict (whether physical or psychological) over teachings that are meant to increase peace and love and spiritual evolution among humankind.

Whatever our personal religious, political, and social beliefs, we all need to remember that every individual religion can appear quite differently to people who have different personalities and rely on different sides of the human brain for their view of mankind and Creation. Left- and right-brained people perceive and process their experience in dissimilar ways, yet both ways of being in the world exist and are "naturally" right and true.

The important thing is that we each follow the path that is ours, all the while acknowledging that there are other just and rightful paths, and that all religious roads have one destination: unity with Creation.

Our Religions

As the human population of the earth grew, cities were founded and with them organized forms of religion developed. Formal religions evolved from tribal beliefs and practices: myth and ritual and magical rites that included propitiatory and sacrificial offerings to nature spirits and deities. The early religious beliefs were primarily transmitted orally and reflected the people's cultures, what they had observed in nature, and what they felt deep within. In those early times people were much more grounded than we are today and spent more time in their inner thoughts, exploring concepts such as the unknowable, their purpose, and the feeling that there was a place where they had come from and would return to. Religious beliefs, rules, and guidelines gave members of the tribe a meaningful, structured pattern to life, death, and postmortal existence, and ensured the tribe's coherence as a unit and its ongoing survival within its immediate natural environment.

As human organization developed beyond small tribes and villages and cities were founded, religion became more codified and metaphoric. Complex pantheons of personified natural forces, at first depicted as animals or mixtures of animals and humans, began to appear, followed by deities that represented archetypal aspects of human life and experience. This was accompanied by an increased emphasis on the ethical, on a personal and social sense of right and wrong, and a moral foundation to the universe.

The polytheistic religions of the ancient Egyptians and Greeks developed well-articulated assemblies of deities and myths. The Greeks even imagined their gods as superhuman men and women.

The monotheism of Judaism was a revolutionary concept. Everything was sourced from one Creator, one overseeing Consciousness, and everything was part of the one unknowable and unfathomable God. There were no separate entities or different gods that represented various aspects of daily life or elements of nature. It was also revolutionary in that there were no idols or physical representations of that One Sovereign of the Universe. The ancient Israelites worshipped God, and entered into a covenantal relationship with God, even though they could not see or touch or physically experience the Divine. This first monotheistic religion with

167

its core belief of oneness also revealed the unknowable's relationship with humanity.

In the next few chapters I will very briefly review the major religions and philosophies of the world, in the chronological order of their establishment. I have tried to differentiate "religion" from "philosophy," in that organized religions attempt to quantify God and interpret what God wishes humans to do, while Buddhism and Taoism, both profound systems of thought and belief, refrain from specifically identifying or describing an individualized god or acknowledging any direct words from a Godhead.

I feel it's important to consult these sources that include thousands of years of thinking and feeling about our purpose, what we are made of, and how we all get along. I also enjoy seeing that all religions and philosophies are heading the same way and really agree with one another. All you have to do to see this is to remove devotion to each iconic prophet and to which one promises the best afterlife. Let us use in our discussion the wisdom and experiences of millions and even billions of people.

Remember that in each of these theologies there are thoughts and passages originating from writers who are right- and left-brained. The major religions have expanded their beliefs through both the right and left filters of their writers, resulting in both a conservative and progressive point of view. Perhaps you will now be able to pick them out as each writes their own truth.

14

JUDAISM

Debate and Dialogue

Over its long history, Judaism has become increasingly diverse, developing many differing perspectives and special points of emphasis among its various denominations while still retaining a core set of beliefs that is at least three thousand years old.

Judaism has traditionally been a scholarly religion, with rabbinical commentaries on the sacred texts reaching back almost to its beginnings. Learned study and written interpretation of the words and actions of God, and of humans' historical relationship with God, have deepened and enriched the religion and created an impressive, wide-ranging literature of spiritual analysis and theological theory. It is a religion that accepts, if not requires, many different viewpoints as true and vital, as evidenced by the famous Talmudic saying *Eilu v'eilu divrei Elohim Chayim*—This and also this are the words of the living God.[1]

Judaism has long had a strong heritage of mysticism that can be defined as the innate desire for a greater union with and understanding of God. The holy texts of Judaism are filled with archetypal humans who often argue with God and wrestle with angels or the divine consciousness within themselves.

It is fair to say that Judaism has always been a religion of "wrestling" with the enigmas of both God and humankind and their everlasting bond. In fact, the name Yisrael (Israel) means the one who wrestles with God.

There is room for scriptural interpretation and debate aided by the fact that the Hebrew Bible, the Torah, is written without vowels. This requires the reader to insert vowel sounds, which can actually change the root meaning of the individual words and give whole stories numerous possible meanings. In addition, each letter of the alphabet has a numerical equivalent, which opens the biblical text to even further interpretation. This can be explored through gematria—the calculation of the numerical equivalence of letters, words, or phrases—enabling us to gain insight into the relationship between words and ideas.

Perhaps the mystery of definition embedded in the words themselves reflects the mystery of God and provides a constant reminder that it is impossible for the human intellect to arrive at one final, single truth about the divine. Interpretation requires imagination and intuition, a co-creation of the text, an intense activity that can become a dialogue with God.

The active human involvement necessary to discover the deepest meanings of the Torah seems especially suited for individuals with a right-brain orientation. By their nature, the right-brained may be attracted to the richness of sacred texts that contain not only multiple but theoretically almost endless numbers of meanings.

Main Covenants

Let's first examine the main covenants by which practicing Jews guide their lives. The Ten Commandments, presented to humanity in the Jewish and later Christian texts, give us wise and important guidelines for choosing harmonious actions and aiding personal and universal evolution. Actually, calling them "commandments" is a misnomer. The Hebrew reads *Aseret Ha'Dibrot,* literally translated as the ten "utterances" of God, not commandments. Calling God's utterances "commandments" may reflect a message of control that demands obedience. As people discover the inner wisdom of the soul, the word "utterance" seems more to the point because it suggests a sense of co-creation with the Creator—of Creation offering wise and generous advice rather than passing down an authoritarian order from on high.

Judaism sees human beings in partnership with God and emphasizes human free will and moral choices in everyday life to partner correctly and fully with God in transforming Creation.

One

And God spoke all these words, saying: I am the Lord your God, who brought you out of the land of Egypt, out of the house of bondage. You shall have no other gods before Me.

The capitalization refers to God and reminds the reader that there is only one God.

Two

You shall not make for yourself a graven image, nor any manner of likeness, of anything that is in heaven above, or that is in the earth beneath or that is in the water under the earth. You shall not bow down to them, nor serve them; for I the Lord your God am a jealous God, visiting the iniquity of the father upon the children unto the third and fourth generation of them that hate Me; and showing mercy unto the thousandth generation of them that love Me and keep My commandments.

The Second Commandment is a clear and powerful admonition not to worship, praise, or endeavor to attain anything except by following the spiritual path that leads to God. God is warning us not to worship anything in the heavens, beneath the earth, or in the water under the earth for itself, apart from God. This all-inclusive commandment teaches us to avoid the deification of created things and to save our desire for God alone, so that our worship of God becomes stronger by being focused only on God.

This lesson is seemingly as old as humankind itself, a truth that we evidently need to keep trying to learn. The worship of money, power, beauty, the new, religious images, and all natural and man-made things deflects our attention from God, who is the ultimate source of all Creation. Our wishes for material things and our intense loyalties to belief systems, which often result in heated conflict with others who hold different beliefs, cause us to shift our attention from God and Creation.

To give priority and power to created things is to forget God and stray from the path that creates harmony within ourselves and within Creation. The Second Commandment empowers the individual to create a state of peace within, and to promote the evolution of the archetypal, benevolent God Consciousness that each of us embodies and that is our truest identity.

The road that leads to the discovery of the divine within and its further development is our most important road, one that allows us to make the experience of life on Earth fulfilling and complete. Concentration on "things" will never bring the human soul a sense of unity and peace but will only spawn an inner chaos that disrupts our enlightenment and transformation and denies us the ecstatic experience of being a consciously divine portion of Creation that lives and breathes in a human body.

The Torah contains many human lessons presented through stories of human fallibility. We can identify with our ancestors' thoughts and actions and learn from their challenges and successes. These stories are filled with a wealth of knowledge and wisdom that can aid us in keeping to the path of greater enlightenment and appropriate earthly actions that help the soul reach its ideal development and become a conscious co-creator with Creation itself.

One can imagine stories from the Torah being told by elders around a fire at night, as they impart to younger family members correct morals and right beliefs that were developed over long stretches of time and were written down by spiritually gifted individuals from many earlier generations. No doubt the Second Commandment received special emphasis, to warn the young against turning from God to idolatry and becoming vulnerable to the seductions of the eye, which hinders the practice of heartfelt acts and personal transformation.

Three

You shall not take the name of the Lord your God in vain; for the Lord will not hold him guiltless that takes God's name in vain.

I believe this commandment speaks to our ethical responsibility to God. Speaking to or about God is a sacred endeavor and requires the believer to acknowledge the solemn nature of such communications and to phrase them with appropriate dignity and seriousness and ethical behavior.

This right relationship with the deity rules out uttering God's name with any expression of profane language, or using God's name to give false authority to any promises or oaths that we might make to others. To rightly speak to or about God means we must search through the intuitions of our hearts and then utter unselfish truth.

The most egregious and frightening violation of the Third Commandment is to use God's name to justify committing violent acts against others. We are reminded of how important our words are and the cruel actions they can encourage or provoke, and that we can never speak for God or assume that we know its final will.

Whenever I hear anyone—a private person, a priest, a rabbi, a politician, or someone over the airwaves—declare what God believes or what God thinks I should do, who is good or bad, and especially whom I should harm or kill in the name of God, I am immediately reminded of the Third Commandment, which forbids us from usurping the place of God or speaking the Unknowable's authority.

My experience is that when someone tells you what God wants you to do, that statement is almost always hypocritical, self-serving, and a lie. Rather than connection to the divine, it reflects human ignorance and selfishness, a willingness to pull God down to an unenlightened human level to be used for immediate human ends. This may seem harsh, but think of all the wars that have been started in God's name and all the Klansmen, terrorists, cults, and even neighborhood clergy who have claimed to receive or know God's will when justifying harmful actions.

There is a simple solution. All of your logical thoughts, intuitions, and feelings about what God wants might be best utilized to inform your own actions and no one else's. If they involve hurting someone, they are not divine. A great guideline is this: if what you're about to say is not positive, don't say it at all.

Four

Remember the Sabbath day, to keep it holy.

This commandment reminds us to keep and honor the Sabbath as sacred time, the holiest of holies. We are reminded that this is a day set apart for internal work, for serious introspection and searching one's innermost heart. The more we do this, the more we can make every day equally holy.

> *Six days you will labor, and do all your work; but the seventh day is a Sabbath unto the Lord your God, in it you shall not do any manner of work, you, nor your son, nor your daughter, nor your manservant, nor your maidservant, nor your cattle, nor the stranger that is within your gates; for in six days the Lord made heaven and earth, the sea and all that in them is, and rested on the seventh day; when the Lord blessed the Sabbath day, and hallowed it.*

The Forth Commandment also presents the proper way to honor the Sabbath. We are reminded that even God set aside one day of the week for rest and reflection.

Five

Honor your father and mother, so that your days may be long upon the land which the Lord your God gives you.

The word *kavod* is often translated as "honor" but it also means to give weight. To me, this means you must do the work to keep this relationship strong. One of the most sacred relationships is that between parents and their children. It is truly one of the relationships that can take the most work but it is foundational for all parties concerned. It can give us strength, purpose, and self-esteem if the relationship is healthy and is not one of servitude on either side. The other common meaning of *kavod* is "glory."

The Second Five

The first five commandments help us understand how we should best interact with God, while the remaining five commandments primarily pertain to human interactions, which of course either further or inhibit our personal evolution and our approach and closeness to God.

Commandments Six, Seven, and Eight are self-explanatory, and I'll make special comment only on the Ninth Commandment, while presenting the Tenth Commandment in the context of its relationship to the other four and underlining the importance and implications of the commandment against murder.

The last five commandments present moral injunctions that are common to almost all of the established religions and moral systems in the world. These admonitions are reminders of shared identities and a spur to increase our empathy and care for others, as aspects of Creation and of ourselves, and to avoid the destructive temptations of our private egos.

Six

You shalt not murder.

Seven

You shalt not commit adultery.

Eight

You shalt not steal.

Nine

You shalt not bear false witness against your neighbor.

Judaism places strong emphasis on truthfulness, constantly warning against telling untruths about others. The rabbis call this *lashon hara,* or evil tongue, which is destructive not only to others but to the bearer of false witness.

Indeed, Judaism insists that acts of gossip harm three personages. The first victim is the person unfairly talked about. The second victim is the one who speaks untruths about another. The third victim is God because Judaism holds that God is within each of us.

Let me conclude my comments on the Ninth Commandment with a Jewish teaching about the ill effects of gossip.

> A man went around gossiping without restraint. Later, when he realized how much his tales had hurt people, and felt remorse, he went to the rabbi seeking repentance. He told the rabbi he would do anything he could to make amends. The rabbi told the man, "Take a feather pillow, cut it open, and scatter the feathers into the wind." The man thought this was a bizarre request, but it was simple enough so he did it. When he returned to inform the rabbi that the task was done, the rabbi said, "Now, go and collect all the feathers and return them to the pillow." Again, the man went to do as the rabbi had asked, but found that the feathers had blown far and wide, and he was unable to retrieve even a handful. He returned to the rabbi, ashamed to admit he was not able to gather the feathers, certain that he should never have released the feathers in the first place. Knowingly, the rabbi rebuked him, saying, "Your words are like the feathers: once they leave your mouth, you know not where they will go, and you can never retrieve them back again. It is always wiser to guard your evil tongue and keep words that you might use to injure others to yourself."[2]

Judaism teaches that bearing false witness breaks one of the holiest and most powerful covenants between God and ourselves and represents a breaking of mutual trust.

Ten

You shall not covet your neighbor's house; you shall not covet your neighbor's wife, nor his manservant, nor his maidservant, nor his ox, nor his ass, nor anything that is your neighbor's.

The last five commandments remind us in specific, literal ways about the dangers of idol worship, about valuing created things and persons, even valuing persons as things or possessions, and not God, who created them. The human ego is tempted by material idols away from the path to God, in the unconsidered belief that what belongs to others will increase our stature, happiness, and security.

Breaking any of the final five commandments always creates at least three victims. Whatever the underlying cause of murder or other crimes against our neighbor, ourselves, and God, the single seed of wrong actions is always an enslavement to the false needs and wants of the individual human ego.

Yetzer Hara and *Yetzer Hatov*

These two opposing Hebrew phrases can be defined as the inclination to do bad (*yetzer hara*) and the inclination to do good (*yetzer hatov*). Judaism has always recognized that humanity has the inclination to do both bad and good and that there is often a conflict between the two within the individual. However, Judaism does not teach that we should try to rid ourselves of *yetzer hara,* because within this "bad" aspect is also the seat of our drive and ambition, which is necessary for good actions.

In Judaism, the human challenge is to discover how *yetzer hara* and *yetzer hatov* can be balanced, and how the power of bad inclinations can be transformed into an ally of good inclinations to create right thoughts and actions.

The Shema

Deuteronomy 6:4, known as the Shema, is the most regularly recited prayer in Judaism: *Shema Yisrael, Adonai Eloheinu, Adonai Echad.* We can translate these words in light of their intention. "Listen all of you God wrestlers. God is our God, God is one." An important meaning of this prayer is contained in the word "Echad," which refers to a special kind of "oneness."

In Judaism, as we've discussed, you are free to look for different meanings in the texts and wrestle with the different interpretations. The oneness that is Echad seems to suggest not just a simple unity of identity but an overarching superunity that takes in all created and uncreated beings and things. This includes all of God, God's works, and the thoughts of which we are a part. Echad teaches that there is nothing that is not God.

Another aspect of the Shema that I especially value is its inclusivity. I understand it this way: "Listen all of you who wrestle with God, religious teachings, and life." It does not say, "Listen, all you Jews." All feeling and thinking people have to wrestle with the concept of God—even atheists, who have to look deeply within and without before they arrive at the conclusion that there is no God.

We all wrestle.

The Tree of Life

Judaism holds dear all extensions of the religion, from the studies of the Orthodox literalists to those of the progressive mystics. All are part of the valued heritage of Jewish teachings and writings.

The study of Kaballah and the mystic influence began in twelfth-century Europe. At the center of this mystical tradition stands the Tree of Life, which within its branches holds all of the aspects of God (see figure 7). One side of the tree represents the masculine and the other side the feminine. The endeavor of the Kabbalists was to aid humanity in embodying all of these aspects of Creation by finding a balance between the tree's two sides, near the tree's center.[3]

Tree of Life Chart

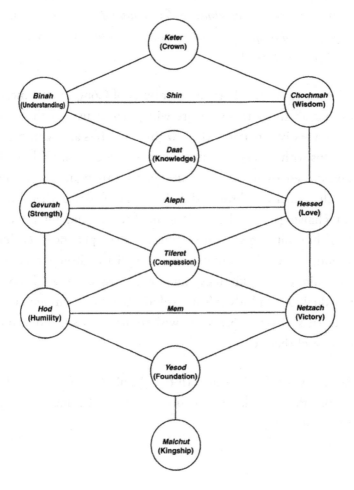

Figure 7.

Mussar Training

Much of the practice of Judaism emphasizes the important of achieving an inner balance. Mussar is a psychospiritual guide for personal/divine growth.

> *Merciful God, merciful God, powerful God, compassionate and gracious, slow to anger, and abundant in kindness and truth. Preserver of kindness for thousands of generations, forgiver of iniquity, willful sin and error, and Who cleanses.*
> *(Exodus 34:6–7)*

These are called the Thirteen Attributes of Compassion, and Mussar teaches that all these attributes are within all of us and that our most important work is to magnify them within ourselves and within our daily relationships with others. The more men and women are able to develop and express these divine aspects through their thoughts and actions, the greater will be their joy, love, and divine awe each day of their lives.

Our challenge as individuals is to discover and integrate within ourselves humility, generosity, grace, trust, patience, enthusiasm, compassion, moderation, order, honor, simplicity, silence, responsibility, faith, equanimity, awe, kindness, and love. Mussar practice helps deepen the individual soul and advance its evolution, and I recommend it to those who value these divine aspects and wish to make them a more conscious, integral part of themselves.[4]

Not far away in Persia (modern-day Iran) and not long after the cultural practice of Judaism had been established came the religion of Zoroastrianism.

15

ZOROASTRIANISM

My Introduction to Zoroaster

In chapter 11 I briefly summarized the general outlines of Zoroastrianism, the dualistic religion of the great Persian Empires, in the context of the individual's internal struggle between order and chaos, which is a microcosm of a cosmic, universal evolution toward harmony and a transformation and integration of disharmonious energies.

As I mentioned earlier, my introduction to this religion began during my teenage years, when my mother was contracted to write and direct a series of films on the history of Iran, from its first Bronze Age societies to the rule of Shah Abbas in the CE 1500s. During this long span of time, there had been a gradual transition from early Iranian pagan religions to Zoroastrianism, which held sway until the Arab invasion of Iran and the country's subsequent conversion to Islam.

Most Zoroastrians either died in the political/religious conflict with the Muslims, were assimilated into the conquerors' faith, or migrated to India, where Zoroastrianism had spread and was still practiced by adherents who are known as Parsees.

I lived and traveled in Iran from 1975 to 1976, a period when the government tolerated all religions including Zoroastrianism, whose practitioners had hidden their beliefs during Islamic rule or had returned to Iran when religious freedom allowed them to once again openly practice their faith. Most of the filming we did concerned the period of the great

Persian Empires that were contemporary with Ancient Greece and through Roman times, when Zoroastrianism, which was tolerant of other beliefs, was the national religion of the Persians.

Such a Happy Woman

One day we were filming an ancient water temple. According to tradition, the last Zoroastrians in Iran had fled into the mountains to escape the Islamic invaders. In their desperate flight, the religious refugees saw the mountains open up before them, leading them to a spring high in the mountains. This place became their sanctuary when the mountains closed behind them for their protection.

The place became a water temple and was called "Chok Chok," named for the sound of the water dropping from a spring that fed the temple. The mouth of the spring could only be reached by climbing a nearly endless set of steps to a high mountain peak.

In the course of filming, there was little conversation between my mother, a strong woman with a strict timetable, and the all-male crew, most of whom were Iranian. Even during this time of greater equality compared to today, it was still hard for them to take orders from my mother, a good top-gun sergeant. Until now, they had been hard working and loyally committed to our project. Now they became sullen and unhappy and were unwilling to continue with the tasks our film work depended on. It was not an easy day and we had been filming for a while when the Iranian crew abruptly sat down and refused to help.

And so it fell to me and the other American crew to carry the heavy camera gear and lights to film the temple's high-mountain spring. Each trip required about a thousand steps—all of them up.

An elderly Zoroastrian woman appeared and saw me struggling with my load of equipment. She went and got her broom and waved it at the sitting men. She firmly informed them that her ancestors had taken care of the water temple for more than a thousand years and that in her own long life she had done the same. She reminded them of their moral obligation to help one another and to work out their disagreements through an even-handed dialogue with all concerned. The woman gave them a brief, informal sermon about the responsibility of humanity to support each other and to end suffering, and to do whatever it would take to find happiness in every day. At no time did she seem angry. All of the wrinkles on her face had come from smiling.

Then she motivated them with little giggles and the motion of her broom as she swept the men from where they sat and pushed them toward the remaining movie gear that had to be hoisted up the tall mountain to the spring. What most struck me about the woman was that she appeared happy, apparently eternally so. She had a smile on her face even as she spoke strongly and coerced the men. At day's end, when we had finished filming on the peak, she brought food, tea, and sweets for everyone.

She was a kind host, often chuckling as she talked to the men she had previously swung at with her broom. As a Zoroastrian woman, she never acted as a subordinate to the men, nor did she assume the role of their superior. She was obviously filled with kind wisdom and true to her tireless endeavor to see good prevail over evil. For me, this episode was perhaps the most delightful moment of the whole yearlong filming adventure. That day introduced me to the heart of the Zoroastrian faith.

The Source

The story of Zoroastrianism begins with Zoroaster, who in an act of ritual purification was gathering water from the middle of a river. As he returned to the riverbank, he had a vision of a shining being on the shore, who revealed himself as "Vohu Manah," a name that means "good purpose." This figure led Zoroaster into the presence of Ahura Mazda and five other radiant beings, from whom Zoroaster received his revelation.

Ahura Mazda explained to Zoroaster that wisdom, justice, and goodness were utterly separate, by their very nature, from wickedness and cruelty. Unfortunately, these positive attributes were coexistent with the negative attributes created by Aurora Mazda, an adversary, a hostile spirit also known as Angra Mainyu or Ahriman.

Ahura Mazda and Aurora Mazda were equal and opposing twins and represented the two primal universal spirits that had created all duality. In Creation there was also a Counter Creation, as there is life and death, good and evil. In combating his bad twin, Ahura Mazda projected direct or indirect emanations of himself and created a series of divine beings who passed his light from one to another, the way a single torch is used to light other torches.

Ahura Mazda and his five subordinates whom Zoroaster met were in league with humanity to further good and fight against evil in a universal battle that took place both in the Heavens and on Earth. Men and women were equal and both had important roles to play in in the ultimate victory of light over darkness.

In Zoroastrianism, the fire temples are masculine, and the water temples, like the Temple of Anaheta, are feminine. Fire represents the Godhead and water the Godhead's wisdom. A main tenet of these forces of goodness and order is the protection of the poor and weak, who should never be abused or become victims of domination. As I noted in chapter 11, Zoroaster demanded that his followers have good thoughts and perform good works.

Three Creations

In the Zoroastrian story of creation there are three specific, different, but interrelated events.

First, Ahura Mazda brought forth all things into a disembodied or energetic state called "Menog," and from this immaterial state manifested physical existence, called "Getig," in which all beings had bodily form as well as consciousness. Once again we see these ancient texts giving us hints about creation that are now proving to be true. It is up to us and modern science to reveal the knowledge of how energy converts to physicality or material things.

Ahura Mazda's created world was immediately attacked by Angra Mainyu, who salted the water and turned productive lands into deserts. He withered all the plants and slew the first man and the first bull that Ahura Mazda had made. Ahura Mazda's evil twin even sullied the purity of created fire as he destroyed the perfection that Ahura Mazda had brought into being.

Ahura Mazda and his lieutenants immediately went to work undoing all the damage Angra Maimyu had done. The destruction and subsequent rebuilding of Ahura Mazda's perfect world make up the second crucial event in the creation of life on Earth.

Now duality had appeared, and with it suffering and pain, and an immense battle began between all the forces of good and evil. In this fight against darkness, humanity is inherently on the side of light but will be severely tested, and after death the deeds of each human soul will be placed on a scale of judgment.

If an individual's good deeds and ethical achievements in combating evil outweigh the bad, he or she will be led across the narrow bridge to paradise by beautiful maidens.

Those who fail to resolve the evil within themselves and whose acts are self-serving, greedy, and uncaring for the weak plunge down into a "dwelling place of the worst purpose," where the wicked endure a long age of misery and darkness, existing on inedible food and in their suffering continually crying out in woe.

In addition, there is a third postmortem destination, reserved for souls whose good and bad human deeds balanced out and didn't tip the scales in one direction or the other. These "neutral souls" are sent to "the place of the mixed ones," a gray world that lacks both joy and sorrow and is reminiscent of Dante's realm in hell for angels who were neither good nor evil and refused to take sides in the battle between God and Lucifer.

Lessons for Today

One can easily see how these ancient stories can represent our own life struggles. If we fight evil within ourselves, it will lead us across a narrow bridge to paradise. This paradise is Heaven on Earth, Heaven in our lives.

Some see heaven as a reward that comes at the end of a physical life well lived. I see it as the reward in this life for doing the often hard work it takes to harmonize one's life.

The narrow bridge reminds us that this is the path less chosen. It takes courage and a strong sense of self and connection to others and the universe to take this path. Although it is hard, refusing to take this path leads to a life that is gray, neither good nor bad. This kind of life lacks the joy and depth of experience that occur when we commit to psychospiritual evolution.

Zoroaster's revelation assures his followers that after a long conflict, good finally overcomes evil. This victory opens a doorway to a third creation, in which men and women will live in perfection as they did in the first creation before Angra Maimyu destroyed it. There will be no hatred, fighting, suffering, or death, only perfection. For all those who have died during the war between light and darkness there is bodily resurrection. The age of duality is over, and human history comes to an end in an eternal state of harmony.

New Humanity

I wonder if the Zoroastrian sense of the end of history suggests that in our earthly, physical world there will no longer be a need for humanity. The victory of light would mean that humankind had finally resolved and harmonized the conflict within itself, replacing darkness with pure, unmixed happiness, laughter, love, and kindness—a prospect that leads me to contemplate a further evolution rather than the disappearance of victorious humans.

Perhaps the future inhabitants of a redeemed Earth will have developed into a new and better species of humankind through a triumph of unified consciousness and the transformation of the ego.

Whatever perfect qualities an advanced humankind might exhibit, it seems to me that our work remains: to follow the good and help prepare this perfect, third creation through our right thoughts and actions. When I asked the Zoroastrians I met in Iran what their primary, immediate, day-to-day goals were, I was always told that they strove to do what was right for humanity at large. Individually, they sought the path or process that led them to being persistently happy.

My Zoroastrian acquaintances were neither naïve nor unthinkingly optimistic and were constantly working to transform those elements within their lives that kept them from reaching a higher state of joy and harmony. Their work was deep and serious and did not consist of just "putting on a happy face." Their laughter was a genuine spiritual event, and their ongoing efforts were not aimed at ignoring life's sadness but toward carrying on the battle within themselves for more light, to diffuse the primordial darkness that we all know to be a part of ourselves.

Influence

When I first heard the accounts of Zoroaster's revelations, in which he learned about the battle between good and evil that had become much more powerful than in Judaism, the existence of a hell, and an ultimate bodily resurrection after the triumph of the light, I often wondered how much Zoroastrian ideas and beliefs influenced the early Christians as they differentiated their new religion from rabbinic Judaism.

If we look at the early bed of Christianity around the eastern Mediterranean and Middle East, where people had been primarily Zoroastrian for hundreds or even a thousand years, it seems very reasonable to assume that these teachings were incorporated.

As Christianity was growing in areas where Zoroastrianism was embedded in the culture, once converts were integrated and became a part of Christianity, Christianity itself might incorporate these philosophies. The last big Zoroastrian-based Persian Empire fell in 632–634 CE. I hope it brings comfort to know that our religions are not so different. The religions and philosophies of the world are brothers and sisters to one another. Within each of the world theologies there are road maps to help us with our human struggle.

I also find it striking that Zoroaster's revelations and Ahura Mazda's creation story parallel the unfolding discoveries of modern physics. The intentions of the Persians' Lord of Wisdom brought forth an unmanifested energetic realm of existence from which physical, sentient beings were created. In both cases—quantum mechanics and the ancient revelations of Zoroaster—we're confronted with a self-creating energy that then enfolds consciousness with physicality, in the form of energized, sentient matter and material being.

16

CHRISTIANITY

Preface

The central aspects of Christianity first require an examination of Gnosticism. Gnosticism was an ancient theological/philosophical system of cosmology that predated the Christian religion by at least two hundred years and provided an important source for many of the core tenets of both Christ's teachings and the later development of organized Christianity.

As I noted at the beginning of our discussion of religious belief, right-brained individuals with a strong desire to approach God tend to seek ultimate truth through personal experience and intuition rather than by following the laws and acts of kindness to others. People with this spiritual, psychological, and neurological orientation have been willing to give up the comforts and securities offered by "mainstream" life in human society in order to devote themselves to religious enlightenment and communion with God. To be "gnostic" means "to know by experience." This pursuit becomes the one important purpose of their lives.

Gnosticism

Gnosticism is a somewhat general name for a varied, interrelated, and cross-fertilized group of belief systems that thrived for approximately six hundred years from about 200 BCE to CE 400. It was a complex amalgam of many pagan religious beliefs and philosophies, including Persian and perhaps Indian.

From its center in Alexandria, then the intellectual capital of the Roman world, Gnosticism influenced not only early Christianity but the Neoplatonism of the Egyptian religious philosopher Plotinus, and Mani, the Persian prophet and founder of Manichaeism, a further dualistic development of Zoroastrianism. Gnostic ideas can be identified among many of the heterodox Christian sects of the Middle Ages. This sense of wanting to connect with or *know* Creation may be as old as modern human consciousness.

Opposing Worlds

One common belief found in most Gnostic communities was that creation was composed of at least two worlds or realms. One was our physical world, an imperfect, ephemeral world constructed of time, space, and matter. The other, upper world (or worlds) was an eternal realm of perfection and light, where one's soul originated and existed before descending to the material world and assuming a body.

Some forms of Gnosticism taught that our lower world was the creation of a "demiurge," an inferior or even functionally evil god far removed from but still a creation of the divine source that ruled the upper worlds of perfection. The demiurge's ineptitude or cruelty was not a result of any innate evil, but rather reflected its distance from God and the emanation of divine light. This concept reveals much of the works and intentions of the Gnostic. In the effort to create more perfection in the lower world, one must not only merge and experience God but must transform into perfection the evil that is a part of the lower world.

The extreme Gnostics were said to believe that matter itself was evil, that the human body and its functions were unclean, and that the soul was entrapped in its body. This was a painful experience for a being that was originally pure spirit and longed to return to the light and its previous immaterial existence.

Christian Gnostics

In December 1945, Egyptian farmers near Naj Hammadi, an ancient city in Upper Egypt, found a sealed earthenware jar containing thirteen leather-bound papyrus codices, along with pages torn from another ancient book. A farmer's mother burned one of the books for cooking fuel, and part of another, but twelve books and the loose pages were saved, including the most complete version of the Gospel of Thomas. These were a part of what are commonly known as the Dead Sea scrolls.

These Gnostic Christian texts, written in Coptic but most likely translated from Greek, provide an important view of the diversity of beliefs that were current in early Christianity.

It remains unclear at what point in the hundred years after the death of Jesus his Jewish followers became known as Christians. The texts found at Naj Hammadi indicate that an ideological fight was occurring between right-brain and left-brain perceptions and sensibilities. Consistent with human history, the left-brained, more conservative or "orthodox" believers most commonly create the rhetoric that their right-brained opponents are heretics who have strayed from the "true" doctrines—in this case those of Jesus.

In any religious controversy, the chosen dogma doesn't necessarily reflect a victory of spiritual truth and a deeper experience of the divine over falsehood or mistaken judgment, but the power of those who make up the majority of a faith's believers. This is how average becomes normal.

What were the ideological differences that separated the Gnostic Christians from their more orthodox brethren? Each group saw Jesus and God in a different way, consistent with the familiar and opposing lines of left- and right-brain thinking.

True Self

In early Christianity, adherents who were left-brained in their thinking and sensibilities believed all of God's creatures to be unique and separate. Each person was a unique individual, unattached and unrelated to other persons or even to God, who was inaccessible and remained in some high, faraway place.

The more right-brained Gnostics believed that by returning to one's true self and the process of spiritual development, the seeker after sacred truth would discover the divine within the human. This belief that humankind was not only closely connected to God, but that God in fact dwelled within each person, was considered heretical by the followers of what was becoming early mainstream Christianity.

In their interpretations of the teachings of Jesus, Gnostic Christians perceived that Jesus had meant to reveal that standard conceptions of human life were illusions, that life itself was in a sense an illusion, and that the earthly work of each man and woman was to undertake a journey of enlightenment. These views of the lessons of Jesus were unacceptable to left-brain practitioners, who believed that Jesus's central message concerned the existence of personal human sin and the need for repentance.

The Gnostic Christian belief that was perhaps most disturbing to the orthodox was the view that Jesus had been a great sage who taught that all of humanity were the children of God, but Jesus had not been God on Earth.

The Gnostic Gospel of Thomas, which is said to contain direct quotations from Jesus, supports the Gnostic belief of an enlightened but still human messenger of the divine. In this gospel, which remained a part of the Apocrypha (early writings about Jesus that were not accepted into the canon of the New Testament), Jesus informs his listeners of his human identity and equality with humankind:

> *I am not your master. But you have drunk, you have become drunk from the bubbling stream which I have measured out . . . He who will drink from my mouth will become as I am: I myself shall become he, and the things that are hidden will be revealed to him.*

Dates

The origins and nature of the accepted Christian gospels are more complex and mysterious than many might realize. Archaeological and linguistic investigations suggest that in all likelihood the New Testament gospels were not written by their accredited authors. Many scholars have shown that single gospels contain various writing styles, indicating that they are a collection of the work of several different authors.

It would be valuable to know with certainty when each Gnostic and Orthodox gospel was written, especially when we view the evolution of Christianity as an organized, codified religion. After nearly three hundred years of Roman persecution, Christianity became the state religion of Rome around CE 312–313 under the Emperor Constantine. According to tradition, the general Constantine had been told in a vision that he would triumph "under the sign of Christ" in a bloody civil war battle with his opponent, Maxentius.

After Constantine's victory, the Roman army was baptized and Christianity became the state religion. The armed forces that had once persecuted the Christians now enforced the primacy of Christianity. It became illegal and often a capital offense to possess any Gnostic texts, and most of these writings were destroyed and disappeared from history, excepting a few remnants like the ones found at Naj Hammadi.

Carbon dating of this particular Gnostic Gospel of Thomas places its origin at CE 140, but that text was probably a copy or a copy of a copy of an original composed sometime earlier. Dating of ancient New Testament gospel texts suggests that they were written between CE 60 and 110. Christian writings that fit within the fifty-year time span in which the New Testament was probably composed mention the Gospel of Thomas as a heretical work, which means that it must have been in existence for at least thirty years before CE 140.[1]

Professor Helmut Koester of Harvard University has found that the collection of sayings in the Gospel of Thomas, although dated at CE 140, may have been written down before the gospels of the New Testament, "possibly as early as the second half of the first century," which would make them as early as or even earlier than the gospels of Mark, Matthew, Luke, and John.[2]

Gnostic/Orthodox

My response to the study of the history of early Christianity is that the Gnostic and New Testament gospels were each intended for a different audience of Christian believers or potential believers, one group right-brained and the other left-brained. These different writings describe the perspectives of two different sensibilities and their alternate paths toward religious understanding and fulfillment.

The Gnostic/Orthodox controversy is an interesting and mysterious real-life story that may enlighten us about the split in religion, politics, and our often opposing ways of looking at the world. With regard to the Gospel of Thomas, current historical evidence would tell us that it may have been the first Christian gospel and that its appearance triggered an ongoing battle for supremacy between the two sects, instigating waves of proselytizing and the dissemination of written advocacy (or propaganda) for one side or the other.

I find it strange that we use the phrase "the gospel truth" to underline the veracity of what we say. The word "gospel" means "good news," but the early Christians were engaged in heated disagreement in defining just what the good news was, where it came from, and the true nature of the person who had delivered it.

I believe it's fair to say that the gospels of the Gnostics and the Orthodox Christians were part of a debate to convince readers that one side of the argument was right and one was wrong, that the two views of Jesus were incompatible, and that the opposing interpretation had completely misunderstood the Christian message.

Scholars commonly agree that all of the gospels were written later than their authors claim, especially when one considers that in the early world of Christianity, priority of authorship was a strong argument for the truth of what was presented. Who wrote first surely must have known best, and there is little doubt that dates of composition were sometimes "backdated" to increase the appearance of authenticity and a firsthand awareness of what Jesus had really said—and most importantly who he really was: God himself or a human child of God.

Why So Many Perceptions?

It seems that in all things, but especially in religion, there are as many "truths" as there are human perspectives. It would be reassuring and convenient if there were only one spiritual truth that we could all agree on and believe in, but that is not how our world and its human societies of individuals with differing psyches are structured. Our personalities and our neurological makeup largely determine our perceptions of what it true and false, real and imaginary.

Although there is human free will, we are all somewhat "prisoners" of our own physiological systems and resulting perceptions. Our bodies filter and choose the stimuli allowed to enter our brains, where the stimuli are coordinated and processed in different ways according to the wiring of each person's unique brain. This simple truth of nature should constantly remind us to not consider our own ideas the supreme and only valid ones, or to try to convince others that our way of being is correct and all others are simply wrong. Everyone sees and experiences the world differently, especially people who are primarily right- or left-brained. This age-old battle points out one of the most important measures of our purpose.

We should also remember that what seem to be "our own" thoughts and beliefs have input from several sources. I believe the greatest filter we see through is the personality that is downloaded into our consciousness. All of reality must go through this interpreter first. Then we receive additional filters from those closest to us: our family, then friends, then associates, and finally society as a whole. Every experience, perspective, and belief will be transformed by all these filters that we collect and hold dear. They are who we are. Much like the picture I put forth of the Creator early on, we are the collection of experiences held in a unified field of conscious. This is why we often identify ourselves according to our beliefs—because that is how we see ourselves. I believe this is why so many people not only align themselves with a religion but say they are a Christian or Buddhist. If you do not follow the same beliefs and ways of thinking that others have engrained and are congruent with, you are shaking their very identity. This in turn can create internal conflict that often becomes external.

Religious truth, like human pain, remains an individual affair and cannot be weighed and compared to or found greater than the faiths of others. In seeking to verify spiritual truths, we cannot rely on numbers or majorities or how many people follow one faith or another.

We need constant reminding that the experience or search for sacred truth is an intimate, individual pursuit, and that criticizing others' beliefs or trying to foist our own beliefs on them is a serious breach of respect. Uninvited, aggressive, adamant proselytizing shows an ignorance of each person's divine nature and the sanctity of the personal struggle toward enlightenment.

In a world with greater acceptance and tolerance, each person might come to religion, rather than religion insistently coming to him or her. Perhaps someday we will all draw upon the wisdom of all the religions and philosophies of the world, finding the aspects that resonate with us and help us in our present struggles, replacing "I am a Jew or Christian or Muslim" identities and the inability to see beyond the walls of our theology, or to see that we all share similar theologies that are simply scripted in different languages with minimal variation in the heart of the message.

Gospel of Thomas

One of the best ways to understand the beliefs of the Gnostic Christians is to read the verses from the Gospel of Thomas. This is not so much a story about Jesus as a collection of what are presented as his direct statements. The following verse is a good example that underscores the emphasis on internal spiritual work:

> *If you bring forth what is within you, what you bring forth*
> *will save you. If you do not bring forth what is within you,*
> *what you do not bring forth will destroy you.*[3]

Thomas's gospel consistently encourages the reader to search for his or her authentic self, a process that will finally return the individual to a true personal identity, which is defined by the divine aspect that resides within every person. The gospel proclaims that the discovery of God within us

195

allows our thoughts and actions to become more godlike, more automatic, and less the playthings of internal conflict and doubt. To know and act from the divinity within reflects knowledge and experience of the "upper world" of Gnosticism.

In this verse there is also the implication that we have no "real" choice whether or not to embark on an interior voyage of spiritual exploration: to discover the God within brings salvation and to not discover it means a "spiritual death." I interpret the Gnostic's upper world as a reference to a realm of consciousness and energy that in its entirety can also be called Creation or God.

The First Three

In the first verse of the gospel, Thomas tells the reader:

> *These are the secret sayings which the living Jesus spoke and which Didymus Judas Thomas wrote down. And he said, "Whoever finds the interpretation of these sayings will not experience death."*

This statement can be understood to mean that those who truly comprehend the meaning of Jesus's words will meet the eternal self within, which is part of God and immortal.

In the second verse, Jesus says,

> *Let him who seeks continue seeking until he finds. When he finds he will become troubled. When he becomes troubled, he will be astonished, and he will rule over the all.*

This message gives us the road map to harmonizing our life. There will inevitably be seeking, troubles, and even struggling but the result will be something you could never have seen before. Perhaps it is a way that you will see and experience life. Once you get through this, it is all good. Life is easy and nothing rules you, not even your ego. You can become the orchestrator of your experience.

Thomas also may allude to the reduction of the filters of your personality and how this alters your reality. It is amazing to see life without any preconceptions from your personality, or your parental and societal teachings. As is stated, there will be troubles ahead but the rewards are magnificent. Take the road that may seem scary and troubled in the beginning and hang in there because it gets really good.

In the third verse, Jesus says:

> *If those who lead you say to you, "See the kingdom in the sky," then the birds of the air will precede you. If they say to you, "It is in the sea," then the fish will precede you. Rather, the kingdom is inside of you, and it is outside of you. When you come to know yourself, then you will become known, and you will realize that it is you who are the sons of the living father. But if you will not know yourself, you dwell in poverty and it is you who are that poverty.*

This statement credited to Jesus is filled with layers of information. He says that the Kingdom is not distant from you, not high above in the sky or deep in the sea, but within you and all around you. The Kingdom is a word that could have many meanings. It appears to remind us that everything is God or Creation. We don't need to look at places we can't see; the Kingdom is all around us.

Next you wrestle with what it is to *know* yourself. This to me is our greatest call, to explore ourselves and find out what we really are. It is to feel, act, and expand our potentials as our radically unique self. At the end of the journey, to know yourself becomes having unconditional love for yourself. The belief in not being good enough would be absent. Your strength comes from the "revelation" of yourself, a deep acceptance of who you are with all of your foibles. What humanity may see as shortcomings are just who you are; there is no need to ever prove or sell yourself to others.

Thomas's recollection of Jesus also says there is another gift in knowing oneself. I believe this means you understand you are a creation of Creation. You will finally know on some deep level that you are an integral part of Creation and its growth. The illusions and tricks of the five senses and separateness are lost forever. Then who you become is very different. Without this you will not only feel poverty, but you will *be* poverty. "Poverty" here is the opposite of richness but not of money: it means a bankrupt life where you cannot see the beauty in every day, every relationship, and every moment. Poverty is the feeling of emptiness that comes from being disconnected, living a life without joy, happiness, or deep love. It is the absence of living in awe, filled with grace. It is indeed a journey to get to this place but it is the highest reward humanity can attain.

Spirit Time

In verse 13 Thomas writes Jesus's words:

> *Jesus said to his disciples, "Compare me to someone and tell me whom I am like." Simon Peter said to him, "You are like a righteous Angel." Matthew said to him, "You are like a wise philosopher." Thomas said to him, "Master, my mouth is wholly incapable of saying whom you are like."*
>
> *Jesus said, "I am not your master. Because you have drunk, you have become intoxicated with the bubbling spring which I have measured out." And he took him and withdrew and told him three things.*
>
> *When Thomas returned to his companions they asked him, "What did Jesus say to you?" Thomas said to them, "If I tell you one of the things which he told me, you will pick up stones and throw them at me, a fire will come out of the stones and burn you up."*

This intriguing verse uses the image of fire, a common human symbol for a state of internal chaos and severe stress. My reading is that Jesus knows that a specific lesson is only understandable and timely for a pupil who has reached a necessary stage of internal development and evolution. Perhaps more important, each personality will wrestle with a certain set of issues and see life accordingly. The wise teacher knows the language of the student's personality and what they can grasp. Imagine the different lessons that are necessary for a right-brained person versus a left-brained person. Accepting the ability of different people to have different perspectives or truths and teaching accordingly is great wisdom.

In this verse, Thomas's isolation from the other followers of Jesus, after Thomas has received a private, individual lesson, seems to indicate the level of his spiritual growth, or perhaps a lesson meant for his journey. In either case this verse tells us that the other disciples would be angry about the information. It is hard to say whether they would have been jealous or that the information would be contradictory to their belief systems. This is a practical fact of spiritual education: the attainment of increased spiritual insight naturally separates the prospective adept from those who haven't yet done the internal work that will allow them to comprehend or benefit from a deeper level of spiritual knowledge. I think this verse alludes to an important and useful paradox to remember: the journey toward unity may at first require a sense of separation from others because of a difference in understanding. In fact, one may become an object of confusion to one's family or friends, of envy, or anger and aggression. People sometimes throw rocks, especially people who don't yet understand.

In verse 113 Jesus speaks of the Kingdom:

> *His disciples said to him, "When will the New World come?"*
> *He said to them, "When you look forward to see it has already*
> *come, but you do not recognize it." His disciples said to him,*
> *"When will the kingdom come?" Jesus said, "It will not come*
> *by waiting for it. It will not be a matter of saying, 'Here it*
> *is,' or 'There it is.' Rather, the kingdom of the father is spread*
> *out upon the earth, and men do not see it."*

Once again, Jesus seems to be referring to perceptions that are the fruit of inner work and the discovery of the divine, which transforms the world and its meaning and appearance. I think the lesson here may be that the New World we wait for someone to bring to us will never happen. The New World will be here the moment we are capable of seeing it. It is humanity's work to create this New World, but we must dramatically change to allow it to happen. This verse reminds me a little bit of *The*

Wizard of Oz. After the journey and quest that Dorothy and her friends undertake through great peril, troubles, and transformation, they learn that what they were seeking was already within them. The journey is important, for without it they could not see the truth or *know* who they really are. The vast majority of humanity goes through the superficial steps most of their lives. Time and time again these verses ask us to do the deep work, welcome the struggle, and remove the illusions so we can live in the "New World."

In verse 6, Jesus's disciples ask about correct ascetic practices:

> *His disciples questioned him and said to him, "Do you want us to fast? How shall we pray? Shall we give alms? What diet shall we observe?" Jesus said, "Do not tell lies, and do not do what you hate."*

Here the students are asking for the steps they must take in order to learn his teachings and a path to piety. As with all mystical texts, there can be many interpretations. From Jesus's response, it appears that his guidance is to help them see that his teachings are not intended to be external, or ways to act that may not be in their nature or are against their traditions. This would be all too superficial and ultimately unimportant for the journey. May I take us back to the first verse that I cited where he calls to his disciples to seek what is within? It is this inward process of awareness, inside and unfolding, that is the path and a connection to one's authentic self.

Modern Christianity

Differences

My formal experience of the teachings of Christianity has been somewhat "one-sided"; the priests and ministers with whom I have studied have been liberal or progressive in their religious, social, and political views and non-doctrinaire in their interpretation of the Bible, which they view as a metaphorical rather than literal word-for-word guide to right action and enlightenment.

These primarily right-brained men and women who continue the teachings of Christianity have expressed their concern and displeasure with the stated ideas and beliefs of many fundamentalists within their faith. They often find the pronouncements of conservative, traditionalist representatives of Christianity strident and narrow, lacking in good judgment and proper measure and reflecting an emphasis on the patriarchal and authoritarian, on sin and punishment rather than on mutual love and individual spiritual evolution.

My Christian friends are disturbed by what they perceive as a consistent tone of anger, condemnation, and superior all-knowingness in fundamentalist sermons, which frequently are delivered before thousands of parishioners in extravagant "megachurches" and widely carried on television. A number of the messengers of a literal and absolutist reading of the Bible have become prominent and influential (and wealthy) public figures. As a group, they are charismatic and photogenic and have been tireless in their efforts to impose their religious views on the widest possible audience and on the American political process itself, which they believe to be generally wicked and atheistic, in need of transformation along lines contrary to the separation of church and state guaranteed in the US Constitution's Bill of Rights.

Many fundamentalists consider America an inherently Christian nation that should officially become so, through laws that will enforce their understanding of Jesus's stern lessons to humanity.

The representatives of Christianity whom I know believe that the majority of Christians are more moderate in nature, and that many "fire and brimstone" evangelicals and other Christian extremists are mistaken in assuming that most Christians share their strict and well-defined viewpoints on religion and the ultimate nature of reality.

Once more, I interpret the opposed positions within modern Christianity as an opposition of left- and right-brain perceptions and processing, an expression of neurological and personality differences as much as a spiritual or theological disagreement. I suppose one's sense of the Christian message depends on an interior, personal emphasis: does an individual experience the words and ministry of Jesus as primarily a call to love and internal spirituality, or a warning concerning sin and punishment and the necessity of combating evil in the outward world?

Neighbors

My friends in the Christian ministry have often suggested specific texts of the New Testament for my study and better understanding of Christianity, especially those chapters in Mark, Luke, John, Romans, Galatians, and Corinthians that describe the gift of love and encourage the discovery of a higher, unselfish love through prayer, meditation, good works, and mutual care and understanding.

When you hear the word "Christianity," how can you not remember the words "Love thy neighbor"? The New Testament strongly emphasizes this message of love, amplifying many passages in the Elder Testament.

The present central challenge for humanity is to work in cooperation with one another, to shed the immediate wants and needs of the personal ego and find an identity with and love of other, through individuals' shared divinity with all of humanity. In the New Testament, this important love for others is often expressed as encouragement to help the poor and those less fortunate in other ways. Generous actions on behalf of others not only aid those in desperate need and create equality, but also result in our own spiritual evolution.

Empathy for others and selflessly acting on that empathy help us gain release from our own egos, which are greedy and self-centered and prone to finding fault with those who require our help: we are drawn to providing ourselves with a "moral alibi," a justified excuse for not sharing our "treasures," whatever they may be.

Temptation

Expressing love and generosity toward others can be seen as overcoming the temptation toward selfishness and the denial of the divine within ourselves and all others. This victory over temptation, the resisting of evil, sin, and Satan, is a constant theme of the New Testament.

In the gospel of Matthew 10:26, we are taught that conquering our own fear helps us defeat the temptations that all of us face in our earthly lives. I interpret Matthew's lesson to mean that the commission of evil acts is usually the result of our own fear that we are inadequate and lacking in personal worth, a forgetting of our divine identity.

To commit and justify an evil act reflects a loss of connection with both humanity and Creation: an awful isolation in which your own immediate survival and security become all important and your intimate spiritual relationship to God and the human community has been lost.

Those who are fearful and insecure within themselves are most tempted to act from the "dark side," from the ego rather than from the divine self.

Heaven Everywhere

The realization of the divine within not only helps us avoid temptation, but also further develops the heaven inside all of us. It advances our communal work of spiritual evolution and the creation of the right and favorable conditions for establishing a heavenly life on Earth, before physical death.

Again, the inescapable, core Christian message is that together we will find inner and outer peace through love of ourselves and others, which requires that we love others as we love ourselves. The final message credited to Jesus is that to discover and act from this love, we each need a direct inner access to God and its love, the universal love that created our world and permeates, and is, all of Creation.

This access to God is finally each individual's sometimes lonely and often arduous journey. Each of us must walk the road to God—no one else can walk it for us. The ultimate meeting between human and God is the most profound, intimate, and private encounter any of us will ever have, although the result of that meeting is an eternal unity with God, all created beings, and the universe, an experience of complete meaning and glorious belonging.

The future spiritual transformation of the human race is a grand and beautiful goal whose reality may be beyond all of our greatest hopes and possible imaginings. However, in our inner and outer search for heaven, we must constantly remember that those who are well studied in religion and faith and who offer themselves as intermediaries between ourselves and the

Creator may be well- or ill-informed, well- or ill-intentioned. Direct access to God was indeed a core message attributed to Jesus.

The effort to acquire and profess spiritual knowledge has many hazards, and those who would lead others on the spiritual path are never completely immune from the temptation to gain power and authority over others.

At best, if a religious guide is truthful and benign and spiritually evolved, he or she can only speak from a personal experience of the Creator, which if genuine and truly deep cannot be fully expressed through human words and actions but remains a divine mystery that each person must individually experience.

Note: I welcome alternative interpretations to the text quoted in this chapter.

At this point in our discussion of many of the world's religions, I ask you whether any of the teachings you have heard resonate with you. My hope in this section is that you may be awakened and activated through the lessons of life that come from thousands of years of human/divine searching.

We now leave religion for a while and seek the view found in two Eastern philosophies. We will start with Taoism.

17

TAOISM

The "Way"

The roots of Taoism go back at least three thousand or even five thousand years, which makes it a contemporary of Judaism farther to the west. The initial philosophers of this enlightened consciousness often lived alone in the mountains and spent intimate time in nature. The exact origins of Taoism are as difficult to pinpoint as any other tradition that started so long ago, and its teachings were often oral. As time went by, writings and canonized Taoist texts emerged, encouraging a journey of self-discovery and transformation along the "Tao," or the "Way," which runs throughout Creation and is responsible for bringing forth all beings and things. The Tao is the flow of the universe, from the infinitely small subatomic world to the outer reaches of our galaxy. It is what is within you and all that exists around you. The Tao operates all actions and being. The person who seriously follows this path increasingly embodies enlightenment and acts naturally and automatically, without forethought, from the divine center discovered and cultivated within the self.

An Introduction to Taoism

Along with many other Westerners, I was introduced to Taoism through the vehicle of television. One of my favorite television series was *Kung Fu*, a show that followed the adventures of the Shaolin monk Kwai Chang Caine as he traveled throughout the American Old West armed with only his spiritual training and marital arts skills. Obviously, the show offered Eastern philosophy in a way that catered to the American television viewing public, but it was a start for me.

Interestingly, the star of the series was David Carradine, a decidedly non-Asian actor. Bruce Lee was considered for the role (and some assert that he even came up with the concept for the show) but the studio did not believe America was ready for an Asian actor to be the star. Luckily, humanity is making progress in this regard as Bruce Lee would no doubt be cast in that role today.

Qigong Master

After this early fascination with Taoism, I became more intimately involved through my practice of the healing art of qigong. Ken Cohen, a Taoist master and qigong teacher, was giving a lecture at a conference I was attending. I went to his lecture and became a devoted student of qigong and of Ken Cohen.

During that first encounter, Cohen demonstrated how consciousness could be used to lock the movement of his elbow. He asked for a volunteer to forcefully bend his elbow while he resisted the action using only his consciousness, without any muscle contraction employed. I jumped in as the volunteer because I had to validate his credibility. My right hand grabbed his fist in order to bend his elbow as my left hand wrapped around his triceps to palpate for muscle contraction.

In order to resist the flexion of his elbow, he would have to recruit or flex his triceps muscle. With great discipline, Ken Cohen focused his mind and directed his consciousness toward his arm. He instructed me to begin bending his elbow.

I forcefully thrust his fist toward his shoulder. With my palpating hand, I didn't feel a single fiber of his triceps contract to restrict that movement. I couldn't bend his elbow no matter how hard I tried. He proved his authenticity and expertise to me right then and there.

I took many classes from him and read books he recommended on Taoism. I also studied with a Shaolin priest and a practitioner trained in medical qigong. Along the way I learned there are many unique strands of Taoism.

Simplicity in Nature

Taoism in infused with the concepts of simplicity, spontaneity, and nature. Its "three treasures" include compassion, moderation, and humility.

The early Taoist lived an almost monastic existence, gleaning all life's lessons from the natural world. By watching and appreciating the beauty found in animals and plants, and by studying natural movements and flow, the Taoist connects to the Tao in nature, in humanity, and themselves. It is very difficult to state exactly what the Tao is; it has greater depth than its simple common translation, the Way, a kind of chameleon term with many different meanings. It is our journey within, a path to enlightenment, peace, nature, and our own true nature. Taoists look to nature for most of the lessons they may need in life. A guiding principle is that it is very important to work with nature and not against it. Many of the exercises, movements, healing arts, and defenses of Taoism mimic the ways of nature and its animals.

Another fundamental teaching of Taoism is to never follow another's path because you will get stuck in their ruts. Taoism stresses the importance of the individual's path and the unique "way" they must experience. My qigong teachers have exemplified this by teaching traditional forms and movements and then opening the doorway to self-expression. Taoism stresses the importance of following a unique path while still working cooperatively together with others, much like symbiotic relationships in nature. This is a teaching that says to think, seek, and feel for yourself instead of merely following. Utilizing your intuition and developing the ability to sense chi—life force energy—are essential to finding your own path as well as to practicing Taoist healing arts. It is not surprising that Chinese communist leaders have attempted to snuff out Taoist practices; this way of being naturally disrupts conformity and encourages individualization.

Sacred Writings

There are many sacred texts in Taoism, the most famous being the *Tao Te Ching* and the *Zhuangzi*.

The *Tao Te Ching* is credited to the author Lao-tse. Like other sacred texts such as the gospels, there is some controversy as to exact authorship. Some historians believe the name itself indicates more than one author; the character depicting the name indicates this is a possibility. The true origins of the work may be lost in antiquity, but stories about this text and its author are very interesting. Some of my teachers have told me that the word "Tao" is used many times in the book but each time carries a slightly different meaning and interpretation. It is also said that Lao-tse never wanted to write the book at all because it would attempt to put into words something that can never be truly described: the Tao is more about the doing of it than reading about it. Capturing it in writing, Lao-tse thought, would limit the very thing he was trying to expand and help people see. This story reveals a man in great conflict, wishing to write about the most extraordinary and rewarding journey he could imagine while at the same time feeling he might harm the very thing he loved.

The *Tao Te Ching* is highly recommended reading, but expect to spend some time with both the text and commentary on the text. The writings are filled with paradoxes that invite the reader to question reality. Commentary is certainly helpful not only for spiritual interpretation of these paradoxes, but for historical and societal context. Fundamentally, these writings help us see the beauty in nature and life that we often take for granted. It is when we can slow down and appreciate the path of nature that we feel enriched and satisfied.

Flowing Like a River

The method of following the Tao is called *Wu Wei,* or natural nonintervention. It is sometimes translated as non-action, but that wrongly implies that nothing is getting done. Wu Wei means living life by going along with the true nature of the world, letting things take their natural course.

To me, Wu Wei means living my life in ways that are effortless. For example, if I get up in the morning and have to force myself to go to a job I don't like in order to make money, I am not practicing Wu Wei. On the other hand, getting up to go to a job that is in my nature and comes easily to me is following Wu Wei. *Wei Wu Wei* is action without action.

To understand Taoist philosophy is to learn to speak in metaphor and understand how the paradoxical writings constantly question your own reality. It is this tearing apart of the established matrix or fabric of your thoughts that gives you the freedom to discover your "Way."

The sweetness of this practice comes in finding effortless action in order to live in balance and harmony. Once again we hear the call to return to one's nature and one's primordial, soul, or radically unique self. It is the ever-important journey of removing all of your nonfunctional issues such as selfishness, greed, and lack of empathy, all of which come from the fear of not being good enough. Once you remove these, you will find yourself. That is your nature and what is often referred to as naturalness. Thus Taoists live their lives in the same way a river flows: finding its natural course.

The concept of *Te* is important within Taoism. Te is often translated as virtue or power but can be better understood as an awareness of the Tao together with the ability and intention to follow the Tao and cultivate all of the Taoist tenets that create a harmonized and synchronistic flow in your life.

Another concept of Taoism, as well as Buddhism, is the dance between the masculine and feminine, known as yin and yang. We have all seen the symbol of two teardrops, one black and one white, wrapped around each other creating a circle. There are many teachings in Taoism where the masculine and feminine interface, life lessons where masculine concepts and energy meet feminine concepts and energy and the attainment of balance begins. Eastern philosophy often sees the masculine and feminine nature in all things, ranging from personalities to medicines and healing practices. The masculine and feminine natures that exist in men and women, independent of their gender, create fertile ground for challenges to be recognized and balanced. If you think masculine energy is by definition stronger than feminine, think again. Both utilize their abilities and assets to spur demonstrable positive change in humanity. Taoist teachings of yin and yang are insightful and transformative.

For me personally, the Taoist practice of qigong is a part of my life. Simply stated, this is a practice that utilizes the self-intentionalized energy or life force known as qi, chi, prana, or dark energy (the unseen living energy that creates the universe) to heal yourself and others. This practice is contemplative and awakens your ability to access the true thoughts and motivations in the subconscious mind. This is a missing key for most of us who wish to get to the bottom of what creates our stress and to understand why we think the way we do. Meditation can include setting the intention of accessing the energetic world of chi, dark energy, and Universal Consciousness (all names for the same thing), opening up the ability to gain insights beyond the knowing of your conscious mind. It is a place where you can help others and gain wisdom about your life. When you return time and time again to this place of receiving, or action without action, the awareness and capacity to know your own underlying motivations and stay on a path that is your own, not your parents' or society's, become easy. In fact, the awareness that comes from the Tao makes it hard to take any other pathway but your own. It becomes self-propelling: Wei Wu Wei.

18

BUDDHISM

Siddhartha Gautama is said to have been born in 563 BCE, which places the rise of Buddhism before Christianity and after Taoism. Siddhartha, who many of us know as the Buddha, spent a lifetime struggling with the concept of suffering. As a young, sheltered prince he had no experience of suffering, but as he grew to adulthood he learned much about it. Siddhartha was not a god or a son of God, but a man who through his struggles found great wisdom that forms the basis of this philosophy. The main teachings of Buddhism do not contemplate God, superpowers, or miracles, which to my thinking means it is not a religion. Its philosophy was created by humans for humanity.

Enlightenment

The Buddhist pathway to enlightenment came from struggle. Buddha faced suffering and disappointments his whole life yet transformed his difficulties into a path of light.

Siddhartha Gautama was born in India near the Nepalese border, a land steeped in the ancient Vedic tradition. As a young, privileged child of royalty living within palace walls, he never wanted or needed anything. When he ventured beyond those walls, though, he witnessed sickness, suffering, and death. His sense of reality abruptly shifted as he empathized with the downtrodden and came to see his own suffering. So began Siddhartha's search for a way to endure struggle and suffering while still living a life of wholeness and well-being. As Siddhartha's profound experiences, wisdom, and teachings were revealed, he grew into the title he acquired: "Buddha, the enlightened one."

Struggle and Nirvana

Buddhism is a practice of dealing with life's struggles as you travel the road to the enlightenment that awakens you to *Nirvana,* a place that can best be described as Heaven on Earth, living an existence of inner peace and infinite possibilities. Some of these possibilities might include people uniting to work together toward a common goal and, most importantly, toward an end to suffering and an understanding of who the self really is.

In order for us to create Nirvana, we must engage in the path of enlightenment. There is a long story of the many steps Siddhartha walked to reach the moment of his enlightenment. I'll offer a condensed version of the parable.

When the Buddha was deep in meditation looking for answers, his greatest struggle was with the demon Mara, who tempted him with all the great desires. There are several versions of this story, some fairly straightforward, some elaborate, some phantasmagorical. Here is a plain version:

> As Siddhartha Gautama sat in meditation, Mara brought his most beautiful daughters to seduce him. Siddhartha, however, remained in meditation.
>
> Then Mara sent vast armies of monsters to attack him. Yet Siddhartha sat still and untouched.
>
> Mara claimed that the seat of enlightenment rightfully belonged to him and not to the mortal Siddhartha. When Mara's monstrous soldiers cried out together, "I am his witness!" Mara challenged Siddhartha: "Who will speak for *you?*"
>
> Then Siddhartha reached out his right hand to touch the earth, and the earth itself spoke: "I bear you witness!" Mara disappeared. And as the morning star rose in the

sky, Siddhartha Gautama realized enlightenment and became the Buddha.

This is a great teaching of how we must not be distracted from the path of internal discovery.

Buddhism separates desire that creates harm from desire that creates a good life. One must examine the motivations underlying a desire in order to determine if that desire will be harmful or employed for good. This deep examination is done through the inward journey of meditation.

Part of this journey includes the Four Noble Truths.

Here is the simple version:

1. Suffering exists
2. Suffering arises from attachment to desires
3. Suffering ceases when attachment to desire ceases
4. Freedom from suffering is possible through practicing the Eightfold Path.

We'll now look a little deeper at the first truth, knowing that we could make an entire life's work out of these Four Truths. We will then return to the short version of Buddha's story.

1: Suffering Exists

The First Noble Truth is often translated as "Life is suffering." The Pali word *dukkha* also refers to anything that is temporary, conditional, or compounded of other things. Even something precious and enjoyable is dukkha because it will end. Related to the nature of life is the nature of self. Are we not also temporary, conditional, and compounded of many parts? We can understand that life is impermanent, but are we also impermanent? The Buddha taught that before we can understand life and death we must understand the self.

2. The Cause of Suffering Is Desire

The Second Noble Truth teaches that the cause of suffering is craving or thirst (*tanha*). We continually search for something outside ourselves to make us happy. But no matter how successful we are, we never remain satisfied.

The Buddha taught that this thirst grows from ignorance of the self. We go through life grabbing one thing after another to get a sense of security about ourselves. We attach not only to physical things, but also to ideas and opinions about ourselves and the world around us. Then we grow frustrated when the world doesn't behave the way we think it should and our lives don't conform to our expectations.

3. Suffering Can Be Ended

This is truly the answer we all seek—how to end suffering. I am sure there are many different answers to this for every individual at different times in their lives. I would ask you to push yourself to the next level of how you will put an end to suffering. For me, the answer has been strengthened by the Buddhist reality that suffering is inevitable. This may sound ironic, but it has led me to realize this: suffering may come but it is not here today. Most importantly, I will deal with it when it comes. I do not have to worry whether it will come because I know it will. It is a free will realm, so there are choices.

If you realize that *all* of your beliefs and interpretations are of your own creation, you can choose whether to keep them or to evolve them into a way that may serve you better. Realizing this and choosing how you will experience suffering are key. I enjoy playing with illusion and reality and my story that I am always telling myself, often in my subconscious mind. My story becomes my reality. When I work with the chronically depressed, I hear their reality story, which they can't wait to tell me and anyone else who will hear them. They repeat the story over and over again, one that is always filled with suffering caused by external sources. They have not done the internal work as yet. Commonly, they receive something beneficial from the story and their beliefs about life that deepens their suffering. In fact, suffering is often part of their personal identity and their beliefs about how the world works.

Yet if you take the time to hear and sink into Siddhartha's story, I believe you will see that *acceptance* was a part of how he diminished suffering in his life. The concept of acceptance is not limited to accepting how people are and how the world is when it does not go your way. It is the acceptance of self and all aspects of life without feeling anger, injustice, malice, judgment, and so on. The mantra is "It is what it is!" The question is, How do you thrive in life *as it is?*

4. The Way to End Suffering Is the Noble Eightfold Path

The Buddha taught that through diligent practice, we can put an end to craving. Ending the hamster-wheel chase after satisfaction is enlightenment (*bodhi*, "awakened"). The enlightened being exists in a state called *Nirvana*.

Following the Noble Eightfold Path means:

1. Right understanding
2. Right thoughts
3. Right speech
4. Right actions
5. Right livelihood
6. Right effort
7. Right mindfulness
8. Right meditation

Balance

Buddha awakened peacefully from his meditative quest. He assured his students that enlightenment was ever present for them if only they could awaken from the illusion of their perceived reality, which kept them from deep wisdom and knowing. In a sense this meant finding themselves or the process of "returning." The gateway to returning included being mindful of all thoughts and actions.

Another part of the Buddhist story is that Buddha failed, just like any other human does. His fallibility and need for return and his repeated attempts to transform himself are delightful reassurance that all of us can move toward enlightenment. If you take the time to read the expanded version of the Buddha's story you will see that time and time again he does not get it right. This is a part of the story that brings comfort to all of us. If you are looking for a magic wand where "poof!" you are enlightened, this story tells you that's not the way it works. The most important part of the story is that he continues to work toward enlightenment, to completely deconstruct the reality of the conscious mind and remove illusions so he gains the freedom to see the world differently. Buddha shows us that the slate must be cleared away step by step so a true reality and belief systems can take the place of those that lead to suffering.

Growth Through Struggle

The Buddha welcomed free will, dissent, and equality. If one of his disciples disagreed with him, he welcomed the discussion and the growth that would follow. Buddha knew that wrestling is an integral part of the journey to enlightenment. Enlightenment is reached through a lifetime of steps: up, down, and up again. The deeper transformative lessons cannot be learned by oral transference; you have to be in the trenches to really get the lesson.

When I was a child I learned that stealing was bad when I saw that others felt bad that I had taken something from them. I had to cross over that line and make the mistake to know what was bad and what was good. Another example of wrestling that is not moralistic can be found whenever we examine our belief systems. Let's take a big one like the existence of a Creator or Heaven. I have contemplated and wrestled with this question for a very large part of my life. Then there's wrestling with accepting others, how they are, and what they believe versus your beliefs of how the world should be, wrestling with how other people should act and the negativity that courses through your veins and the stress it creates. We find suffering and the wish to escape in many of the things we wrestle with.

Another of the qualities Buddha possessed was being gender and status blind when he welcomed students into his realm. It didn't matter if the student was male or female, rich or poor. This was especially remarkable considering the pressures of the Indian caste system.

This environment of openness and understanding was fertile ground for Buddha's teaching. He taught that instead of running away from negative emotions, one must engage and investigate them because not until we understand where these emotions come from can they be resolved. This is the constant mindfulness of Buddhist practice that helps resolve suffering and disappointment. The Eightfold Path is always available if you get lost.

Three Poisons

The Three Poisons are usually listed as greed, hate, and delusion. My Buddhist teacher interpreted them and taught them to me as grasping, aversion, and ignorance.

Grasping

This is the ego chasing after what we desire. But what we desire most often covers up the fears and insecurities that the ego runs from. For most of us, this incorporates the majority of our daily actions. We may be best served by adopting a practice of not wanting. This may help us separate grasping from wanting to experience a life of unbridled joy, without a secondary payoff for the ego.

Aversion

This means pushing things away. The more we push things away, the more entangled with these things we become. When aversion is based on anger toward others, aversion stimulates the laws of attraction. The more we hate someone, the more we see that behavior in people around us.

This can take many forms. We may see someone who looks like the person we wish to avoid. We may begin looking in every crowd to see if that person might be there. Clearly, we are more connected to them now than ever before. Aversion is the mechanism by which we create shadows within ourselves: the things or thoughts we dislike about ourselves or the qualities and actions of others that hurt us. They often don't fit in with our morals or belief systems, and we avoid or bury them deep inside. But it is there that they fester, waiting to erupt, often manifesting as extreme behaviors. It is for these reasons that the path to harmonization does not include aversion. We must listen to and work through the things we wish to hide from.

Ignorance

This could be described as forgetting that we are spiritual beings in a physical form, having a spiritual experience. Nothing in life makes any sense unless we see that there is a bigger whole that we are part of. The only thing that gives us persistent happiness is the de-junking of our emotional baggage. This is the harmonizing of our life and this is what we do. Chaos makes us angry, stressful, and fearful. Internal chaos is reflected in negative emotional dynamics and takes us away from our godlike side. We have the capacity to scoop the chaos out of creation and harmonize it. When we harmonize these feelings, we also harmonize our personal environment. Unfortunately, we often lose sight of the fact that we are an integral part of creation. This is ignorance.

So Far Apart, yet So Alike

Absent the concept of God, there are many similarities between Judaism and Buddhism along the road to finding inner peace.

Studies show that 30 percent of American Buddhists were Jews by heritage.[1] This resonance between traditions is likely because the struggles and belief systems are similar. Both traditions acknowledge a brokenness in our world, and it is through suffering and the life journey of dealing with such suffering that we learn how to heal. Jews are very comfortable with Buddhist practice and teachings because Buddhism lacks the judgment, blame, and hate that emanate from some Muslim and Christian teachings toward Jews. Even though the history of the time is in direct conflict with the Christian biblical account when it comes to the death of Jesus Christ, the longstanding erroneous teaching that Jews are responsible for Jesus's death is difficult to overcome. Over the centuries, that teaching has become the source of anti-Semitism, leading to hatred and slaughter of Jews. In 1965, Pope Paul VI took a great step in making the declaration known as *Nostra Aetate* to heal the deep hurt of blaming the Jews for killing Jesus, who was one of their own. Hinduism and Buddhism were also mentioned in this declaration of the unity of all God's people.[2]

More recently, an Episcopal priest, Reverend Susan Auchincloss, launched a campaign called "Faith Not Fault: Affirming Christianity without Faulting Judaism." Rev. Auchincloss is dedicating herself to education and working to encourage Christian churches to stop reading texts that were prejudicial to Jews and Judaism in Sunday worship services. As we have discussed, when others do not follow our beliefs, internal chaos can result, leading to a new story to justify our beliefs and needs. The undoing of this self-serving agenda points to our greater humanity—our ability to overcome this chaos and replace it with acceptance.[3]

This was groundbreaking work in 1965 and it continues to be brave work today. But it is absolutely essential to bring about healing to people of faith and to the whole human community.

19

ISLAM

The Starting Point

Islam begins with Muhammad, who lived on the Arabian Peninsula, known today as Saudi Arabia, and introduced the initial teachings of the religion around 610 CE. Islam incorporates many of the practices of both Judaism and Christianity, believing in the information given by the principle people in the Judeo-Christian lineage but seeing them as prophets. Muhammad himself is seen as the last of the prophets who will be given to humanity, and a continuous thread is found between Judaism, Christianity, and Islam.

Muhammad claimed to be a direct descendant of Ishmael, the first son of Abraham. To recall the story, Abraham was unable to have children with his wife, Sarah, and in the custom of the day, she suggested that Abraham create a child with Hagar, her maid or servant. The translation for the name Hagar is "the stranger." She bore a child named Ishmael, but was not treated kindly by Sarah and was sent away. Later she was told by God that she must return because she would give rise to a great nation.

Then by the graces of God Sarah was made fertile, and she and Abraham gave birth to their son Isaac. The children of Isaac are the Jews and their story is found in the Jewish Bible. After Isaac was born, Abraham sent Hagar and Ishmael away. When Abraham died, Ishmael returned to bury his father with Isaac. The boys reconciled with one another but neither fully reconciled with their father: one child had been prepared for sacrifice and the other had been cast away twice.

With Muhammad laying claim to the lineage of Ishmael, you can understand why there have been many times in history when Muslims and Jews got along quite well, as brothers. Both can even sit at the same table because they both follow the same kosher (or halal) guidelines for the foods they eat.

The current division between Muslim and Jew is much harder to understand, and there are divisions within Islam as well. The majority of Muslims are of the Sunni branch. My own introduction to Islam was in Iran, where the Shia denomination is practiced. The other main expansion of Islam is found in Sufism, and there are also some other smaller denominations that I will not delve into here.

Humanity's Purpose

Humanity's purpose, according to Islam, is to worship and connect to God. Everything we do is in service of this. A spokesperson for my local Islamic community once told me that God's greatest delight is when humanity asks for forgiveness and He gets the chance to grant it.

When a person acknowledges their shortcomings and sincerely dedicates themselves to changing their actions, God will surely grant mercy and forgiveness. Then follows repentance, which is done not just for the sake of receiving that compassionate forgiveness but with the intention of not repeating the wrongdoing again.

In Islam, it is commonly believed that a good deed done with intention and deep commitment erases a bad deed. And when the ultimate day of judgment arrives, the net effect will be weighted in favor of good versus bad. Islam teaches that God enjoys granting forgiveness, especially to those whose hearts are so clear that they can see the light of God. Asking God's forgiveness is also a sacred undertaking because it is one way for humanity to draw nearer to God.

What the Heart Knows

The *Hadith* are teachings of the prophet Muhammad, passed on through the oral tradition and along with the holy text the Koran. These constitute the major source of Islamic religious guidance.

Muhammad taught that human righteousness or corruption starts with the heart. If the heart is righteous, the person becomes righteous, and if the heart is corrupted, the person becomes corrupted.

In another Hadith, the prophet taught that the reason for the goodness or evil of the heart lies in how we handle sin. If the heart accepts sins and embraces them, a dark spot is left behind in the heart. If the heart rejects those sins, a bright spot is left behind. The prophet said:

> Trials are presented to the hearts like a mat, one stick at a time. If any heart accepts it, a dark spot is left in it. If any heart rejects it, a bright spot is left in it. Consequently, the hearts become two types: Bright heart that gets no harm from any sin as long as the skies and the earth exist, and a dark heart that does not know any good deed and does not reject any evil unless it is from its whims and desires.[1]

The more darkness covers our heart the more difficult it is for us to see or receive the light and wisdom that God offers. God realizes that humans are imperfect and that making mistakes is part of the learning process. It is important, however, to be mindful of those mistakes so you do not make them over and over again.

Form and Meaning

Like Hebrew, the Arabic language contains words derived from a three-letter base root. Many words share the same root but have different meanings. Yet they are still connected in a fundamental way.

For example, the words Islam, Muslim (one who follows the religion of Islam), salaam (peace), tasleem (submission), and salamah (well-being and wholeness) all come from the same three-letter root, Sa-Li-Ma. The triliteral root of Islam represents wholeness, safety, and peace.

Heavenly Battle

The pathway to being a good and holy person is the central practice of this faith, informed by the Five Pillars, which I'll present shortly, and other spiritual practices.

Three of God's creations were the angels, human beings, and Satan, who came from the category of the Jin (smokeless fire). Human beings have within their ranks messengers, prophets (such as Muhammad), and the rest of humanity. After God blew spirit into all of His creation, He asked that it be respected, but Satan did not align with this hierarchy. Instead, Satan arrogantly explained to God that he was made of fire and that man was made of clay: why should Satan bow down the same as a human being? Consequently, Satan was expelled from God's mercy and thus promised to devote all of his energy to derailing the descendants of Adam and Eve from their eternal quest to worship God and follow God's ways. The prophet Muhammad taught the way and the laws to assist human beings in clearly differentiating the path to God from the one to Satan.

The Five Pillars

The Five Pillars of Islam are:

- Reciting the Koran and testifying that there are no other deities other than God alone and that Muhammad is the messenger of God
- Praying five times a day in order to create a personal relationship with God and draw near to God
- Charitable giving intended to help the poor and ensure that there is not great inequality between the rich and the poor
- The Hajj or pilgrimage to Mecca, the place where God was revealed to Muhammad
- Fasting from dawn to dusk during the month of Ramadan. For thirty days, the spiritual journey is elevated above physical desires and needs.

The greatest spiritual quest is to submit to God by being of service to God. This satisfies humanity's desire to draw close to God.

Spiritual Action Through Tradition

While in Iran, I watched people enter the mosques for daily prayers. At the entrance to the mosque they washed their eyes, ears, noses, and mouths to cleanse themselves of anything that they had seen, heard, smelled, or said that was impure. This is a physical embodiment of the spiritual desire to connect with God and to steer one's course, led by God's moral compass.

As with Judaism and Christianity, Islam has a mystical tradition, Sufism, that appeals to the right-brained thinker. Sufis follow the same tenets and pillars of Islam but represent the internal, esoteric, and mystical dimension of Islam.

Despite the fact that Sufism is accepted by the vast majority of Muslims as a legitimate theology within Islam, conservative or fundamentalist Muslims do not recognize Sufism as Islam. Sufism is perhaps too spiritual and not traditional enough for the orthodox and self-proclaimed true believers. We have discussed this phenomenon of rejecting mystics with other religious traditions, so it comes as no surprise.

Sufi Muslims believe that through their practice, it is possible to draw even closer to God, which they believe to be the singular expression of life. Their practice enables them to abandon dualism and separateness and replace it with oneness or divine unity.

I was introduced to Sufism by coincidence, while attending a seminar with the Noetic Society that just happened to be sharing a conference space with a Sufi group. Their practice seemed similar to other mystical traditions I was familiar with. Meditation, dancing, and prayer were predominant. These are intuitive practices that right-brained individuals employ to merge with or draw nearer to the Creator.

Just as with any Islamic practice, Sufi mystics work to uncover actions and behaviors that are adorned by Satan. Their practice works to constantly overturn ego-driven motivation disguised as right action in order to find the path to God.

Our Big Family

We have just explored most of the major religions and philosophies that have created a wealth of wisdom to help us in our journey through life. The big question becomes, What do they all have in common? Even if there is some quibbling over what God looks like and what it is thinking, the underlying reality is that the vast majority of people on the earth believe in an organism or entity that is a force of creation. This creation is sentient and has greater knowledge and wisdom than what we are capable of. Though people from different lands with different languages give this overseeing consciousness different names and attributes, this does not change the true nature of this organism. We will never completely understand its capacities or potentials. For this reason I like names for it such as "the Unknowable," which does not carry with it limiting descriptions. It is humanity's nature to continue our tireless search for and learning about God/Creation. We will get close but we will never comprehend it all. Science will surpass religion and its knowledge about God. We will see how long it takes the new views of Creation to sink in. My guess is that it will happen much faster than the time it took for the masses to recognize that the world is not flat.

So what do all these religions and philosophies tell us that will help us find connection and choose love and acceptance instead of hate and judgment? What common helpful advice do they offer on how to orchestrate our lives without major pitfalls, and reduce if not eliminate stress and suffering?

They all tell us that we are vitally important to each other and that we are really one big entangled family. They tell us to search within for our radically unique self or to *return* to what might lie behind the illusion of the conscious mind. If we find what is within us, we may envision a new reality that is beyond our current understanding. We may find that we were made with great potential to heal the planet and help co-create a messianic age that makes relevant the terms "Heaven," "Heaven on Earth," and "Nirvana": simply stated, a utopian society where we all work together as one because we *are* one. We are told to draw closer to our own concept of a Creator, whether we use the word God or Mother Nature. This can be done in many ways, by following the guidelines within the religions for the higher good or a Gnostic quest through prayer and meditation. There is always a road for every personality and for every individual.

Suffering exists. It can also be abruptly diminished and perhaps stopped if doing so is your deepest intention and you do the work. Some of our oldest guidelines include not stealing, lying, coveting, killing, or spreading gossip with an evil tongue. It is important that you become capable of going within to find the motivation for all of your actions. This will ensure that they are all harmonious and not at the direction of the ego. It is important that we walk this world with kindness, love, inner and outward peace, and willingness to help the downtrodden. We are requested to increase our own humanity in the direction of how we want Creation to be. We are a part of that Creation and our actions matter. I ask, How will you help write the book of life for your big family? By all accounts and from all religions, *this is the most important thing you can do with your life.* This is our purpose; nothing else comes close.

20

TRANSFORMATIVE HEALING

Our complex world operates on many levels. Deep within this interspace may be the consciousness of Creation, where there exists a process that can convert energy consciousness into the building blocks of our physical world. We know these building blocks as subatomic particles, atoms, and molecules. At this level it appears that these subatomic particles exist in the energetic realm and at the same time in our physical world or our perceived reality. What we will look at is the interplay between our thoughts and our physical reality.

Our early modern minds logically felt there was no connection between the two. This was the world of magic and miracles that once frightened people of science. But now everything is changing. New frontier science appreciates and investigates the transformative nature of our physical reality and the impact our consciousness has on it. It is all conceivable when we realize the stepwise process from energy to physicality, from micro to macro.

By the time the energy of consciousness has transformed into physical reality, that energy has become quite specialized and dedicated in the physical realm. This is why you can't transform an elephant into a jellyfish. That example may be far-fetched but the same thing occurs in less dramatic fashion in everyday life. Imagine a person who is a chronic worrier. They fret and stew and often hold their stress and anxiety in their stomach and intestinal tract. Over the years, this person can develop irritable bowel syndrome, a chronic inflammation of the intestinal lining. This in turn leads to cellular changes and detrimental alterations in DNA. The intestinal cells begin to transform into cancer cells after years of chronic inflammation resulting from continual stress. This is the effect of negative structuring in your cells that we learned about in the chapters on epigenetics; cells structure themselves in positive or negative ways in accordance with our thoughts.

These changes can occur because the cells of your body are constantly re-creating themselves throughout your life. Some tissues can change rapidly. The tissues of the mouth and the eyes can re-create themselves in one or two days, for example. It is good news that all of the organs of the body are in constant re-creation because we are afforded the opportunity to use consciousness to effect positive change in our regenerating bodies.

Imagine the physical body receiving input from the conscious mind, the subconscious mind, and soul consciousness. Imagine that some or all of this consciousness exists in a large realm beyond our own scope. Though our conscious mind thinks it is capable of the best answers as well as giving us the best direction, soul consciousness, with its greater capacity to see the big picture, has greater clarity. If we can draw on this database of information as we use consciousness to effect changes in our personal beliefs and ways of dealing with life, we will be much further along.

Let's return to the example of the person with irritable bowel syndrome and possibly colon cancer resulting from a constant state of anxiety. The logical mind hears the diagnosis: "You have colon cancer." But the subconscious mind and soul consciousness receive this information in a different way: as the signal to wake up and transform the belief systems that lead to chronic worry and stress. The words are received as invaluable energetic information that becomes the impetus to do the emotional and psychological work needed to curb the damaging behaviors and thought processes leading to illness and disease. This person must tackle the hard work of changing behavior that comes from a deeply imbedded belief system and shifting to a more functional belief system and way of dealing with what is going on around them. You can choose to change your habitual responses to stimuli that result in anxiety and worry. But while this is logical, it is very difficult to do. We often come up with rational if not honorable reasons to avoid changing or confronting the fears that created the existing behavior. Disease can be what motivates us to do that difficult work.

When we do the work, positive changes in emotional and psychological responses lead to physical changes in the body. We change our old behavior patterns and responses, the gastrointestinal system is released from the constant barrage of damaging neurochemicals, and transformation occurs on a cellular level. The receptor sites for negative neurochemicals in the gastrointestinal tract are no longer needed. The cells now have the opportunity to regenerate back into healthy tissues that existed before the negative thought patterns, behaviors, and mutations were present. With the dysfunctional patterns now replaced by harmonious patterns, the cells undergo positive structuring and mutations.

We assume that regenerating our cellular makeup is impossible because we wake up every day and look in the mirror, and outwardly nothing seems to change. But we are amazing creatures who change for the positive and negative all the time. When we eat toxic chemicals, our digestive system tissues suffer damage, but when we stop that toxic habit the large intestine can revert to its normal healing. The more quickly the negative effects—whether emotional or chemical—are halted, the faster the return to good health.

Let me make a point of clarification on the causes of disease. Though they are a key factor, the chronic deteriorating effects of stress are not the only reasons for disease. Toxins, allergens, trauma, genetics, and radiation are also common culprits, and they can search out weak areas in the body—areas often made weak by getting stuck with the job of processing negative emotional issues. The corollary to this is that if you are emotionally and physically balanced, consistently working on the emotional issues in your life that trigger you, your chances of getting organic diseases are greatly decreased. In the case of idiopathic diseases—illnesses that have no apparent cause—there is probably something emotional going on. The other red flag is chronic conditions that don't seem to want to heal correctly or completely.

In my early introduction to Vedic medicine, it was said that a person who is emotionally and physically balanced can eat poison without effect because their internal fire is burning so hot. We see examples of this with people who are extremely healthy and do not fall prey to the colds and flu that most people get.

Dysfunction and disease that seem to stem from a deep emotional traumatic event or from chronic repetitive emotional trauma can be rapidly altered by changes in consciousness. I often tell the story of a film I saw in a psychology class of a woman with a multiple personality disorder. The most important aspect of this film to me was not her behavior. It was that when she demonstrated her first personality, she had all of the symptoms and laboratory findings of systemic lupus erythematosus. Then, when she jumped into the next personality the malar rash, joint pain, and other symptoms associated with lupus quickly vanished and in the new personality she presented, she had a heart valve problem. Our logical mind says the body is still the same and only the subjective personality has changed. Moreover, the different personalities are still the same person. But this is not the case. The belief systems and filters through which that personality sees their reality have dramatically changed the body. The posture, chemical makeup, and even disease processes align themselves with the different personalities. All of this supports the idea that emotions, personality, and consciousness are integral parts of our health profile. If consciousness creates reality, this would have to be true.

Manifesting Physicality

What does it mean to manifest? It means that in order to make room for new thoughts and new actions, you need to change the way you think. It takes effort and imagination to change your old thoughts and behaviors, but it's a powerful tool for changing your physical makeup. The next step after that is to use your consciousness to manifest changes outside of your body.

There are many people who are masters of manifesting. One of these is Wayne Dyer, who has written extensively about the miraculous changes that can occur through manifesting.

I have personally experienced amazing changes through manifesting: changes that have gone beyond what my rational scientific beliefs tell me are possible in the everyday world.

In order to understand this process, we must delve deeper into the question of the nature of personal consciousness and how it relates to Universal Consciousness. As a result of my experiences, I believe that we exist in several realms simultaneously and that all of these experiences create a collective consciousness that may indeed be our soul. This would mean that the soul coordinates experiences from the earthly physical realm, the energetic realm we commonly call heaven, and the creator realm where souls individuate and can function with free will. If you are experiencing other realms, all of this input is part of a collective experience that you may not be fully aware of while you live in the earthly realm. At the same time, you are intimately entangled or connected to the much larger consciousness of Creation. There is no hierarchy to these three levels as they are all one thing, but from what I have heard, there is always a greater oversight that coordinates the growth and expansion within itself.

This is important because your conscious mind might tell you that you really need a new sports car with shiny chrome rims and a great stereo system. Because the conscious mind is where the ego resides, getting the sports car seems of the utmost importance, but the soul consciousness has different thoughts about what is important. It might create situations that keep you from buying that car in order to keep you on another track in life.

Then there is the Universal Consciousness that binds you to the rest of humanity and all things that exist in Creation. The soul consciousness and the universal Creation Consciousness are bound together seamlessly. The two together have been called the "oversoul." Within this construct, manifesting can only occur for the common good and for personal growth.

We return to the sports car. Your conscious mind believes owning the sports car will prove you are successful so it chants the mantra "The car would be good for me. The car would be good for me." But there is a bigger thought form lurking in your subconscious mind: "I am afraid of not having the car. Without it I am not special and people will not see me as special." The subconscious mind has greater input, so chances are you will attract what you fear. Fear makes a lot of noise when it comes to manifesting. So if you really want that sports car, you must first change your deep thoughts and motivations about the importance of showing "success" and the even deeper work of self-worth not being based on what others think. You must wrestle with the ego to arrive at a place of internally feeling worthy *without* owning the car. Then things will flow much better for you to acquire and keep the car. Just remember that the greater thought form will win the day.

Let's use a very common example of people wanting to manifest more money. The conscious mind thought form is I want more money, more money is what I deserve, I would feel better about myself if I had more money, I really need more money. The subconscious mind is swirling with thoughts like I am so afraid of not having money, I am so afraid of not having money, I hate my life because there is never enough money. So what gets created? Right: not having any money or enough money and the view that my life stinks because I don't have enough money. The soul is always looking to give us opportunities to transform our fears into gifts. The chance is that you will either not bring more money into your life or if you do it will not stay around long. The soul will try to create lessons where you become okay without the money. Self-acceptance is job one as far as the soul is concerned. It is here that you no longer need stuff in order to be okay with yourself. If you want to manifest more money in your life, the most important thing you can do is to be okay without it. That's right. Then your greater thought form emanating from the subconscious mind is infinitely open to the possibility. As always, it must also be in alignment with your life's journey.

I would like to share with you these next three stories in order to expand on the concept of manifesting.

I was fifteen years old when my mother started looking for a place to spend her retirement years. We left Los Angeles and drove up the California coast all the way to the Oregon border. On the last night of our return trip home, we landed in a small coastal town, set up camp in a nearby state park, and sought out a realtor. We took the list of her available properties but none of them caught our eye. So we returned to the realtor to report this and found she had just listed something fifteen minutes earlier that she thought could be perfect. We went to the property and immediately knew it was the place. Interestingly enough, the cost of the property was exactly the amount of money in my mother's budget. We signed the papers the next morning and as we were leaving, another person came in to purchase the property we had just purchased. It seemed like everything had aligned itself for us to own that perfect spot.

This may be an example of manifesting but it is not the most striking example in this story. Just before we entered the park to pack up our campsite, I pointed to the side of the hill, a lovely wooded area with a beautiful ocean view. I told my mother that was where I wanted to live someday. Years later, after all my professional schooling was complete, I started to investigate locations to begin my chiropractic practice. I traveled throughout the state and did a lot of soul searching but in the end, I decided that the best place would be the same sleepy little coastal town where my mom lived. I moved to the town and started my practice. Six months later, I began looking for a place to build my own home. One day I was having a casual conversation with a patient who happened to be a realtor. I told her I wanted a small piece of property on the coast or a larger parcel inland with lots of trees. She told me about a piece that had been for sale for some time, had been taken off the market, and had recently been listed again. It was very close to my mother's home and had an ocean view. At my next free moment, we rushed out to get a quick look at the mysterious piece of property. It was the very parcel of land I had pointed to when I was fifteen years old.

I had lodged the intention in the energetic world to live on that land, and here it was years later coming back to greet me. It is possible that I always knew I would live on that land. Often manifesting involves a game with time that we cannot imagine.

It was one thing to be reunited with the property but money was an issue. I was just starting out so I would need a partner in order to buy the land. My friend Pat magically filled that role, but we found ourselves part of a bidding war. Pat and I went to visit the parcel, and I sat down on the ground and asked myself intuitively what price we should offer as a bid. The number came to me, we agreed on it, and we made the offer. We won by a very slim margin and the dream I'd had years ago came to fruition.

I've asked the skeptic in me if this scenario could be explained by chance. It is conceivable but highly improbable that all of the potentials would align without some help. It was more likely that this was the situation I needed in order to create experiences that would allow for my growth. I also believe I had to be okay with not having the property while still being passionate about it, and it had to be in my highest and best good for the rest of my life as determined by my soul's perspective.

I've had some adventures in New Zealand that have also brought amazing insights into manifesting. I love backpacking alone and giving my thoughts the freedom to roam as I travel the trail. I have found it's one of the best ways I can access my subconscious thoughts. This practice may be the reason manifesting comes easily for me in places I hike.

There was one hike that stands out. After a long day, I reached the "hut," a communal group of cabins conveniently located along the trek. Upon readying my dinner, I discovered I had forgotten my spoon. It's the only utensil I usually bring, so I was in a real bind. Luckily, a kind Swiss couple loaned me a spoon that night. After dinner and through the night, I kept thinking how I might be able to fashion a spoon to use for the trip. "I need a spoon. I need a spoon," kept cycling through my head. I sent this thought form unknowingly out into the universe without even trying.

The next morning I started off early and decided to take a slight detour to another hut that was off the beaten track. I could have my lunch there and rest a bit before the remainder of the day's journey. I arrived at the hut and there was no one to be found. I walked into the kitchen and there, sitting in the center of the small table, was a spoon. I believe it was a little gift from my soul. I don't know how this was arranged or if the spoon had been left the previous night or even earlier, but I was extremely grateful for whatever mechanism had brought this spoon—not a fork or a knife—to rest on the center of the table inside a hut I'd had no intention of visiting when I started hiking the previous day.

The next year, I traveled deep into New Zealand's fjord lands for an eight-day backpacking trip. This time, I brought along an iPod, a new contraption for me that my son had gotten me up to speed on before I left. The iPod was a welcome addition as the music kept me going at the end of a long day's hike. My problem was that as I walked or jumped from rock to rock on the hike, the music reshuffled. I'd be hiking along, just beginning to groove to a new song, and off it would go to a different one. This became more and more frustrating throughout the day. I tried to figure out how I could hold the device in such a way that I wouldn't jar it; in fact, for three entire days I tried to walk as softly as I could. It didn't help much, and I began to obsess on the thought "I wish I had an iPod carrier, I wish I had an iPod carrier." Once again my subconscious mind sent out to the universe that I needed an iPod carrier. The other criteria for expeditious manifesting were also in place. My wishes had no detrimental effects to my life's journey and were not placating the needs of the ego. The story continues on the very next day.

I was on a particularly beautiful track, and one morning I could see the sun rising on Lake Alabaster, which was slightly off the trail. I walked over to the lake, looking for the perfect place to take a picture of the beautiful clouds reflecting on the calm water. I decided to shoot the picture from a low perspective so I could include the shoreline rocks in the foreground.

Figure 8.

I got down on my knees and then lay on my side, trying to find the right angle for the shot. I looked at the ground to set my camera and there, partially covered by the grass, was an iPod carrier. I pulled it out and once again wondered, *What are the chances?* Out of the millions of things that someone could drop and the thousands of places where I could have taken a picture, how could this be? It seemed to me that these very improbable— if not downright bizarre—experiences were teaching me about the capacity of human consciousness to manifest what most would call little miracles. My experiences have shown me that if something is in your highest and best interest, if it does not feed the ego, and if it is complementary to your life and often the emotional issues that you are here to harmonize, the answer is *yes.*

Examine your own life experiences and see what has manifested for you in the context of these guidelines. Did the spoon or the iPod carrier appear after I recognized the need for them, or is time nonlinear or creating itself so far in advance that it can work ahead of the request? I can only imagine that that iPod carrier had been there for days or longer.

Placebo: Manifesting Within Our Own Body

It seems we spend more time and effort researching how harmful things can happen to our body than how to effect positive changes. Could harnessing the power of the placebo effect bring about a new era of medicine? A placebo is a benign substance given to an experimental subject in lieu of an actual medication: a sugar pill instead of a drug, for instance. The placebo effect occurs when a person experiences the desired effect of the drug without taking the drug and often without any negative side effects. This happens to an average of 30 percent of the people who take that sugar pill. The body somehow mimics the effect of the drug because we believe we're taking the drug.

The power of the placebo effect has not been widely studied, likely for a couple of reasons. First, if we were able to take sugar pills and receive the benefits of the perceived drug, it would put a big dent in the income of the pharmaceutical industry. Second, it takes a leap of faith for many people to move beyond their comfort zone and accept concepts that are not part of their foundational experiences and beliefs in order to self-create the placebo effect within their own bodies. Interestingly enough, it doesn't matter whether you believe in the placebo effect for it to work; if you believe in the authority of the people telling you the sugar pill will work, there's still a 30 percent chance that your body will manifest the changes you've been told to look for.

Let's not forget the research done in Japan where thirteen people who were highly allergic to poison ivy were used in a placebo experiment. When the plant was rubbed on their arms, all thirteen of them broke out with allergic reactions. On the other arm researchers rubbed a neutral plant and two out of the thirteen broke out in a rash. The interesting part of this experiment was that what the researchers called poison ivy, wasn't, and the so-called "neutral" plant actually was poison ivy.[1] The body created the response to what it believed it should do based on its past. It created the same response to what it believed was happening. This is much like what we do with emotional stimuli or various situations in our lives. I'd be interested to learn whether the body created the *substance* or just the expected *outcome*.

Mankind could utilize the placebo effect, or positive internal manifesting, to cure and prevent disease as well as to reduce the effects of aging. Placebo research reminds us how flexible and recuperative our healing powers are. Here is one example of some of the research that has been done.

Shawn Achor is a nationally known researcher and author. I first learned about him from a TED talk and later read his book. His research is all about how we can change the lens of our perception, and he proposed that we become desensitized to the wondrous miracles that exist all around us by converting everything we see to just average. Once the miraculous is reduced to average, or the norm, life can quickly become disappointing. In other words, if an experience usually rated a "10" is experienced as just average, and "10" is at the top of the experience rating scale, life is mundane even when your experiences are exceptional. This also can make an average day a bad day.

Achor discovered that you can train your brain to highlight positive things in your life and in so doing, effect great changes in your health and productivity. His research study asked subjects to recognize all the wonderful things that happened in their day—appreciating and feeling grateful for events that were positive instead of letting them slip by as average or even unnoticed altogether—for a few minutes, three times a day, for a period of twenty-one days. The results in improved quality of life and increased productivity were significant. The subjects were 31 percent more productive, 37 percent better at sales, and 19 percent more accurate at doing their job. In addition, they had an increase in intelligence as measured by IQ tests and an increased ability to learn systems and be more adaptable at work and in life.

Achor believed that these changes were the result of an increased output of dopamine. This neurochemical plays a part in pleasurable reward-based behavior, cognition, and our ability to pay attention as well as many other functions.[2]

Frequent expressions of gratitude are not the only technique found to increase quality of life and well-being. Journaling, exercise, meditation, and random acts of kindness have all been studied and proved to make a significant impact. Achor quoted additional research on gratitude by Emmons and McCullough in 2003, journaling by Slatcher and Pennebaker in 2006, exercise by Babyak et al. in 2000, meditation by Dweck in 2000, and finally, random acts of kindness by Lyubomirsky in 2005.

After encountering Shawn Achor's research, I decided to employ the same technique, but with one change. If expressing gratitude three times a day made this kind of impact, what would happen if I did this practice ten times a day? I set the alarm on my watch to go off hourly throughout the day, and I noticed a change in my outlook and attitude within just a few days of starting the practice. Coincidentally, I had just had a full blood panel done prior to starting this practice to evaluate my liver enzymes, sedimentation rates, and C- reactive protein (an indicator of inflammation in the body). I then repeated the blood panel six months later after doing the stepped-up gratitude practice. Though I'd had fairly normal blood work to begin with, there were little improvements in several areas.

I recommended this practice to a patient of mine who was recovering from metastatic breast cancer that had spread to her lumbar spine, brain, and abdominal organs. I had been working with her for several months, helping her become aware and harmonizing her emotional beliefs. The cancer had stopped spreading and her cancer markers had fallen but had now stabilized along with her progress. She was becoming a little frightened and frustrated that she was not seeing the progress she'd hoped for. I told her about Shawn Achor's study and about the fact that my blood work improved after employing this gratitude practice

As a chiropractor herself, she was not a stranger to alternative care so she began the gratitude practice, seeing the beauty in all things, every hour of the day, just as I had done. Her outlook improved and she began to look for the little miracles in life. One month later, her blood work was repeated and the cancer markers had gone down once again. She told her own patients about her experience, and those who tried it expressed appreciation for this new way of looking at life and how much better they felt.

Her body had changed: the cancer cells had slowed or halted their reproduction as a result of her new view of life. She was restructuring the cells of her body as well as changing her neurochemistry. All this magic was occurring as her consciousness shifted. I see harmonizing one's belief systems and the resulting positive changes in my patient's health as a positive feedback mechanism to keep us moving in this direction. This is one of the many ways I see verification of our life's purpose. And this is one of many stories that teach us that our consciousness has great control over how we create our bodies and perhaps the world around us.

I think it's time to take the word placebo off the list of unimportant words and put it front and center in our research as part of the cure for many organic diseases.

Passing on Learned Knowledge

Just before my son was conceived I was an avid waterskier. I had competed in local tournaments and had increased my abilities to where I could begin to compete on the national level. Unfortunately for my waterskiing career, I sustained a vestibular injury that took me out of the sport. When my son was six years old we decided to teach him how to waterski. He quickly jumped from two skis to one. He enjoyed his time at the lake so we went out often during the summer. In just a few years he was making cuts where his shoulder nearly touched the water. When he was in junior high school I decided to take us on a course along with a friend of mine who had also competed in years past. The object of waterskiing through this course was to work your way up to a speed of thirty-six miles an hour while skiing through the course. Then, while staying at that speed, we shorten the line to make it more difficult to reach around the buoys. For most people reaching that speed takes years of practice as well as mature strength, but on my son's first run, he made it through the course at thirty-two miles an hour and we began to cut the line shorter.

My friend and I watched in astonishment, never having seen anyone make it through the course the first time through. Even after we shortened the rope fifteen feet, he was still able to ski the course successfully. The story of his continued gains goes on, but the point is that his abilities were far from being explainable unless we can conceive that learned abilities are transferable to our children. There exist countless examples of children who are phenomenally good at the same professional sport as their parents. It's easy to think that it is physical genetics, but whereas many other people may be more physically fit, the children of trained athletes bring something more to the table that allows them to go further. The incidence of this goes way beyond chance, indicating that there is something more to it. Perhaps it happens along the lines of epigenetics: somehow the learned experiences and perhaps more are passed on in our DNA or some other carrying mechanism. The other possibility is that the parent and child have DNA so similar that some form of communication exists that allows the transfer of knowledge.

The reason I bring this up here and not in the earlier section on epigenetics is that it speaks to our potential. As humanity's abilities progress and we become more open to ways we can manifest change in our world, these abilities will be passed on to our children. This will expedite the process of human evolution and bring into view the human purpose that may still be hidden from our sight. We may not be capable of comprehending that purpose until we have become different.

AWAKENING OUR HIDDEN POWER

Human evolution is an ongoing process. As our capacities for greater consciousness and intellect grow, our physical form changes as well. Our evolution from Neanderthal to *Homo erectus* shows some of these changes. We talked a little bit about what the next step might look like. More importantly for this discussion, what will our capacities be in the future? If we were to go back a few steps in our evolution and look through the eyes of those individuals, our current form would look strange and alien. Our present mental capacities would be unimaginable. This reminds us that we are not at the end of our evolution. Instead, we are headed toward times that will call for new answers, capacities, and levels of awareness. And the evolutionary changes that occur during our lives will be passed on seamlessly from generation to generation.

Figure 9.

The more proficient we become at transforming or manifesting energy into physical outcomes, the quicker our adaptive and positive evolution will be. It is my hope that as we gain information about our ability to interface between energy and physicality, humanity will be compelled to prioritize the teaching of arts that will expedite our ability to heal ourselves and the planet and advance our evolution. Walking down this leg of the road of human evolution may even bring about a capacity to interface between the realms we've explored in this book. It's not that hard to conceive if we realize that through meditation today we are creating a conduit through which information passes. In this chapter we will look at the interplay between energy and matter as well as the current research that proves the efficacy of our abilities to effect positive changes in our world.

We can define Creation Consciousness as energy. This energy is transformed into physicality, also known as mass, through the *intrinsic process* we call creation.

Albert Einstein showed us that energy and matter are interchangeable. $E=MC^2$ translates to energy equals mass times the speed of light squared, or E divided by C^2 (something really fast times itself) = Mass. So it stands to reason that all energy, whether divine or otherwise, divided by the speed of light squared (34,701,132,550 miles per second) equals or becomes matter. Conversely, a little bit of matter can become an unimaginable amount of energy. Through science we can see that the two are one and the same, and are just different forms or states of being. We talked about the fact that scientists are trying to better understand this process and mechanism in which energy is altered to become something that functions as a solid. We now give this process names such as M or string theory. The good news is that scientists have recognized and are working to better understand how this process actually occurs. The very creation of CERN in Switzerland is to better understand the process of how energy is converted into the matter that creates the realm we live in. This work will no doubt get us closer to finding out who or what is strumming the strings of creation or how the intention and breath of Creation animates our existence. Just as important is the research that shows the power of human consciousness in this process of creation. *We are a part of the evolution that exists between energy and matter.*

Creation is an ongoing process that requires the physical realm. Without physicality, there would be a missing piece in the catalyst for change. From what I have been told, change must occur in this realm in order for the organism that some call Creation, the Unknowable, Nature, or God to grow and evolve. If we look at how the system is set up, we see that there are many feedback mechanisms for positive change. When we move toward kindness, acceptance, and helping each other, we always feel good inside, disease can disappear, and the world (humanity and Creation) is more stable and happier. These actions again highlight and perpetuate our purpose.

The Unity of Two Realms

I often work with people who want to engage in therapy free of interaction with the people in their life who present difficulty. They just want to set their intention for changed behavior, and they hope this is enough. While this is a good first step, my experience shows that change does not occur unless those changes are actually carried out in the external, physical world as well. Engaging with the unique situations and people in our lives is essential in transforming our emotional issues and belief systems. This process can't be done by just thinking you have changed, without walking into the fear and integrating new actions with the people and situations that create the difficulty or set the stage for your own stress.

I am the first to admit that it is not easy to change behaviors and unravel inner story lines that have taken a lifetime to create. It is difficult, and it can sometimes be scary, but it is the most important thing you can do to bring about real change and growth in your life. This work requires acknowledging that the actions you have taken thus far are not working and that in order to change, you must make a commitment to a different path.

Often my patients ask for some kind of help with creating a new path. A simple guideline is to do the opposite of what they have usually done. For example: if you are afraid of conflict and run away from it, never stating your opinions and letting people run your life, the opposite is to become okay with conflict and state your opinions, wishes, and feelings.

Our physicality is a reflection of our emotions. In order to re-create a healthier body and humanity, we must change our action and our personal beliefs that add to our stress, suffering, and lack of *awe* in life. This is the fundamental process of humanity's evolution. This is what we are here for. There is more good news: the more you utilize this process, the easier it gets. This is just another gift to humanity to remind us of our path.

As I said, this kind of transformation is not easy. It takes attention and strength. It's not uncommon for particularly sensitive patients to want to run away altogether or return to a previous life in an energetic heavenly realm where things were easier and there were no confrontations. Some tell me this is their last life, their last incarnation, so there is no need to resolve issues in preparation for the next life. All of this reveals the frustrations and disappointments they feel; it also acknowledges an underlying sense of connection to realms where they feel life is much easier and not filled with so much turmoil: i.e., "Heaven." This is also a logical story line designed to justify their aversion to confronting the "teachers" they encounter that can help bring about change and transformation in the physical world.

We must do more than rehearse change in our thoughts; we must do the work. If we don't effect changes at defining moments in the physical world, within ourselves, and with the important people in our lives, Universal Consciousness will remain unchanged and we ourselves will not get the real rewards.

Proof in the Pudding

Much research has been done surrounding this relationship between energy/consciousness and physical outcomes in the human experience. Many people have read *The Power of Prayer* by R. A. Torrey. Also, Daniel J. Benor, MD, has edited two volumes about research into the power of intention-focused consciousness, carefully selecting studies conducted under the highest scientific standards.[1]

One of these studies selected children between the ages of twelve and fifteen who were diagnosed as nearsighted enough to need glasses. The children were randomly assigned in four groups. Group 1 received no therapeutic treatment at all. Group 2 received placebo eye drops containing no therapeutic agent. Group 3 was taught and practiced qigong meditation, a Chinese meditation practice with a focus on healing, breathing, and alignment. Group 4 was treated by qigong masters.

The results were significant. Groups 1 and 2 (no treatment and placebo eye drops) showed no improvement in their vision. Two subjects in Group 3 showed vision improvement. The most improvement was in Group 4, where sixteen showed improvement in their vision. Qigong masters use focused intention in healing their patients. There are certainly different variations depending on the master; however, these people utilize the energy or life force that is all around us and then, through positive intention, focus their healing on the area that needs care.

Dr. Benor highlighted another experiment examining how focused intention affects seedling growth.[2] The seeds were soaked in salt water, which was expected to suppress growth. Before the soaked seeds were planted, they were divided into two groups. Half of the seeds were treated with positive energy intention by healers, and the other half were planted without any further intervention. The result? Plants from the treated seeds grew much taller and healthier than those from the untreated seeds.

The study also involved a third group of seeds. In this group, the seeds were neither soaked in salt water nor treated with intentional healing before planting. Instead, they received water that was kept in a psychiatric hospital filled with chronically depressed patients. Plants from these seeds grew much smaller and failed to thrive, unlike the control group that was watered directly from the tap. The point of this research is to expose the power of human consciousness on our physical surroundings.

Further research was done into the power of healers. The next phase of the study involved laboratory animals that had cancerous tumors induced into their bodies.[3] The experimental group of animals received treatment by healers while the control group received no treatment at all. The group treated by the healers showed significant decrease in tumor growth, and their mortality was significantly delayed.

Research on human subjects is also part of this focused intentional healing research. Ninety-six patients with high blood pressure were selected and divided into two groups. One group received no treatment while the second group was treated by healers using intention. The healers were instructed to visualize or meditate upon three things: First, they were to visualize a sense of well-being and relaxation. Second, they were instructed to imagine connecting to a higher power. Third, they were asked to visualize perfect health for the patient they were treating. The treatment was completed with an expression of gratitude to the Source.

Neither the patients nor their doctors knew who was receiving the treatment, and the healing work was done at a distance from where the patients resided. Every one of the patients who were being treated showed significant improvement as evidenced by objective measures such as decreased blood pressure and heart rate and less need for medical intervention. One of the healers even had a 92.3 percent improvement rate with his patients. This was a great improvement, especially considering that these patients had already received medical treatment.[4]

I interpret these results in the following way. When the practitioners begin their meditation and create a sense of well-being and relaxation, their brain activity is altered in such a way that they can access other aspects of their brain. There is a consistent change in the brain wave state that indicates greater access to the subconscious mind and our own wisdom, often attributed to accessing our soul consciousness. This allows the healers access to areas of the brain that have greater healing impact. When the conscious mind is less in control and these other areas come to the fore, the healers have greater access to their soul self; perhaps that can open the potential of the energetic realm and human consciousness, the catalyst of change.

When the healers visualize connection to a higher power, this helps to shift to right-brain function, which gives them a greater sense of oneness and interconnectedness, and consequently a greater bond with patients. Using visualization for health and well-being is a powerful tool because you imagine this state of being to be true and present. All of this together generates a sense of awe and wonder that is ideal for creating positive structure in the cells of the patient and the practitioners who are doing the healing work.

The final step of expressing gratitude inclines the mind toward positivity, which in turn aligns the cells of the bodies of both the healers and the patients toward positivity. This study and many others recorded in Benor's books illustrate the correlation between intentional healing and stress reduction and physical healing.

Intentional Healing and Autoimmune Deficiency Syndrome

Before the advent of effective drug therapies, receiving a diagnosis of HIV/AIDS was a death sentence. During the search for anything and everything that could possibly treat this deadly virus, intentional healing was put to work and studied as a method of treatment. One study looked at forty male patients between the ages of twenty-two and thirty-four who were HIV positive.[5] The subjects were divided into two groups, both of whom wore noise-cancelling headphones and sleep masks so they could not hear or see anything that was happening in the treatment room. The experimental group consisted of twenty men who were treated by a therapeutic touch practitioner using intentional healing. The other twenty subjects in the control group received fake treatment, consisting of the healer just sitting in the room but doing nothing. The study involved two measurements: levels of CD4, a white blood cell that is deficient in AIDS patients, and the stress response of the patient measured through psychological testing. These factors were tested before the study took place and then at three, six, and nine months post study. The research showed a significant increase in the CD4 blood count of the experimental group and an improved ability to cope with stress. This study clearly showed the healing effects of intentional healing.

Another study was done on the AIDS population, this one examining healers from different faith traditions and schools of thought and the efficacy of intentional healing.[6] Twenty patients with end-stage disease were studied. Ten subjects were placed in the experimental group and ten in the control group, which received no treatment. The healers were Christian, Jewish, Buddhist, Brennan school graduates, Native American Lakota, or Chinese qigong masters with an average of seventeen years' experience. These practitioners had also treated an average of 117 people with distant healing. The study lasted six months.

The experimental group was treated with distance intentional healing for one hour per day, six days a week for ten weeks with one healer before switching to the next. White blood cell count and T-cell count were used as the measure of success, as were the incidence of associated diseases such as Kaposi's sarcoma and the incidence of medical services used to treat these diseases or other complications.

The results of the study were significant. All ten of the patients in the experimental group showed improvement in blood counts and a decrease in associated diseases and medical intervention rates. In the control group, four patients died and the remaining six patients showed a worsening of their blood work and an increase in the incidence of associated diseases. While the subjects in the experimental group were of younger age on average, all twenty of the patients were at the same progression of the disease process. The results were staggering: the power of intentional healing surpassed every modern treatment for the virus. Not only did all the patients live, but they did better than they had prior to the treatment in terms of stopping progression of the disease.

Because these results showed promise, an additional study was done, this time with forty patients, all of similar age and disease progression. The measurement in this study was T-cell counts, need for medicine or medical intervention, hospitalization days, associated illness, and psychological well-being. The study design was the same as the earlier one and again, the results were just as impressive as the former study. Seventeen out of twenty patients in the experimental group showed significant improvement in blood counts, a decrease in associated diseases, and improved psychological well-being. In the control group that received no treatment, twelve of the twenty patients had increased associated illnesses and needed additional medical intervention and hospitalization.

The results of these two studies taken together should be a wake-up call for the medical community about how we treat disease. Intentional healing for just one hour a day made a significant if not dramatic impact on the course of the disease and on the patients' psychological well-being.[7]

Healing Energy

Researchers wanted to learn more about how this intentional energy is generated and communicated. Elmer Green, PhD, is a pioneer in the field of biofeedback training. He designed what is called "The Copper Wall Experiment," constructing a room with copper walls to measure changes in electrical voltage of the body during meditation.[8] The healing practitioners in this experiment sat in the room in front of the copper wall, isolated from the floor on glass blocks. The voltage of their bodies was measured as they began meditating or healing. Green stated that a normal body voltage would be in the millivolt range with little fluctuation attributed to static electricity buildup. But when the meditator was doing a healing, the voltage shot up by as much as 200 volts from baseline. The healer voltages were a thousand times above normal. This study adds to the body of evidence that intentional energetic healing exists and is effective, giving an indication of increased energetic output. Voltage is one of the few ways that we can measure electrical energy but it may also be an indicator for other types of healing energies that are taking place.

Skepticism and Intention

A study sponsored by the Institute of Noetic Sciences was done to assess whether or not a person could sense, either consciously or subconsciously, that someone was thinking about them or visualizing them from a distance.[9] Researchers utilized electrical readings on the muscles that raise the hair on the back of the neck, a way of measuring the sympathetic nervous system, which responds to being observed. First they placed the observer behind the person in the same room and registered the sympathetic response. They then moved the observer to a distant location where he or she watched the person on a television monitor. The results showed that the person being visualized knew it was happening 85 percent of the time. It didn't really matter how far away the observer was from the person in the study; the hair on the back of the neck indicating the sympathetic response was triggered.

A group from Idaho who were skeptical of this research repeated the study and came up with the exact opposite results: the person being visualized did not know they were being visualized approximately 85 percent of the time. These skeptics confronted the Noetic Science group with these findings, and both groups agreed to reproduce the experiment, but this time using the locale and the same equipment the skeptic group had used.

The results were the same as the first round of experiments—in direct opposition to each other. These results were beyond coincidence; they had to have stemmed from intention. One group wanted to prove people could sense being observed and the other wanted to prove they could not. The belief system or intention of the investigator conducting the experiment had an impact on the outcome of the experiment.

This was some of the first research to revolutionize the scientific method, and what it indicated was staggering. It meant that much of our research is tainted by the people overseeing and conducting the experiments. Human consciousness has that much impact. This means that if a drug company is doing research on one of its drugs and the company and its employees even remotely want a positive result, the drug will have a more positive effect. If not for the oversight of the skeptic group and the cooperative effort of the two entities, this underlying bias would never have been revealed. We are now realizing that the world we live in is the result of a self-fulfilling prophecy. We must be mindful of our thoughts for they have the potential to create two different worlds. This reminds us of the power of our consciousness and its effect on everything we encounter.

Delving into Collective Consciousness

Much of the research I have cited demonstrates that an inherent part of human nature is the ability to heal ourselves and others. What happens when that healing ability moves from individuals to a group consciousness? The power increases exponentially.

In 1998, Roger Nelson, in conjunction with the Institute of Noetic Sciences, set out to research the phenomenon of human collective consciousness with the Global Consciousness Project (GCP).[10] Nelson conducted this study by placing Random Event Generators (REG) or Random Number Generators (RNG) in seventy host sites around the globe. The study describes these REG machines as high-speed coin flippers, only instead of heads or tails, they produce pulses that are then converted into

1s or 0s. Normally, RNG produce completely random and unpredictable sequences of 1s and 0s. The study wanted to determine whether a great event could collectively unify the feelings and consciousness of millions of people, thereby causing a change in the RNG sequence. Would this prove the existence of a collective human energetic consciousness? The data from the RNG are transmitted to a central archive, which now contains more than fifteen years of data.

Over the course of that time, events occurred that caused the data to show some organization, but it wasn't until the death of Princess Diana that the number sequences were sustained as nonrandom. But the largest sequential event of numbers occurred with 9/11. The most interesting part of this was that the numbers became sequential *several minutes before* the first plane crashed into the World Trade Center and lasted four hours after the event took place. I believe this indicates that our consciousness, whether soul or subconscious, is aware of things before they physically happen. This may also be an indication that this event had already collapsed in time and that the future was already knowable.

This research teaches us that there is indeed a global field of consciousness that at a minimum circulates all around the world. The picture that comes to mind is much like the electron field of an atom; the electron is a probability cloud that allows it to be everywhere. This is an amazing way to prove that all of our individual consciousness is connected, which creates a very special feature allowing humanity and perhaps all living things to move in a coherent fashion. This might indicate that if enough people are working toward a common goal, it helps to pull others with them. I have heard it said that we do not need everyone to reach a messianic age or state of Nirvana. It just takes a critical part of humanity to champion peace, love, and kindness to get us all on the bandwagon.

Other research has been done to assess whether group consciousness can cause societal healing and change. "Super-radiance" is a term used to describe the extraordinary and positive effect radiated out into society by a group of specially trained meditators. Such a group was formed in Washington, DC, in 1993.[11] Four thousand people meditated for two months, setting their intention on peace, and after two months, violent crime decreased 24 percent instead of escalating as it had been doing before the meditators went into action.

Another group, which practiced Transcendental Meditation, organized intentional healing groups in twenty-four large cities around the United States. Their results were similar to the Washington, DC, group. An increasing crime trend was reversed and violent crime decreased 22 percent.[12]

During one of the heated Arab-Israeli conflicts, a group of people in Israel intended peace there for two months, resulting in a 76 percent decrease in deaths and dramatic reductions in local crime, traffic accidents, and set fires.[13] Again, less than 1 percent of the population had a wildly significant outcome. I wonder where the tipping point would be when all of humanity turned toward peace. Looking at the impact of less than 1 percent makes me believe that the percentage of people it would take to create peace or even Heaven on Earth would be less than half. If the numbers were that big, I believe people who defaulted to aggression would be turned by the group consciousness and become more tolerant and less violent. My guess is that it takes fewer people to turn the world toward good than it does to turn the world toward bad. We have seen in our history where the masses turned toward evil and generated their beliefs from fear. This is the only way I can explain for myself how Hitler in Germany and McCarthy in the United States were able to turn the collective consciousness in such a way that they could cause so much destruction. We must always endeavor to keep our thoughts positive with peace and love and kindness and divorce ourselves from the fear, anger, revenge, and judgment that are so tasty to our ego. We must always clearly see that our political leaders who utilize these tricks and the self-proclaimed news agencies such as Fox that sell the propaganda of fear are really seeking to control our way of thinking.

Developing Our Ability and Potential

We human beings have a highly developed ability to heal our physical bodies and our collective community. We can even impact the physical nature of our planet, all through intention and consciousness.

However, our capacity to do this is being underutilized. Few people choose to see beyond the five senses and recognize the power of an interconnected oneness. Through that sense of connection, we can replace an existence often based in fear with the enriching sense of cooperative humanity.

Perhaps as more people become aware that we can create great healing and peace in our world through focused healing intention, the numbers of people doing so will increase and we will find the critical mass of humanity necessary to bring about positive change. If intention can impact crime levels, what would it take to reverse climate change and heal our planet? Perhaps if the group is large enough, we can create change that seems impossible now. Maybe we can change the harmful effects of pollutants, herbicides, and other contaminants. This is a stretch but I think it's important to entertain the unforeseen possibilities. As time goes by and we continue to alter the earth for our needs, we may just need to see if these powers can help us. What will be the impact of a collective focused consciousness? The more we experiment, and the more we see positive results from this practice, the more people may be willing to embrace this untapped capacity.

Imagine the Possibilities

The potential impact of collective focused intention is like a bud waiting to blossom. Imagine the possibilities for change. Government and economic systems would run more efficiently and harmoniously when operating from a right-brain perspective that sees us all as one and realizes that anything negative we do has a negative impact on ourselves. This would be very different from the current ego-driven world where we see ourselves as separate and have the obsessive wish to have more than the next guy or girl. When we can separate from the egotistical symptoms of greed, narcissism, hierarchy, and hatred as our motivators, we can erase corruption and create a system of economic equality and fairness. It is only here that true capitalism could work without corruption, and socialism would not lead to taking advantage of the system.

Everyone who could contribute to the community would do so according to their special gifts and abilities, all for the common good. This seems like a far-off utopian concept compared to our current societal trends, but this is a future we can envision if we employ communal consciousness for the sake of the greater good. This, our greatest possible evolution, may be forged by self-created hard times. I believe our hardest challenge will come from our exponential growth. With our population doubling every twenty to thirty years, we are looking at our population going from 7 billion to 56 billion in a hundred years. We have mass starvation now. I cannot even imagine how such growth could be possible without lots of human suffering. The problem will not be limited to starvation but will include all the effects of having that many people with all of their needs living on the planet. All of the filtration systems that the earth has within it will be overrun. Our need for energy will require energy production that has extreme detrimental effects on the earth and the human population. Large distribution centers that hope to take food to places where it cannot grow will make the system more fragile. The more scarce food, resources, housing, and space become, the more frightened and thus aggressive we will become.

Somewhere in this progression will be our defining moment. If we choose to remain unaware of our oneness with all living things and our connection to our soul wisdom, it will lead to great human suffering and loss. Maybe that is what we need to make the shift, or maybe there is a call to make the positive changes that will allow us to transform our egocentric views into a view that sees humanity and all living things as *one* living organism. Along with the reality of oneness will come a stripping away of the illusions of the five senses and a return to the knowing that we are spiritual beings in a physical body, expanding and harmonizing consciousness. This knowledge of who we are and what our journey is has echoed through time, but the majority have not listened or chosen to do the work. These numbers will be forced to grow because it is the only alternative that assures our survival in this realm.

It will be hard if you are one of the few on this journey, but as the numbers grow you will have good company. We have seen great changes when less than 1 percent of society has this awareness. It is my belief and hope that the system is set up for thoughts to work synergistically and it may only take 20 percent of society to change to bring about change so that all may see, feel, and enjoy a new way of living. An integral part of the human process is the need to have "pain" to motivate change. Great growth has always come to humanity after difficult times. If this is what is to be, let us be aware of our purpose and begin to find the path that serves us and all living things—which are simply *Creation*.

The future is wide open in terms of our potential for change and growth, and the field of epigenetics is the new frontier for this work. It is exciting to imagine what we will look like, how much more intelligent and adaptable we will be when all of the co-evolution between our consciousness and our physicality occurs. How much more peaceful we will be? How much healthier will we be, and what will the impact be on our longevity? How will our planet thrive when its inhabitants all work together to create a healthy organism called Earth? Will the diversity of animal and plant life return as we unselfishly volunteer to limit our population growth to reduce the burden on Mother Earth?

Our Infinite Potential

So here we are on the threshold of a new dream. We are nearing a time of great change no matter how hard we try to ignore it. We are smart enough to know that the sooner we change, the easier it will be. I foresee great positive change, although the longer we wait the more human loss and suffering will occur. It is in these moments that we do our best work. As our consciousness and emotional makeup change, so will our physical makeup; we know this from epigenetics. As we think differently we will look differently. Slightly changing the quote from Jesus in the Gospel of Thomas: the more we discover what is within us, the more it will save us. We may find within us the capacity for cognitive hypermutation, allowing us to adapt to the difficulties that will be set forth in the time to come. If Lamarck could only hear us now as science informs us that we are co-engineers in our own evolution. (See figure 10.)

Figure 10.

How will we write our future? What will it look like? Will the new medicine include intentional self-healing and the healing of others? Will we utilize the placebo effect instead of being afraid of it? Will we utilize a vision of the oneness of all living things and learn to share the planet with a diversity of life that helps sustain all of us? This means we would not place humanity first, and that we would choose to limit our population to a sustainable level.

Here is one thing I hope you appreciate after reading this book:

We have the potential to engineer our own evolution in order to assist our bodies' adaptation to a changing environment. For example, as I mentioned earlier in discussing epigenetics, a mother who senses the world as stressful and unsafe will create a son who is a fighter with large, muscular legs and arms and a mind that is reactive rather than logical. But a child who is born in a world that is safe and loving and who is taught to connect to their inner soul wisdom for the common good will look and act completely differently. This child's evolution will accentuate the physical attributes and abilities needed to thrive in a world of cooperation and acceptance as all things work as *one* but each person offers their own abilities to support the community as a whole.

We are reminded by evolution and its constant target of our direction and purpose: intelligence and connection. Whales and dolphins have been around much longer than humans. In some ways I think they typified direct evolution. The more modern whales, porpoises, and dolphins work intimately together with a much more complex language than we can comprehend. They seem to communicate beyond sound as they connect across oceans. Sound can travel long distances in water; however, it would be impossible to discern complex communication with all of the background noises of animals, waves, and human mechanization reverberating throughout the oceans. Logically, there simply has to be more to it than meets the ear. I have never seen or heard of reports of fighting among blue whales, or blue whales fighting humpback whales. They are by all definitions peaceful, and these whales on the cutting edge of their own evolution are mostly vegetarian, eating only some micro and macro animal plankton. Despite the fact that we have barbarically harvested them, killing off their families and children to near extinction, they wish us no ill will. From all accounts all they wish to do is understand and communicate with us. How would humanity look if we were to adopt the intentions of these animals that have much larger brains than we do and have been involved in the game of co-evolution longer than humans?

The question remains: what will be our next jump in evolution? What will we look like and what will be the special gifts we bring with us into the next generations?

My hope is that we will learn more about our connection with our own self-creation and all of the capacity that holds. We are not just a collection of physical systems separate from our surroundings. Buddhists speak of the Three Poisons, of which the final one is ignorance. This is when we forget that we are spiritual beings in a physical form. We traced our physical nature of the macro world down into the subatomic world where all things are energy. This is our transition point, where the greater reality of who we are is found. Here we realize that energy is another word for consciousness: our consciousness and Universal Consciousness. We are energetically and therefore physically a collection of all of our experiences in a unified field with and without the filters of our human personality across many realms. We are an infinite-potential field. The possibilities of what we are and what we can become are increasingly within our human grasp. Thanks to frontier science, guidance from the prophets within our religions, and the personal growth that each of us works on every day, we are increasingly aware of who we will become: a humanity that is part of a grand organism whose flesh is consciousness and space.

Our greatest and only purpose is to transform the energy of consciousness within ourselves and therefore the greater organism. Intrinsic within all of creation is the wish to live with internal harmony and peace. We touch it when we feel love and connection. We do not feel it when we are filled with anger, hatred, and fear. I was alarmed to hear that 50 percent of our war veterans attempt suicide in their lives. This clearly tells us the path we should never take. We go against our prime directive when we kill, hate, and see ourselves as separate from our fellow humanity. Physical manifestations of stress, pain, and disease loudly show us the wrong direction for our lives and humanity. When you feel stress, elevated heart rate or blood pressure, irritable bowel syndrome, headaches, chronic symptoms that don't heal, ulcers, and so on, this is often a message to you that there is something different you need to do or your beliefs need to be amended. When a day is filled with beauty, tenderness, and connections with friends and loved ones, and there are no tensions, just love and awe, you are definitely on track to your greatest purpose. We all have work to do in this endeavor, and we will never feel pure grace every day of our life, but we are getting closer and closer.

Let's see what we can do together. By strongly committing to the real work of acceptance, harmonizing and creating peace within, we can heal ourselves, stop wars and killing, and ultimately do our part to heal the *oneness*. Never forget that you are a collection of your experiences extruded through your beliefs. You were in charge of the beliefs when you adopted them and you have complete control of evolving them now. You are not trapped in old, harmful, fearful beliefs and actions. It is just a matter of choosing to change despite the fears that you put in your way so you can opt out of changing. Remember: we can easily come up with a logical if not honorable reason not to change our actions and confront our fears. It is helpful to remember that 99.9 percent of the horrible things in your life will never happen. They are just fears and are rarely physical reality—rather, they are emotional reality. It is your purpose to find peace and love where you once felt anger and fear. The moment you change, everything will change. As you find peace and love within, so will the world, little by little. The little snowball will become massive as it rolls downhill. We as humanity have been doing our part and have made much progress, but these times demand more. This is our defining moment of great change. We are a part of the energy and sentient consciousness of an infinite-potential field. Self-evolution, healing, and transformation are what we do best. I hope you enjoy the ride as together we write an amazing chapter in *The Book of Life for Humanity.*

NOTES

Chapter 1: Background and Foundational Experiences

1. William D. Mehring, *Finding Peace in Chaos* (Bloomington, IN: Balboa Press, 2012).

Chapter 2: Multiple Lives

1. Brian L. Weiss, *Many Lives, Many Masters* (New York: Simon and Schuster, 1988).
2. Michael Newton, *Destiny of Souls: New Case Studies of Life Between Lives* (St. Paul, MN: Llewellyn Publications, 2000).

Chapter 5: Science—The Evolution of Consciousness

1. Harold E. Puthoff, "Everything for Nothing," *New Scientist,* July 28, 1990: 52–55.
2. Margaret Wertheim, "Buckyballs and Screaming Cells," *LA Weekly News,* April 3, 2003.
3. Fritz-Albert Popp and Jiin-Ju Chang, "Mechanism of interaction between electromagnetic fields and the living systems," *Science in China* (Series C), 2000; 43:507–18.
4. Lynne McTaggart, *The Field: The Quest for the Secret Force of the Universe* (New York: HarperCollins, 2008), 39–44.
5. Bruce Lipton, *The Biology of Belief: Unleashing the Power of Consciousness, Matter & Miracles* (New York: Hay House, 2008).
6. Popp and Chang, "Mechanism of interaction between electromagnetic fields and the living systems."
7. Lipton, *The Biology of Belief.*
8. McTaggart, *The Field,* 92–95.
9. Ibid.

Chapter 6: Surprises Revealed in the Crystalline Matrix

1. Jeremy Narby, *The Cosmic Serpent: DNA and the Origins of Knowledge* (New York: Tarcher/Putnam, 1999).
2. Bruce Lipton and Steve Bhaerman, *Spontaneous Evolution: Our Positive Future and a Way to Get There from Here* (New York: Hay House, 2009).
3. Rupert Sheldrake, *A New Science of Life: The Hypothesis of Formative Causation* (London: Paladin, 1987), 23–25.
4. Candace Pert, *Molecules of Emotion: Why You Feel The Way You Feel* (New York: Scribner, 1997).

Chapter 7: Epigenetics and Our Living Evolution

1. Ananda Zarin, lectures on homeopathy, Santa Barbara, CA, circa 1998.
2. Karl S. Lashley, *Brain Mechanisms and Intelligence* (Chicago: University of Chicago Press, 1929).
3. Ibid.
4. Michael Talbot, The *Holographic Universe: The Revolutionary Theory of Reality* (New York: HarperCollins, 1991), 26.
5. Masuro Emoto, *Messages from Water* (Tokyo: Hado Hyoikusha, 1999), 90–113.
6. Ibid.
7. Both experiments, Bernard Grad, "Some Biological Effects of the 'Laying-on of Hands': A review of experiments with animals and plants," *Journal of the American Society for Physical Research,* 1965; 59: 95–127.

Chapter 8: Consciousness—The Bridge Between Energy and Physicality

1. Kim, Yoon-Ho et al., "A Delayed 'Choice' Quantum Eraser," *Physical Review Letters* (2000) 84: 1–5.
2. Lance Pollard (2014, Sept 14), "How Does the Electron Jump Across 'Gaps' in its Orbital?", http://physics.stackexchange.com/questions/135520how-does-the-electron-jump-across-gaps-in-its-orbital, 9/14/2014.
3. Richard Newrock, "What are Josephson Junctions? How do they work?", *Scientific American*, November 24, 1997, http://stilton.tnw.utwente.nl/people/eddi/Papers/PhysRevLett_TUNNEL.pdf,

Chapter 9: Dimensions Versus Realms

1. Ker Than, "Dark Matter Detected for First Time?", *National Geographic News,* December 18, 2009.
2. Malcolm W. Browne, "Far Apart, 2 Particles Respond Faster Than Light," *New York Times,* July 22, 1997.
3. Translations by Rabbi Janice Mehring.

Chapter 12: Fear and Awe

1. Lipton, *The Biology of Belief.*

Chapter 14: Judaism

1. Babylonian Talmud, Eruvin 13.
2. Joseph Telushkin, *A Code of Jewish Ethics: Volume 1: You Shall Be Holy* (New York: Crown, 2006).
3. Melinda Ribner, *New Age Judaism: Ancient Wisdom for the Modern World* (Deerfield Beach, FL: Simcha Press/Health Communications, Inc., 2000).
4. Alan Morinis, *Everyday Holiness: The Jewish Spiritual Path of Mussar* (Boston: Trumpeter Books/Shambhala Publications, 2008).

Chapter 16: Christianity

1. Elaine Pagels, *The Gnostic Gospels* (New York: Vintage, 1989), xvii.
2. Ibid.
3. Ibid., xv.

Chapter 18: Buddhism

1. Pope Paul VI, "Nostra Aetate: Declaration on the Relation of the Church to Non-Christian Religions," October 28, 1965, http://www.vatican.va/archive/hist_councils/ii_vatican_council/documents/vat-ii_decl_19651028_nostra-aetate_en.html
2. Ibid.
3. Faith not Fault: Affirming Christianity without faulting Judaism, http://faithnotfault.org/welcome.

Chapter 19: Islam

1. Deenislam.co.uk: The Western Sufi Resource Guide, http://www.deenislam. co.uk/Sufism.htm.

Chapter 20: Transformative Healing

1. Sandra Blakeslee, "Placebos Prove So Powerful Even Experts Are Surprised; New Studies Explore the Brain's Triumph Over Reality." *New York Times,* October 13, 1998.
2. Shawn Achor, *The Happiness Advantage: The Seven Principles of Positive Psychology That Fuel Success and Performance at Work* (New York: Random House Audio, 2010).

Chapter 21: Awakening Our Hidden Power

1. Daniel Benor, *Spiritual Healing: Scientific Validation of a Healing Revolution* (Southfield, MI: Vision Publications, 2001), 211–12.
2. Grad, "Some Biological Effects of 'Laying-on of Hands,'" 95–127.
3. Bernard Grad, "Healing by the Laying-on of Hands: review of experiments and implications," *Pastoral Psychology,* vol. 21, issue 7 (1970); 21: 19–26.
4. R. N. Miller, "Study on the effectiveness of remote mental healing," *Medical Hypotheses,* 1982; 8: 481–90.
5. C. Garrard's experiment; "The Effect of Therapeutic Touch on Stress Reduction and Immune Function in Persons with AIDS," doctoral dissertation, University of Alabama, Birmingham, 1996.
6. McTaggart, *The Field,* 189–90.
7. F. Sicher et al., "A randomized double-blind study of the effects of distant healing in a population with advanced AIDS," *Western Journal of Medicine,* 1998 Dec; 169(6): 356–63.
8. E. E. Green, "Copper Wall research psychology and psychophysics: subtle energies and energy medicine: emerging theory and practice," *Proceedings,* First Annual Conference, International Society of the Study of Subtle Energies and Energy Medicine, Boulder, Colorado, June 21–25, 1991.
9. From lectures presented by the Noetic Society, late 1990s.
10. "Terrorist Disaster, September 11, 2001," Global Consciousness Project website: http://noosphere.princeton.edu.
11. J. S. Hagel et al., "Effects of group practice of the Transcendental Meditation Program on preventing violent crime in Washington DC: results of the

National Demonstration Project, June–July, 1993," *Social Indicators Research,* 1994; 47: 153–201.

12. M. C. Dillbeck et al., "The transcendental Meditation program and crime rate change in a sample of 48 cities," *Journal of Crime and Justice,* 1981; 4: 25–45.

13. David W. Orme-Johnson et al., "International peace project in the Middle East: the effects of the Maharishi technology of the unified field," *Journal of Conflict Resolution,* 1988; 32: 776–812.

Printed in the United States
By Bookmasters